Exegesis at Qumran

Journal for the Study of the Old Testament
Supplement Series
29

Editors

David A. Clines
Philip R. Davies

Exegesis at Qumran
4QFLORILEGIUM IN ITS JEWISH CONTEXT

GEORGE J. BROOKE

Society of Biblical Literature
Atlanta
2006

To the memory of
William Hugh Brownlee
(1917–1983)

Christian, Scholar, Friend

Library of Congress Cataloging-in-Publication Data

Brooke, George J.
    Exegesis at Qumran : 4QFlorilegium in its Jewish context / George J.
Brooke.
        p. cm.
    Originally published: Sheffield, Eng. : JSOT Press, 1985 in the Dead Sea
Scrolls Project of the Institute for Antiquity and Christianity, v. 2 and in the
Journal for the Study of the Old Testament Supplement series, 29.
    Includes index.
    ISBN-13: 978-1-58983-237-4 (paper binding : alk. paper)
    ISBN-10: 1-58983-237-X (paper binding : alk. paper)
    1. 4QFlorilegium. 2. Bible. O.T.—Criticism, interpretation, etc., 3. Bible.
O.T.—Criticism, interpretation, etc., Jewish. I. Title.

BM488.A13.B76 2006
221.60933—dc22

2006012823

Printed in the United States of America
on acid-free paper

CONTENTS

v

Preface

This book is an extensive revision of a dissertation
submitted in 1978 to the Department of Religion of Claremont
Graduate School, California. Much in this book is the result
of the careful guiding interest and attention to detail of
Professor William H. Brownlee; it is to his memory that it is
dedicated in gratitude. As Director of the Dead Sea Scrolls
Project of the Institute for Antiquity and Christianity at
Claremont he generously welcomed this study as Volume Two in that
project's series of publications, his own *The Midrash Pesher of
Habakkuk* (SBLMS 24; Missoula: Scholars Press, 1979) being
Volume One. I am also grateful to the Editors of the JSOT Press
for accepting this book into the JSOT Supplement Series.

Among many other scholars to whom I am grateful I would
mention Professor R. P. Knierim whose methodological insights
are evident in many places, Professor J. A. Sanders who offered
much helpful criticism as the dissertation was in the final
stages of production, Professor J. A. Emerton whose discerning
eye has prevented many minor errors and immeasurably improved
the consistency of the book's presentation, and Professor
J.P.M. van der Ploeg, O.P., for encouraging the book's
publication. To all these scholars I am especially indebted,

though naturally the responsibility for the content of
this book remains mine.

I am also very grateful to all who have helped me
meet the cost of publication: the trustees of the
Sarum St. Michael Educational Trust and their chairman,
the Very Rev. Dr. Sydney Evans; the trustees of Salisbury
and Wells Theological College and the College Principal,
Canon Reginald Askew; the trustees of the Kennicott and
Pusey and Ellerton Hebrew Funds of Oxford University and
their chairman, Professor James Barr; the trustees of the
Bethune-Baker Fund for Theological Studies and their successive
chairmen, Professors Henry Chadwick and Morna Hooker.

I also thank those who have helped produce this book:
Sue Langford for many hours of painstaking typing,
Geoffrey Annas for proof-reading, Michael Morris for proof-
reading and the preparation of the indexes, and the staff
of the JSOT Press for their care in publishing. To many
other people, scholars, friends and members of my family,
I am grateful for encouragement over the years it has taken
for this work to come to fruition; not least among them is
my wife, Jane.

Abbreviations

AJSL   *American Journal of Semitic Languages and Literatures*

ALGHJ   Arbeiten zur Literatur und Geschichte des hellenistischen
            Judentums

ALUOS   *Annual of Leeds University Oriental Society*

AnBib   Analecta biblica

AOAT   Alter Orient und Altes Testament

APOT   R. H. Charles (ed.), *Apocrypha and Pseudepigrapha of the
            Old Testament*

ASTI   *Annual of the Swedish Theological Institute*

BA   *Biblical Archaeologist*

BASOR   *Bulletin of the American Schools of Oriental Research*

BDB   F. Brown, S. R. Driver, and C. A. Briggs, *Hebrew and
            English Lexicon of the Old Testament*

BETL   Bibliotheca ephemeridum theologicarum lovaniensium

BHS   *Biblia Hebraica Stuttgartensia*

BHT   Beitrage zur historischen Theologie

Bib   *Biblica*

BibOr   Biblica et orientalia

BJS   Brown Judaic Studies

BO   *Bibliotheca orientalis*

BTB   *Biblical Theology Bulletin*

BWANT   Beitrage zur Wissenschaft vom Alten und Neuen Testament

BZAW   Beihefte zur ZAW

CBQ   *Catholic Biblical Quarterly*

CBQMS   Catholic Biblical Quarterly Monograph Series

ix

ConBib   Coniectanea biblica

ConNT   *Coniectanea neotestamentica*

DBSup   *Dictionnaire de la Bible, Supplément*

DJD   Discoveries in the Judaean Desert of Jordan

EncJud   *Encyclopaedia Judaica* (1971)

ETL   *Ephemerides theologicae lovaniensis*

EvQ   *Evangelical Quarterly*

HSM   Harvard Semitic Monographs

HTR   *Harvard Theological Review*

HUCA   *Hebrew Union College Annual*

IDBSup   *Interpreter's Dictionary of the Bible Supplementary*

            Volume

IEJ   *Israel Exploration Journal*

Int   *Interpretation*

JANESCU   *Journal of the Ancient Near Eastern Society of Columbia*

            University

JBL   *Journal of Biblical Literature*

JBLMS   Journal of Biblical Literature Monograph Series

JBR   *Journal of Bible and Religion*

JJS   *Journal of Jewish Studies*

JNES   *Journal of Near Eastern Studies*

JNWSL   *Journal of Northwest Semitic Languages*

JQR   *Jewish Quarterly Review*

JR   *Journal of Religion*

JSJ   *Journal for the Study of Judaism*

JSOTSup   Journal for the Study of the Old Testament Supplement

            Series

JSS   *Journal of Semitic Studies*

JTC   *Journal for Theology and the Church*

JTS N.S.	*Journal of Theological Studies* (New Series)
KB	L. Koehler and W. Baumgartner, *Lexicon in Veteris Testamenti libros*
LD	Lectio divina
LQR	*Law Quarterly Review*
MHUC	Monographs of the Hebrew Union College
NFT	New Frontiers in Theology
NovT	*Novum Testamentum*
NovTSup	Novum Testamentum Supplements
NTS	*New Testament Studies*
OJRS	*Ohio Journal of Religious Studies*
OTL	Old Testament Library
OTS	*Oudtestamentische Studiën*
PAPS	*Proceedings of the American Philosophical Society*
PEQ	*Palestine Exploration Quarterly*
PTMS	Pittsburgh Theological Monograph Series
RB	*Revue biblique*
RechBib	*Recherches bibliques*
REG	*Revue des études grecs*
RGG	*Religion in Geschichte und Gegenwart*
RHPR	*Revue d'histoire et de philosophie religieuses*
RQ	*Revue de Qumrân*
RSR	*Recherches de science religieuse*
RSV	*Revised Standard Version*
SBLDS	Society of Biblical Literature Dissertation Series
SBLMS	Society of Biblical Literature Monograph Series
SJLA	Studies in Judaism in Late Antiquity
SP	*Studia Philonica*
SPB	Studia postbiblica

STDJ	Studies on the Texts of the Desert of Judah
SUNT	Studien zur Umwelt des Neuen Testaments
TBl	*Theologische Blätter*
THAT	*Theologische Handbuch zum Alten Testament*
TLZ	*Theologische Literaturzeitung*
TS	*Theological Studies*
TZ	*Theologische Zeitschrift*
VC	Vigiliae christianae
VT	*Vetus Testamentum*
VTSup	Vetus Testamentum Supplements
WUNT	Wissenschaftliche Untersuchungen zum Neuen Testament
ZAW	*Zeitschrift für die alttestamentliche Wissenschaft*
ZTK	*Zeitschrift für Theologie und Kirche*

Chapter I

THE JEWISH EXEGETICAL CONTEXT

A. Introductory Remarks

The purpose of this study is to provide a comprehensive analysis of one text from Qumran, 4Q Florilegium.[1] 4QFlor is a fragmentary text containing several quotations from the Hebrew scriptures: 2 Samuel, Exodus, Amos, Psalms, Isaiah, Ezekiel, Daniel and Deuteronomy. These quotations are variously interlaced with commentary that attempts to show the interrelationship of the various texts and their significance. It appears as if the quotations from 2 Samuel, Psalms and Deuteronomy determine the general argument of the text; their relative positions and the formulaic phrases that either precede or follow them or both suggest as much.[2] Yet it must be acknowledged from the outset that we do not know how the scroll began or how it finished and that the text that remains is in a poor state of repair.

Indeed the fragmentary nature of the text forces one to conclude that the methods of higher criticism which presuppose that the scholar is working with complete units of text are in need of supplementation when a partial text is under consideration. If it is the concern of historical criticism to describe and explain the intention of an author as it can be

discerned from the one predominant organizing principle
behind the entity of the literary form,[3] then it must be the
case that a text with no clear beginning or end will only
yield imperfect results to the critic. This realization has
had two interrelated consequences for this study.

The first and more obvious is that it has become
necessary to consider much background material from the intertestamental period. The general conclusions of these theological,
traditio-historical and other investigations are given in the
appropriate sections of the next chapter. However, and perhaps
more significantly, since 4QFlor contains scriptural texts and
interpretation such general appreciation of 4QFlor is
supplemented or rather is necessarily preceded in this chapter
with very particular investigations of the ways in which
scripture was treated in Judaism in the first centuries B.C.
and A.D. This first chapter, then, argues that exegetical
techniques akin to those set out in various lists of rabbinic
middôt were used widely, if not universally, in Jewish
exegesis of the late Second Temple period, and that their use
was more, rather than less, precise. The results of the
acknowledgement of this exegetical methodology for our understanding of 4QFlor are discussed in the proper sections of the
next chapter. Chapter three contains further examples from
Qumran texts of a variety of genres in support of the contention
that an understanding of the exegetical methodology being used
considerably aids our understanding of the text at hand. The
approach is thus clear from the outset: without appreciation
of exegetical devices and techniques at use in early Judaism,
any analysis of 4QFlor is as fragmentary as the text itself.

Indeed in one or two cases knowledge of the technique in
use enables the text to be more probably restored.

Some few remarks need to be interposed at this point
concerning the terms "hermeneutic" and "exegesis." In a
book that shares many concerns with this study D. Patte has
attempted to show, particularly in relation to the targumim,
that the Jews of the first century A.D. accepted scripture as
"canonical," reckoned that everything in scripture was
meaningful, and that scripture could be interpreted by
scripture.[4] Patte prefaces his study, therefore, with some
remarks as to the necessity that the modern critic understand
that for the early Jew there was no difference between
exegesis and hermeneutic,[5] that is, no difference between
his encounter with the text as object *per se*, and as it
related to himself as subject. Such is to say that the text
presented itself to the early Jew as immediately relevant.
So Patte's understanding of the early Jewish encounter with
scripture leads not unnaturally to a traditional account of
the place of revelation within the early Jewish use of
scripture; through continual revelation all Jews, but the
apocalyptists (including the Qumran covenanters) in particular,
are brought to understand scripture.[6]

Admittedly we must accept Patte's contention that the Jew
was concerned not with objective exegesis in the modern sense
but with prolonging "in a new discourse the discourse of the
biblical text,"[7] but initially in whatever vague fashion it
must remain that he encountered the text as object. Even if
it is a slightly artificial distinction for the first century
Jew, the hermeneutic, the result of the individual's making

contemporary a particular text, depends upon the exegesis,
the application of a method to achieve a result that enables
any canonical text to remain authoritative in some way. So
a correct understanding of the hermeneutic depends upon a
correct understanding of early Jewish exegesis and especially
that exegesis' technical methodology.[8] The missing ingredient
from the modern scholar's point of view for understanding any
commentary, including the fragmentary 4QFlor, is the exegetical
methodology that was applied by its author.

   The second consequence of supplementing the traditional
methods of higher criticism by reference to early Jewish
exegetical methodology concerns the validity of any interpretation.
It seems that the use of any particular exegetical technique
was not arbitrary. Any interpreter of scripture who wished
his interpretation to be accepted is likely to have used
particular interpretative techniques because they were reckoned
to be valid ways of producing a meaningful interpretation.
Though we may be unable to discover in every case what technique
was used, nevertheless we can better gauge the acceptability
and the possible impact of any interpretation if we appreciate
how an interpreter has reached his conclusion.

   The history of scholarship illuminates how it is important
to consider the part played by the exegetical skill of the
author in any assessment of the authority and meaning of any
interpretation. Thus the traditional clash between the understanding of a text as inspired, over against it being solely
a human production has long been seen to be a false dichotomy.[9]
For example, in relation to Qumran exegesis, W. H. Brownlee
early proposed[10] treating 1QpHab as a midrash employing some

of the exegetical techniques of the later rabbinic midrashim.
K. Elliger opposed this view,[11] though adopting some of its
conclusions, and proposed rather that the Habakkuk pesher be
seen in the light of the inspired dream interpretations of
Daniel. Several scholars have since pointed out that these
views are not necessarily mutually exclusive. Writes
L. H. Silberman: "It may be wondered whether these distinctions
as they stand are not irrelevant to an understanding of the
texts; indeed, whether they may not impede and frustrate any
attempt fully to understand the materials at hand;"[12] and
M. P. Miller adds: "If pesher is the revelation of prophetic
mysteries, these mysteries are exegetically discerned. They
are the product of a meditative study on biblical texts."[13]
So the determination of the way in which the commentary on a
biblical quotation is written and connected is the means
whereby a text can be seen to be valid, to have authority in
itself apart from but also in conjunction with the biblical
quotation; valid commentary is linked to scriptural citation
through the use of certain principles applied in particular
describable exegetical techniques.[14]

   In light of what has been said in these introductory
remarks, a proper understanding of 4QFlor depends upon the
identification of the exegetical techniques used in the
construction of the argument of the text. Since not all
scholars recognize the use of these techniques in Judaism
of the late Second Temple period and so as to demonstrate
that the Qumran scribes were not acting independently of
contemporary Judaism the rest of this chapter is a brief
consideration of early Jewish exegetical method, the necessary

preliminary to any analysis of 4QFlor itself. The following
discussion includes a description of some of the influences
upon Jewish education in the period to which 4QFlor is dated,
a consideration of the age and origin of the *middôt*, the
provision of some examples from Philo and the Targums of
various exegetical devices used by Jewish commentators at
this time, and some few remarks about Qumran exegetical
method based largely on the history of scholarship.

B. Early Jewish Use of the Bible

1. Judaism and Hellenism in the late Second Temple Period

In relation to the general cultural background in
Palestine in 100 BC - AD 70, a Palestine which contained
forever changing varieties of Judaism together with non-Jewish
elements, the work of W. D. Davies has been most influential
in stressing the interpenetration of Hellenism and Judaism
both in Palestine and in the Diaspora. He writes: "Palestinian
Judaism is not to be viewed as a watertight compartment closed
against all Hellenistic influences: there was a Graeco-Jewish
'atmosphere' even at Jerusalem itself . . . . There is thus
no justification for making too rigid a separation between the
Judaism of the Diaspora and that of Palestine."[15]
More recently M. Hengel has completed a closer analysis
of Judaism and Hellenism in pre-Christian times.[16] He examines
early Hellenism as a political and economic force, noting,
for example, the Hellenistic war tactics used in 1QM;[17] he

points to the apparent similarity of Jewish and Spartan
governmental structures in early Hellenistic times[18] and he
discusses the LXX translation of Isa 58:6, "undo the thongs of
compulsory treaties, release the broken ones by letting them
go free, and *shatter every unjust treaty*,"[19] as indicative of
a change in the 'social climate' ascribable to Hellenistic
influences, the rational and technical order of the Greeks.[20]

The pervasiveness of the Greek language, occurring even
among Essene documents at Qumran[21] was enhanced among educated
Jews by the fact known in Alexandria and elsewhere that many
Jews participated to the full in Greek gymnasium education.[22]
Indeed the establishment of Greek institutions in Jerusalem
in the second century B.C. could only have taken place, Hengel
maintains, if there had already been a portion of the more
influential Jews who were prepared for such innovation.[23] Even
the Maccabean revolt was just a temporary break in the increasing
hellenization of Palestine, though at no time, except perhaps
under Antiochus IV, was there any major attempt to assimilate
Judaism to Greek ways; rather, all that was learnt was put to
serve the Jewish cause.

In education Hengel traces to a Greek background the tradition
of naming of teachers, the master-pupil relationship, the dia-
lectical form of instruction, the *middôt* and the purpose of
haggadic exegesis.[24] The education of the professional class was
thus permeated with Hellenistic elements.[25] Indeed in relation to
Qumran, Hengel states that "der Ausgangspunkt der bei den Essenern
geübten Gelehrsamkeit waren die palästinisch-chasidischen Weisheits-
schulen in der 1. Hälfte des 2. Jh. s v. Chr., in denen - wie auch
bei Ben-Sira - schon eine gewisse Kenntnis »griechischer Weisheit«

im Sinne popularphilosophischer, volkstümlicher Anschauungen
vorausgesetzt werden darf."[26]   That this was so is perhaps
most clearly exemplified from the descriptions of the Essenes
in Hellenistic terms by such contemporary observers as
Josephus, Philo, Pliny, Solinus and Porphyry.[27]

It is not possible, nor is it necessary, to list further
the findings and the viewpoints of M. Hengel here. Rather,
in sum, it can be said that his detailed analysis of source
materials of a greater variety than those normally considered
demonstrates that Hellenistic influence was in many ways as
widespread in Palestine as it was in Alexandria and Diaspora
Judaism. Though there is still some considerable debate
concerning the extent of this Hellenistic influence, Hengel's
views have been widely supported, explicitly by J. A. Fitzmyer,[28]
G. Vermes, F. Millar and M. Black,[29] and implicitly by
D. E. Gowan[30] and M. E. Stone[31] amongst others. It is, therefore,
no longer proper to assert that Hellenistic Judaism can be set
over against Palestinian Judaism in, say, the first century
B.C., though of course there were different emphases in
different areas.[32]

2. The Age and Origin of the Middôt

Once the interdependence of Hellenistic and Jewish thought
is recognized in Palestinian Judaism of the late Second Temple
period then a fresh perspective can be given to the debate
concerning the age and provenance of the *middôt*, the so-called
"rules of exegesis." Undoubtedly our understanding of the
Jewish use of scripture of this period will be enhanced, if
light is shed on early Jewish exegetical method. Two schools

of thought persist concerning the *middôt*.

On the one hand Hengel, following D. Daube and others,
supposes the use of the *middôt* to be dependent upon Hellenistic
influence; more narrowly that they are largely derivable from
the methods of Alexandrian philology as applied to demonstrate
the absolute authority and sufficiency of Scripture, the Torah.[33]
D. Daube himself, in an oft-quoted article,[34] has long insisted
on the Hellenistic rhetorical basis of the *middôt* as ascribed
to Hillel. Rather than there simply being a coincidence of
method in Hillel's principles and those of Hellenistic rhetoric,
Daube shows that the Hebrew lists of principles follow the
order of those found in the earlier sources of Aristotle
(*Rhetoric* 2:23:4f.), Cicero (*Topica* 4:23) and Auctor ad
Herennium (2:13:18) amongst others:[35] first the inference
a minori ad maius (qal wahōmer), then the inference from
analogy *(gĕzērâ šāwâ)*. The list of seven *middôt* is attributable
to Hillel himself, according to Daube.[36] Although Daube's work
is recognizably noteworthy in its insistence on the Hellenistic
basis of Hillel's principles, even though they became judaized,
he pays little attention to a detailed analysis of the sources
in which the lists occur attributed to Hillel.[37]

On the other hand the second school of thought is most
forcefully represented by the work of J. Neusner. He bases
his work on two suppositions: firstly, that the Mishnah-Tosefta
as embodying the oral law in no way tries to show its dependence
on scripture exegetically, that being the task undertaken by
the early midrashim;[38] secondly, that the rabbinic sources
are to be treated with all the available methods of higher
criticism: a tradition attributed to a generation older than

the source in which it is written down must not be taken at
literal face value, but, rather, its tradition-history must
be revealed as best as possible to determine the way in which
the form and content of the particular tradition developed
over the years.[39]

In relation to the list of *middôt* in *t. Sanh.* 7:11[40]
which are there attributed to Hillel, Neusner supposes firstly
that the pericope is making reference to the exegetical
traditions of Hillel's encounter concerning what should be
done when the Passover falls on a Sabbath;[41] then, following
Lieberman, in that the passage does not necessarily ascribe
authorship of the seven *middôt* to Hillel, stating simply that
he used them, Neusner points out that on the one hand the story
of Hillel's encounter with the Bene Bathyra hardly bears out
that Hillel used all seven principles,[42] and on the other hand
a pattern can be discerned in the formation of tannaitic
materials in which as many well-known sayings and stories as
possible were attributed to Hillel. When one considers the
extremely composite, even self-contradictory, content of the
description of Hillel's encounter with his opponents in the
temple courtyard[43] and the fact that it seems incredible that
no one can remember what to do should the Passover occur on
a Sabbath, an event which must have occurred several times
in the lives of Hillel's opponents, it is most unreasonable
to attribute any of the story of the encounter as we now have
it to a time when the temple was still in existence.[44]

Thus for Neusner the *list* of seven *middôt* finds its best
setting in the Hellenistic Jewish world of the second century
A.D. The story of Hillel's encounter in the temple is designed

to demonstrate the superiority of tradition (oral) over
deliberate exegesis, but at the same time it also shows the
correct application of certain exegeses. It could be suggested
that in a world where many varieties of Judaism existed, the
rabbinic kind allowed only a limited number of exegetical
methods. And, because of the rabbinic understanding of the
nature of oral law, these exegetical methods were applied
predominantly in other writings more clearly of tannaitic and
amoraic origin wherein a certain attempt was made to demonstrate
the exegetical relationship of oral law to scripture. The
adoption and use of the seven *middôt* thus appears as a
delimitation of exegesis by the rabbis rather than a broad
acceptance of Hellenistic methodology.[45]

A point of view midway between these two schools of
thought is represented in the work of S. Lieberman.[46] Although
his chapter on the rabbinic interpretation of scripture was
written without reference to Daube's work, he reaches conclusions
similar to those of Daube concerning the use of exegetical
techniques in the Second Temple period and their Hellenistic
provenance. He gives examples of what he argues are the Greek
terminological equivalents of the rabbinic terms which antedate
the Tosefta,[47] and he sees the technical use of some parts of
the terms as clearly antedating Hillel.[48] The same can be said
for the haggadic terminology of the rabbis: there are pre-
rabbinic Greek parallels as far as content is concerned but
little or no evidence that there was a current precise terminology available to the interpreters of Homer or whomever.[49]

Lieberman's study provides the rabbinic examples that
Daube does not fully cite, alongside those of classical authors.

Yet in investigating whether or not Hillel himself was
responsible for the terminology that the later sources
attribute to him in the list of *middôt*, Lieberman concludes
that it is "very possible that . . . . it is the editor of
the *Tosefta* who designated Hillel's arguments by the later
terminology."[50] With such a conclusion we have seen Neusner
agree. Put another way this suggests that Pharisaic Judaism,
once stripped of the Temple, was forced by that very event
to see the justification of scriptural interpretation, and in
varying degrees allowed the application of certain Hellenistic
methods. Thus, while the content and methodology of the
rabbinic interpretations may in some cases date from well
before 70, the formation of the actual body of rabbinic
literature as we now have it, including the *lists* of *middôt*,
depends primarily upon the Pharisaic struggle for domination
of Judaism after the temple's destruction.[51]

It is not surprising, therefore, to discover a list,
very similar to that attributed to Hillel, in the introduction
to *Sifra*.[52] That list of thirteen principles expounded by
R. Ishmael follows the order of the seven; it contains five
exegetical principles that are variations on the twofold
principle of "the general and particular" and "the particular
and the general." This longer list, therefore, makes no
pretence of having been adopted in rabbinic Judaism before
the second century. If anything is surprising, it is that the
thirteen principles are attributed to Ishmael and not to
R. Akiba, for *Sifra* is most frequently associated with the
school of Akiba.[53]

Along with these halakic exegetical *middôt* are to be found

the thirty-two principles of R. Eliezer ben R. Yose Ha-Gelili
which are largely concerned with haggadic exegesis.
H. G. Enelow, the editor of *The Mishna of Rabbi Eliezer*,[54]
maintains that these thirty-two rules, possibly without the
examples and the complete work that follows them, may in fact
have originated with the second century Eliezer to whom they
are attributed, and he supposes that where talmudic passages
agree with materials in the main body of Eliezer's midrash, it
is the talmudic literature that is dependent and not the other
way around.

Whatever the case may be concerning the actual list of
thirty-two[55] *middôt*, it is clear that there are many examples
of the use of particular principles in the early rabbinic
literature, such that if the list was only adopted later, it
would have been adopted under pressure from already existing
exegeses, rather than as a demonstration of acceptance of a
new dimension in the rabbinic use of scripture: thus, once
again, the delimiting nature of lists of exegetical principles
can be observed, especially since the three lists of rules
mentioned are far from representative of all the principles
at work even in early rabbinic literature.[56]

If the conclusion is right that although the clearly
formulated lists of *middôt* are all tannaitic the methods they
enshrine were being actively used in Judaism of the late
Second Temple period, then it is necessary to give some
particular examples of these exegetical principles at work.

Three sources seem inappropriate as quarries for such
examples. The first is the corpus of rabbinic literature.
Lieberman gives examples from rabbinic literature of *māšāl*

(parable), *gĕmatrĕyā'*(computation of the numerical value
of letters),*'atbaš* (letter substitution) and *nôtārîqôn*
(abbreviation), but although he mentions materials that in
content could antedate the destruction of the temple,[57] their
form cannot be demonstrated as earlier than A.D. 70. Since
the actual form in which an exegetical result is stated is
important in determining which exegetical method was used,
then if the form is datable with certainty only to tannaitic
times it cannot be used to argue the use of exegetical
principles in an earlier age.

The second body of material which cannot be dated with
certainty is the apocrypha and pseudepigrapha. These texts
can usually only be found in a later translation and often
only in a translation of a translation. Again, since the
actual wording of the text is important in identifying a pun
or word-play,*gĕmatrĕyā'*or *nôtārîqôn*, it is not justifiable to
use texts that are largely versions or which are available only
in forms which are very likely to be later than the fall of
the Second Temple.

A third source that is not to be used here is the New
Testament. Although the New Testament contains explicit and
implicit use of the Jewish scriptures, the hermeneutical presupposition of all the writers and usually of their readers as
well is clearly the centrality of the figure of Jesus recognized
through faith as the Christ.[58] The authority of the Jewish
scriptures rests in their finding their correct fulfilment in
Jesus. The various literary forms of the NT do not for the
most part set out to justify the faith in the Christ, crucified
and risen (matters only poorly demonstrable from scripture),

but rather they work to proclaim that faith. The aim of the
NT books is dependent on the twofold presupposition of faith
in the Christ and the authority of scripture.[59]

Undoubtedly, however, the scriptures do receive treatment
in the NT similar in method to the Jewish use of scripture.
It is noteworthy that those authors (and sometimes their
audiences) most closely associated with demonstrating (or
hearing), consciously or unconsciously, some continuity with
the Jewish tradition more clearly use exegetical methods
acceptable to Jewish ears. Thus there has been considerable
scholarly work done on Matthew's use of scripture[60] and Paul's
epistles have also been studied for their exegetical forms,[61]
especially in relation to rabbinic texts. Matthew is often
considered the most Jewish of the Gospels, while Paul appears
to have been among the best educated of the NT writers. Other
scholars have variously attempted to assess both the form and
content of much of the NT in terms of rabbinic traditions;
most notably, in English, D. Daube[62] has amassed and analyzed
considerable parallel material, and in German the work of
H. L. Strack and P. Billerbeck remains unsurpassed.[63]

Yet although these three sources are inappropriate for
providing particular examples, they all suggest that during
Judaism of the late Second Temple period there was widespread
use of exegetical principles. Lieberman concludes that the
rabbis, in attempting to expound and preserve the viewpoint
of just one part of Judaism of the time, undoubtedly utilized
exegetical principles accepted all over the critical world of
the time; this they did in order to be understood and appreciated
by their contemporaries,[64] that their interpretations should

be seen to be valid.[65] It is this conception of the prior
existence and use of these principles of exegesis, especially
in the Hellenistic literature before A.D. 70, that has led to
use of the terminology of the lists of *middôt* and other
exegeses in this study. This is not necessarily to suggest
that the technical terms for the principles used in our
examples were current in Judaism of the first centuries B.C.
and A.D., but from convenience the examples cited are
categorized according to the later Hellenistic Jewish
(rabbinic) terms to save us from having to invent our own
anachronistic terminology. The strength of the examples
cited here lies in their demonstrating clearly the use of
principles of interpretation that are the immediate progenitors
of the later rabbinic principles as embodied in the various
lists of *middôt*; these were used more widely and earlier than
rabbinic sources would lead us to believe.

It is the works of Philo and the interpretations of
scripture suggested in the Targums as well as the various
materials from Qumran that support the conclusion that just
as the fall of the Second Temple forced Pharisaic Judaism to
delimit the canon so it forced it to delimit how the canon
was to be interpreted. This was no simple step forward in
an obvious process but rather it was the recognition by early
tannaitic Judaism of what was already largely the case. So
in Philo and in the targumic texts that more certainly predate
the fall of the Temple are to be found various exegetical
techniques some of which were later named and officially
recognized in tannaitic Judaism and some of which were not.
Of the precise age and origin of the *middôt* we cannot be sure,

but of their use, though without technical categorization,
in the late Second Temple period, there seems to be increasing
evidence; the following examples from Philo and the targums
are adduced in support of such a conclusion.

3. Exegetical Method in Philo and the Targums

  a. Philo

    1) Introduction

Given what has been said about the interpenetration of
Judaism and Hellenism, discussion of Philo's exegetical
methodology is not out of place. Indeed such discussion
may be part of a necessary corrective to much that has been
written about the methods of Palestinian Jewish exegesis
contemporary with Philo. This is supported by three factors.

Firstly, it is no longer possible to dismiss Philo
simply as an allegorist.[66] On the one hand at least in
relation to the laws of the Pentateuch, Philo was not an
allegorist alone; he did not set aside the literal practice
of the Law while attempting to unravel its inner truths.[67]
On the other hand Philo attacks those who restrict their
method of exegesis to allegory and likewise he rebukes those
who hold to a literal meaning without asking further questions.[68]
This "two-level view"[69] of scripture needs to be put alongside
Philo's own statements concerning the allegorical style of
scripture[70] for although he might have agreed with Heracleitus
who defined allegory as "a style speaking certain things and
meaning something other than what it says"[71] nevertheless he
had regard for scripture's plain meaning. Even if Philo
considered scripture as pure allegory that does not answer

the question as to what methods of exegesis he used in
order to describe its meaning.

Secondly, it is no longer possible to describe Philo's
exegetical method either as essentially Greek[72] or as most
closely paralleled in the works of the rabbis[73] or as a
mixture of both.[74] In a historical perspective these
categories are too narrow, since it is quite possible to
trace the allegorical method to the Near Eastern milieu of
the early Stoics,[75] and to assert that, except for the
presence of traditional Judaism in a variety of forms, the
general Hellenistic culture prevalent at the time of Philo
would not produce very different trends of exegesis in "Greek"
Alexandria and "Jewish" Palestine, the whole geographical area
being Hellenistic.[76]

Thirdly in light of these two points it is not surprising
that much recent Philonic scholarship has emphasized the
centrality of scriptural exposition *per se* in Philo's works.
J. Cazeaux[77] and V. Nikiprowetzky,[78] amongst others, both
stress the dependence of Philo's exegesis on particular phrases.
B. L. Mack has proposed a thorough examination of the Philonic
corpus with the supposition that "Philo used traditional
exegetical methods and materials. These materials are diverse
and may reflect stages of exegetical history or 'schools' of
exegesis which are in debate with one another. Philo employed
these traditions with degrees of acceptance and he reworked
them with varying degrees of consistency."[79] R. D. Hecht and
H. Moehring are amongst those who have tried to work out the
implications of Mack's program. Hecht has attempted to analyse
Philo's use of scripture in *De Specialibus Legibus*;[80] Moehring

has considered arithmology as an exegetical tool.[81]

2) Examples

Philo's use of etymology is perhaps his most frequently
discussed exegetical method. Of the two examples of philonic
etymologies to be considered here, the first occurs in
Fug 213[82] where Philo writes that βαράδ means ἐν κακοῖς. In
Quaest Gen 3:36 Philo is clearly aware that the Hebrew word
means "hail" and so to brush aside his interpretation in
Fug 213 as "very faulty etymology"[83] is hardly sufficient.[84]
A. Hanson notices that Philo is deriving his meaning from a
combination of the preposition ב and the adjective רע but he
fails to see that Philo is in complete control of his derivation:
not ἐν κακῷ but ἐν κακοῖς Philo therefore wishes to understand βαράδ at this point as representing ב + רעות whose
pronunciations approximate one another. Furthermore the
context of *Fug* 213 demonstrates that Philo was concerned not
with a "faulty etymology" but with finding an antithesis to
his exegesis of Kadesh as ἄγια; as Colson translates: "'Bered'
means 'in evils', and Kadesh 'holy', for he that is in gradual
progress is on the borderland between the holy and the profane,
fleeing from bad things, but not yet competent to share the
life of perfect goodness."[85]

A second example of Philo's careful and exact use of
Hebrew or a Hebrew tradition for his own purposes is to be
found in his understanding of Abram and Abraham.[86] In both
Cher 7 and *Mut* 60-76 Philo treats Ἀβράμ as meaning πατὴρ
μετέωρος, "uplifted father," dividing the word, the two parts
of which he then translates. When, however, Ἀβράμ is changed
to Ἀβραάμ, Philo has to undertake some elaborate exegesis.

Once again Hanson[87] identifies the Hebrew that Philo is using
without seeing that in translating the meaning of Abraham's
name as he wishes it, Philo is understanding actual forms of
Hebrew words and not simply their roots. So for Philo Abraham
means πατὴρ ἐκλεκτὸς ἠκοῦς, "elect father of sound,"[88] a
translation of אב ברור המון. By taking the first letter or
two of each word, the name Abraham (אברהם) can be reconstructed.

In Genesis itself (17:5) when Abram's name is lengthened,
the reason is given that היית לאב המון גוים , as if the last
syllable of the name is taken to be the first of המון . In
fact, the rabbis took Abraham's name-change as the biblical
rationale for the use of *nôṭārîqôn* in exegesis, a method whereby
words are broken up and each letter or syllable is treated as
an abbreviation: "How is *noṭarikon* deduced from Scripture?
We know it from this: And THOU SHALT BE AB HAMON the father
of a multitude of nations, the *resh* being lacking."[89] This
section of Genesis Rabbah makes it clear that אב המון was
itself considered to be an example of *nôṭārîqôn* and this
resulted in the application of *nôṭārîqôn* to the phrase itself
(*b. šabb.* 105a). The reasoning of the rabbis is that since
scripture itself provides the interpretation of the lengthened
name Abraham through *nôṭārîqôn*, it must be the case that *rêš*
be ignored.

R. Aḥa solved the difficulty of interpreting the name in
another ingenious way. By expounding the name-change of Sarai
to Sarah and by alluding to Prov 12:4 and Gen 21:12, which,
taken together, detail the crowning of Abraham by his wife,
R. Aḥa holds to the tradition that the *hē'* in Abraham's name
comes from the fact that the *yôd* of Sarai requires two *hē'*'s

to make up its numerical value: Sarah has one, Abraham the other.[90] Or again the Talmud offers another interpretation perhaps closer to the Bible's own: Abraham's position is changed with his name from that of father "to Aram" to father "to the whole world."[91]

In considering Philo's etymology of Abraham, therefore, several factors need to be kept in mind: 1) there is no consensus in Jewish (or Christian) tradition that the name be interpreted in any one way;[92] 2) there is evidence, albeit late, that Abraham's name was used as the rationale for the use of *nôtārîqôn* as an exegetical method; 3) *b. Šabb.* 105a witnesses to the fact that "chosen" or "elect" (root: בחר) was to be applied to the *bêt* in interpreting the phrase אב המון; 4) Philo is familiar with a tradition based upon the Hebrew since he scoffs at the godless man who expounds the addition of *alpha* to Abram's name and in a self-satisfying way notes that the same man ended up dead not long afterwards - surely Philo is concerned not just that the man scoffed at the name change but that also he misunderstood the nature of that change by basing his remarks on the Greek text.[93]

This is not the place to attempt to settle the question whether or not Philo knew Hebrew and, if he did, how much;[94] rather the aim of the use of this example is to suggest that Philo considered himself to be using valid exegetical method; yet, it is worth including some remarks on Philo and the Septuagint. The evidence of the Septuagint seems to support the thesis that Philo was well acquainted with both Hebrew and Greek texts at this point, and in general. The Septuagint renders the phrase under discussion in Gen 17:5 as πατέρα πολλῶν ἐθνῶν (המון → πολλῶν). Elsewhere the Septuagint translates

המון by ἦχος seven times.[95] Nowhere is המון rendered by
φωνή or any of its synonyms that could have served Philo
as suitably for his purposes; rather, המון is restricted by
its Hebrew meaning to ἰσχύς, πλῆθος, πλοῦτος, δύναμις, μέγας,
φόβος and πολῦανδρίον - once it is homoeophonically translated
as ἁρμονία.[96]

Philo's choice of ἦχος to represent המון is, therefore,
not based solely on a good acquaintance with the Septuagint
but on knowledge of how the translators had rendered המון
elsewhere in the scriptures. Unless Philo obtained his
tradition of the meaning of Abraham from another source, his
interpretation would suggest that he was competent in handling
both Greek and Hebrew texts, but that he normally chose the
former, since that was the medium in which he himself normally
worked. Whatever the case may be, the presence of the two
etymologies discussed above in the writings of Philo helps
make the point that not only might he have known Hebrew, but
also Philo used the exegetical methods of wordplay and
abbreviation.[97]

In other places than in his etymologies did Philo use
exegetical methods akin to those associated with the rabbis.
Although I. Christiansen has demonstrated clearly that in
De Agricultura Philo's method most closely approximates that
of the Greek *diairesis*, in which a basic idea is divided into
its opposite secondary ideas and these ideas are in their turn
divided,[98] that alone does not necessarily substantiate her
claim that the diairetic technique is the basis of the whole
of Philo's allegorical method. Indeed, as Hammerton-Kelly has
pointed out,[99] *De Agricultura* itself is in part constructed
around the use of *gězērâ šāwâ* in its rabbinic mode, whereby

biblical verses can be juxtaposed in commentary or interpretation
simply because they share a common word or two.

   Thus in *De Agricultura* the section beginning with talk
of the combination of horse and rider (72) contains a quotation
of Deut 20:1: "If thou shalt go out to war against thine
enemies and see horse and rider (ἵππον καὶ ἀναβάτην)   and much
people, thou shalt not be afraid, because the Lord thy God is
with thee" (78). Taken with *Agr* 72-77, which is presupposed
in the discussion following the quotation,[100] Philo continues
to develop his commentary by discussing another biblical verse
before he cites it with its common words: "Let us sing to
the Lord, for gloriously hath he been glorified; horse and
rider (ἵππον καὶ ἀναβάτην)   He threw into the sea" (Exod 15:1, 21;
Agr 82). In *Agr* 84, as Hammerton-Kelly points out,[101] ἵππος
alone enables Philo to introduce Deut 17:16: "because he shall
not multiply horses to himself, nor turn the people back to
Egypt." While what follows in the commentary elucidates Egypt,
it also presupposes the diairetic distinction between rider
(ἀναβάτης)   and horseman (ἱππεύς) which is one reason for
Philo's citing of Gen 49:17 at *Agr* 94, again with the use of
gĕzērâ šāwâ, ἵππος , and that biblical quotation is the basis
of the discussion until the end of the unit at *Agr* 123.

   A similar construction, the use of *gĕzērâ šāwâ* within a
diairetic framework, can be seen in *Sac* 1-10. This section
is a commentary upon Gen 4:2: "And He added (προσέθηκε) to
this that she brought forth Abel his brother."[102] After an
explanation of the terms that Philo says he is about to use,
in which the distinction is made between addition and subtraction
and their necessary separation in philosophical discussion,

Philo talks of Abraham, citing Gen 25:8, "his is added
(προστίθεται) [103] to the people of God," of Jacob who "is
added (προστίθεσθαι) to something better, when he left the
worse,"[104] an allusion to Gen 49:33, and of Isaac who "is
added (προστίθεται) and allotted to another company."[105]

All these are then diaıretically contrasted with Moses
about whom προστίθημι is never used (*Sac* 8-10) and Philo
concludes the unit: "such ıs the meaning of the words that
God added (προσθεῖναι) to the mind the birth of the perfect
good. The good is holiness and the name of holiness is Abel."[106]

These examples from *De Agricultura* and *De Sacrificiis
Abelis et Caini* illustrate how Philo composes his exposition
of bıblical texts along chains of analogous biblical phrases,
the analogy often beıng maintained through only one word. In
that way the reader is guided away from a solely literal
understanding of the text to the allegorıcal meaning.

Other exegetical techniques are in evidence ın Philo's
work. Although more interested in content than form, S. Belkin
has pointed to other ways in which Philo uses exegetical methods
that are more frequently associated with the rabbis. He cites
examples of Philo's use of *qal wāḥōmer*, inference from the less
to the more important and vice versa,[107] and of *binyan 'āb*, the
generalization of a special law.[108] In respect to tautology
Philo seems to have held a similar view to that of R. Ishmael
who denied that tautology was possible in scripture - each
repetıtion must have a new significance.[109] Belkin also cites
a lıst of passages from Philo that in his view depend upon hıs
having used a Hebrew text, such that Belkin can only conclude
that if Philo knew no Hebrew, "he must have been informed of

the Hebrew text by Alexandrian adepts of Hebrew Scripture."[110]

3) Conclusion

From these brief comments that include some considerable elements of detail on specific points, it no longer seems possible to confine Philo solely to the role of an exponent of Greek philosophy in the Alexandrian Jewish community. At the least some interaction with contemporary Judaism has been demonstrated and it seems as if Philo was an author "equally at home in the Hellenistic and the Jewish conventions of exposition"[111] - if indeed they are different and distinguishable. For the purposes of this study it is sufficient that such "conventions of exposition" have been seen to have existed in Philo's time and that the methods used included but also went beyond those attributed in formulation to his near contemporary, R. Hillel the Elder, to whom rabbinic literature assigns the seven *middôt* of interpretation.[112]

b. The Targums

1) Introduction

The recent growth of interest in the study of the targums[113] has come about largely because of the publication of fragments of the so-called Palestinian Targum by P. Kahle,[114] because of the discovery of a nearly complete copy of a targum to the Pentateuch by A. Díez Macho[115] and because of the presence of written targums among the finds from Qumran.[116] The interrelationship of the various targum recensions, the dates of their composition and redaction, and the establishment of the trajectories into which fit the various traditions reflected in those recensions are complex questions indeed and

beyond the scope of the present study. A few introductory
remarks are appropriate, however, as justification for
including a section on the targums in this book.

Firstly, although *Tg. Onqelos* is often considered apart
because of its Babylonian provenance and its apparent word
for word translation, recent studies[117] have demonstrated
that it contains considerable haggadic material and that sometimes it overlaps considerably, even in the use of whole
phrases, with the targum tradition represented in the various
Palestinian recensions. Evidence from *Tg. Onqelos* is thus
included in the examples that follow.[118]

Secondly, arguments concerning the date of the targums
are based on the linguistic evidence for which Qumran Aramaic
is taken as the fixed starting point. But there seems little
agreement amongst scholars. In relation to *Neofiti I* Díez
Macho has refined his original proposal that it is to be dated
early[119] by arguing that its Aramaic is in many places similar
to that of Qumran; where it differs, the difference is not
necessarily one of time but rather is that of a spoken popular
Aramaic *(Tg. Neofiti)* over against a literary Aramaic (Qumran).
On the other hand J. A. Fitzmyer supports a more rigid
evolutionary approach to Aramaic;[120] he insists that the
language of the Palestinian targum in all of its recensions
is later than Qumran Aramaic and must be recognized as such.[121]
Thus whilst the dictum that whatever disagrees with the Mishnah
is pre-mishnaic cannot be applied across the board, it can be
argued that in actual phraseology and morphology the targums
may have preserved *forms* dating back to the late Second Temple
period. At the least from the point of view of *content* the

targums definitely have a place in discussion of first
century B.C. and first century A.D. exegesis; ever since
the pioneering work of A. Geiger[122] evidence has been
accumulating for pre-tannaitic traditions of interpretation.[123]

Consideration of the date of the targums makes some remarks
about the place of the LXX in all this pertinent as a third
point. Although there appears to be on occasion a certain
correlation between the LXX and the targumic interpretations
of scripture,[124] there seems to be little evidence whereby
septuagintal material can be used directly to date targumic
traditions or *vice versa*. For example, the LXX renders what
is written as לב קמי in the MT (Jer 51:1) as χαλδαίους. It
is impossible to determine whether the LXX translates and
interprets by '*atbaš*[125] from a text similar to that of the MT
or whether in a Babylonian recension the MT represents a
deliberate concealment of כשדים; the targum in all recensions
follows the LXX tradition and speaks of the land of כשדאי. It
is not necessary, therefore, to conclude from this that the
LXX and the targums have "les mêmes méthodes targumiques,"[126]
except coincidentally, if indeed there is any interpretation
taking place.

Lastly, bearing in mind that absolute contemporaneity
with Qumran materials is not at the moment provable, it is
worth venturing to investigate the method of exegesis that
the targumists use, for clearly all scholars now agree that
there exists such a method. R. Le Déaut has attempted to outline the targumic methodology which, he mentions, overlaps
that found in the "genre midrashique."[127] He lists six

tendencies:

    1. The Bible is treated as a whole which is
complete in itself and which can be clarified
from the juxtaposition of biblical texts one
with another.

    2. The targum has a synthetic view of the whole
of the unrolling of the history of salvation.

    3. Everything in the text is of value and has
significance.

    4. The popular nature of the targum means that
it employs correspondingly popular methods:
"étiologies; histoires drôlatiques, voire salaces;
souci de préciser et déterminer d'ajouter des
détails, de trouver un nom aux lieux, aux personages
pour mieux concrétiser un récit."[128]

    5. Occasionally texts are isolated from their
contexts and treated more freely.

    6. The overall aim of the targumist is to render
the Hebrew text intelligible.

Le Déaut's list is an important pointer to what might be
expected to happen in a targumist's treatment of his Hebrew
but it fails to distinguish clearly between the presuppositions
that the targumist may have had, the aims which he hoped to
achieve and the methods by which he hoped to achieve those
aims.

    In making more precise the exegetical methodology of
the targumist especially as concerns Le Déaut's fourth point,
it is worth considering certain verses as they are treated in
the targums. Of necessity the expositions in the examples

given depend on minutiae but that should not invalidate
their use in the discussion since the targums intentionally
stay closer to the text of the Hebrew scriptures, as they
translate-interpret, than do those texts solely interested
in interpretation.[129] It will become clear that the most
evident technique of interpretation used by the targumists
is that of *'al tiqrē'* whereby the Hebrew text is understood
in a slightly different way from the tradition represented
in the consonantal MT.

What is proposed in the following examples is put
forward with extreme caution, since one cannot be exactly
sure from what form of Hebrew text the targumist was translating.
Because of this, all the examples are taken from the Pentateuch,
for scholars are fairly certain that for the Pentateuch at
least Qumran (and therefore Palestine?) possessed, among
others, copies of a text often closest to that represented
by MT; also the variety of recensions of the Palestinian
Targum to the Pentateuch provide more comparative material
from which the history of the tradition of certain targumic
interpretations can be better reconstructed.

2) Examples

The first example concerns ויכל in *Genesis 2:2*. The
MT implies that God in creating worked on the Sabbath. The
LXX altered the text so that God completed his work on the
sixth day; the Peshitta and Samaritan versions agree with
the LXX. *Genesis Rabbah* 10:9 unfolds the manifold ways in
which the rabbis tried to skirt the issue: God had finished
his work just as the Sabbath commenced; it only *appears* as if
God completed his work on the seventh day; the sabbath itself

was created to complete creation (but it was not created,
of course, on the sabbath); the sabbath is the perfection of
the world.[130]

Of the targumic versions of Gen 2:2, *Tg. Onqelos*
renders ויכל by ושיצי. B. Grossfeld takes the use of this
particular word to demonstrate that *Tg. Onqelos* is understanding
it in the sense of cessation (from creation) rather than
completion (of creation).[131] Although it is difficult to
date the tradition of interpretation as represented by *Tg.
Onqelos*, it is noteworthy that a similar interpretation does
not occur elsewhere in rabbinic literature.

Among the Palestinian recensions both *Tg. Pseudo-Jonathan*
and *Tg. Neofiti* render ויכל of Gen 2:2 as ואשלם, thus remaining
close to the MT, though attempting to create in their choice
of words an ambiguity of completion/perfection, the latter of
which is akin to rabbinic understanding. The *Fragmentary
Targum*, however, reads וחמיד at this point: "and on the
seventh day the word of the Lord was *filled with desire* for
his work which he had made."[132] The targum has thus understood
that ויכל comes from כלה, "to desire, long for, pine," as in
2 Sam 13:39 but always with a *lāmed* since this verb only occurs
with that particular meaning in the idiom כלה ל.[133] What is
of especial importance is that one manuscript of *Tg. Onqelos*[134]
also at this place reads וחמיד, suggesting that an ancient
Palestinian interpretation has at some point influenced *Tg.
Onqelos* as they encountered one another. The absence of this
interpretation from any rabbinic understanding of Gen 2:2 and
its distinctiveness over against the other recensions of the
targum at this point suggest that the deliberate use of *ʾal*

tiqrē' in the *Fragmentary Targum* and the interpretation that
results from its use are pre-tannaitic.

A second example of *'al tiqrē'* concerns the understanding
of בני אלהים and נפילים in *Genesis 6:1* and *4* respectively.
Until the middle of the second century A.D., it can be reasonably ascertained that the בני אלהים were identified as angels;
indeed, 1 Enoch 6-11, a midrash on Gen 6:1-4, is dependent on
this identification.[135] After R. Simeon b. Johai[136] every
effort is made to exclude the connection between בני אלהים
and angels from Jewish literature; where angels are mentioned
they appear to be merely parts of old interpretation that have
not been removed and none of them has any link with Gen 6:1-4.[137]

The targum recensions reflect such a development in the
tradition. *Tg. Onqelos* renders בני אלהים by בני רברביא and
הנפילים by גיבריא; *Onqelos* is followed in the former by *Tg.
Ps.-Jonathan* and in the latter by *Tg. Neofiti*.[138] But the
Palestinian Targum represents the older understanding which
R. Simeon rules against, in that *Tg. Neofiti Margin* reads
מלאכיא, "angels," instead of *Tg. Neofiti*'s בני דיינא, and
more interestingly, at least as far as exegetical method is
concerned, *Tg. Ps.-Jonathan* renders הנפילים by the phrase
שמחזאי ועזאל הינון נפלו מן שמיא. By the application of *'al
tiqrē'* the targumist reads נְפוּלִים for נְפִילִים. This is not to
suggest that that understanding of the text is necessarily
original to the targumist,[139] but merely to assert that here
seems to be a clear indication that the targum represents an
early, even pre-Christian, interpretation through the application
of a particular exegetical method to the Hebrew text; P. Alexander
concludes, indeed, that of the three traditions of fallen angels

which he discusses[140] *Tg. Ps.-Jonathan* represents the oldest
form of the story.

   Another example involving angels suggests the use of
hilluf (anagram)[141] in the interpretation of *Genesis 32:25* as
represented in *Tg. Neofiti*. There the angel who wrestles with
Jacob is named specifically as Sariel;[142] he describes himself
in v27 as "chief of those who praise."[143] This secondary
description is common to the whole Palestinian Targum and
also occurs in Pseudo-Philo (1st C. A.D.).[144] G. Vermes has
pointed out that Sariel is the angel named at 1QM 9:12-15[145]
who has not appeared among lists of the four archangels prior
to Qumran literature.[146] As well as providing a parallel to
1QM 9:12-15, which with Pseudo-Philo helps date the tradition
represented in *Tg. Neofiti, Neofiti* also helps toward an
understanding of the name of Israel in intertestamental
tradition.

   Over against the MT etymology "for you have striven (שרית)
with God and with men and have prevailed," which is variously
explained as from the root שרה,[147] or the understanding of the
versions,[148] the targumists render the Hebrew with the Aramaic
רב *(Tg. Onqelos)* or אתרבב (Palestinian recensions), "to rule,
dominate, act as a prince." "In other words," concludes Vermes,
"they attribute to the root שרה the sense of שרר, 'to be a
prince, rule,' a denominative verb from *śar*, 'prince'."[149]
Aquila and Symmachus support this in their use of ἄρχειν, "to
rule." So Vermes justifiably translates the etymology of
Tg. Neof. Gen 32:29 as "for you have conducted yourself as a
prince with angels before the Lord, and with men, and have
prevailed against them."[150]

The targumist, therefore, is understanding part of the
etymology of Israel as dependent upon associating it with
the root שרר, but that derivation and his complete understanding
rests upon his association of Israel and Sariel. Sariel
interprets Israel, firstly through the exegetical method of
hilluf (anagram) which justifies the juxtaposition of the two
names, and secondly through *nôṭārîqôn*[151] whereby the name is
seen to be an abbreviation for its explanation. This use of
anagram may go a long way in explaining why in 1 Enoch 10:1
the archangel's name appears as Οὐριήλ in one Greek manuscript
(G^S), as Ἰστραήλ in the other Greek manuscript (G^g) and as
ă-să-ré-yă-lé-yē-r(e) with many variations in the Ethiopic
manuscripts.[152]

In the targumic treatment of *Exodus 15:8* there seems to
be another example of a pre-tannaitic use of *'al tiqrē'*. The
phrase of interest is נצבו כמו נד נזלים. *Tg. Neofiti* renders
this phrase by קמו צרירין היך זיקיא דמיא נזליא, "they stood
bound like water bags of flowing water;" this is also the
phraseology of *Tg. Ps.-Jonathan* and the *Fragmentary Targum*.
A fragment from the Cairo Geniza published by W. Baars reads
קמון להון צרירין בזיקיא מיא נזליא,[153] "They stood for them
bound by bags of flowing water," which detracts somewhat from
the miraculous nature of the event even though Yahweh provides
the water-skins.[154] All the recensions of the Palestinian
Targum, therefore, agree on reading זיקיא for the Hebrew נֵד,
which is thus being consistently understood by means of *'al
tiqrē'* as Hebrew נֹאד.[155]

That this is an ancient traditional interpretation not
necessarily primarily dependent on the originality of the

targumist appears from its occurrence in the LXX,[156] the
Peshitta and elsewhere.[157]

Further attestation that this tradition in the Palestinian
Targum is pre-tannaitic comes from *Tg. Neofiti*'s reading of
the very next verse, Exod 15:9. E. Levine has pointed out
that the unspecified hand of the MT is specified in *Tg. Neofiti*
as the right hand against normative rabbinic tradition.[158]
B. Menaḥ. 36b-37a rules, through the application of Isa 48:13,
Judg 5:26 and Ps 74:11, that all unspecified hands in the text
are left hands: "Our Rabbis taught: *thy hand*, that is the
left hand."[159] The indefinite "our Rabbis" suggests that here
is an ancient tradition that did not require any particular
name for its validation.

Exod 22:4 provides a final example of pre-tannaitic
interpretative method. This *locus classicus* for the study of
targumic interpretation serves as a good illustration of the
dictum that a text that contains a tradition which goes against
standard mishnaic codified law, most probably antedates the
Mishnah. Not surprisingly *Tg. Onqelos* agrees with the mishnaic
position on this text and renders the disputed word, בְּעִירֹה, by
בעיריה, "cattle."

P. Kahle was the first to notice, however, that the
Geniza Fragment for this verse understood בעירה as יקידתה,
"fire,"[160] whereas the understanding of the Mishnah (*B. Qam.* 6:4)
is that the words from the root בער in Exod 22:4 are to be
taken as "cause to be eaten," "beast" and "feed" whereas in
v5 they are taken as "kindled" and "fire."[161]

J. L. Teicher voiced the loudest objection to Kahle's
interpretation of the text.[162] He made three points: that

יקידתה is feminine but the verb depending on it is masculine; that the targum fragment renders only the noun (בעירה MT) as "fire"; that יבקר cannot mean "to visit" as Kahle suggested, but rather is an alternative spelling of יפקר, "to abandon one's rights," "to disregard." In the second edition of his book[163] Kahle ignored Teicher's criticisms[164] whilst commending the work of G. Schelbert.[165]

Schelbert answers Teicher's first objection by arguing convincingly that the verb יוכל can only be an 'aph^{c}ēl and that, therefore, יקידתה is no longer its subject: there is thus no conflict in gender. For the second objection Schelbert proposes from the photographs that in fact יוכל should be better read as ייוקד, 'aph^{c}ēl, meaning "brennen machen, anzunden, verbrennen."[166] This then means that Cairo Geniza Fragment A agrees with *Tg. Neofiti* at this point. For the initial occurrence of בער in Exod 22:4, which Fragment A translates as יבקר, Schelbert offers for the Aramaic the meaning "säubern," that is, to purify or cleanse the field by means of fire.[167] *Tg. Neofiti* again supports this conjecture by understanding all three occurrences of the root בער in Exod 22:4 as to be translated by יקד.

Thus Fragment A and *Tg. Neofiti* have the same understanding of Exod 22:4 throughout. Since the LXX represents the understanding of בעירה as "beast" rather than "fire,"[168] it can only be supposed that in encountering the ambiguous unpointed Hebrew text the targumist deliberately decided not to read (*'al tiqrē'*) בְּעִירָה but rather chose to interpret the whole verse as being about fire, בְּעֵרָה; it is possible that he was influenced by the only other use of this word in the Hebrew text, at the end of Exod 22:5.

Not only the anti-mishnaic interpretation of the targum
recensions but also the occurrence of that interpretation
indirectly in *m. B. Qam.* 6:4 and overtly in *Mekilta,*[169]
shows that this exegesis of Exod 22:4 is indeed old.
J. Heinemann concludes that here the *"Targumim* have undoubtedly
preserved an ancient pre-tannaitic halakhic *midrash,"*[170] "un
derecho pretannaitico."[171]

3) Conclusion

Thus it seems evident that throughout the targumic
material available for study there can be located very specific
uses of particular exegetical methods for rendering the Hebrew
text more intelligible according to a particular tradition of
that text's interpretation, and that these exegeses belong in
many instances to pretannaitic times. Furthermore, the targumic
use of such exegetical principles shows that they belong not
only in Alexandria, as Philo's work has shown, but also in
Palestine. The use of the Bible at Qumran confirms the
pervasiveness of these principles in Judaism of the Hellenistic
era.

4. *Exegesis at Qumran: Some General Remarks*

It would be rash to suppose that all that has been written
on the use of the Bible at Qumran, and on Qumran biblical
exegesis in particular, could be summarized and presented here
in a few short pages: some terse remarks must suffice.

It is clear that the scriptures were used in a variety
of ways at Qumran:[172] "with the exception of the Copper Scroll
and a few fragments, all the texts discovered in the eleven

caves are either biblical manuscripts or works based on
Scripture: exegetical therefore, in the broader sense of
the word."[173] In many of the non-biblical manuscripts there
are direct citations of scripture which are interpreted or
used as support for the content of the particular document,
and the part played by implicit citation of scripture, allusion
to biblical texts and the use of biblical imagery is no less
important (e.g. in 1QS, 1QSa, 1QM, CD). For the rest, alongside the pesharim, commentaries on biblical books in the form
of text citation followed by interpretation, there are works
which expand and retell biblical narrative (1QapGen), pieces
of targums (4QtgLev, 11QtgJob), texts fashioned after biblical
books (1QH) or perhaps containing traditions for some reason
excluded from the normally accepted ("canonized") scripture
(4QPrNab, 4QPssJosh), texts with midrashic features (1QSb,
4QPB, 4QFlor, 11QMelch) as well as other non-biblical texts
(4QTestim, 4QOrd). Any consideration of the use of the Bible
in the Qumran texts must, therefore, be based on this broad
spectrum of texts with their multiple use of the biblical books.

In seeking to identify in some small way wherein lies
the unity of approach to the Bible of the Qumran covenanters,
if there is unity as such, it can be ascertained that, lacking
a fixed canon, certain books were held as more or less
authoritative by the sect. These included the Pentateuch,[174]
the Prophets,[175] almost certainly the other books that were
later included in the authorized canon, as well as certain of
the Apocrypha and Pseudepigrapha (Ben Sira, Tobit, *Jubilees,
Enoch, T. Levi* and *Naphtali*). It is these texts that are used
as the basis of the ordering of the community, and it is these

texts, especially the Pentateuch and the Prophets, that are
interpreted in detail and appealed to or alluded to in support
of that ordering.

Although a case can be made for the existence of a
specialized vocabulary used by the sectarians in their
discussion of both halakic[176] and prophetic materials (e.g.
formulae of introduction), such a word-study approach to the
materials already limits the number of texts that can be
considered and possibly imposes an unwarranted classification
upon the texts themselves. In fact, the largest part of the
literature devoted to the use of the Bible at Qumran has
concerned itself with attempting to define the term פשר in
the hope that that would be the key to any understanding of
what the commentaries in particular may contain.

It is in the definition of פשר that some have seen the
best answer to the question of how the text of the commentary
relates to that of the biblical citation. Yet since 4QFlor
contains both the word מדרש and the word פשר in relation one
to the other, the only Qumran document so to do, a detailed
discussion of these terms and the way in which they function
in Qumran literature, and also their possible use for
designating generic categories, will be postponed until
treatment of 4QFlor. Of note at this point is that the
discussion of the pesharim has, in general, followed either
one of two approaches. Summarily these are on the one hand
the stress that the pesharim are to be considered within the
development of intentional scriptural interpretation on the
basis of the use of certain exegetical techniques,[177] a type
of interpretation that is evident in the Bible itself and

which culminates in the medieval Jewish commentaries; on the
other hand there is a more general understanding of the pesharim
as reflecting literary compositions based on a revelation
given to the interpreter: rationalistic explanations are
then false, irrelevant or incomplete.

The first approach has been supported by W. H. Brownlee
in various forms for many years[178] and has been further
enhanced by the work of L. H. Silberman and A. Finkel.
L. H. Silberman[179] proposed many more or less precise ways
in which the commentary (pesher proper) of 1QpHab was related
to the biblical citation through certain deliberate exegeses
involving various interpretative techniques. Silberman
reckons that the closest analogy to the pesharim is to be
found in the structure of the rabbinic midrash in which occurs
the formula פתר קריא followed by the "interpretation of
individual words or phrases within the verse in terms of the
specification of the meaning of the whole verse."[180] The
interpretations themselves are not revealed but they are
interpretations of revealed material (dreams or visions) and
the correspondence between commentary and citation is worked
out systematically. It is the belief of the interpreter that
it is valid to make the revealed vision contemporary that is
the starting point of the Qumran pesharim.

A. Finkel[181] adopted a similar line in understanding the
interrelation of scripture and commentary but he relies for
the most part on dream interpretations for his extra-Qumran
examples since he maintains that the pesharim are closely
linked to the dream interpretations of the OT, though also to
the interpretations of the visions of Daniel. He too allows

that beyond the allegorical method of dream/vision
interpretation,[182] the interpreter deliberately employs
interpretative techniques: dual-reading *('al tiqrē')*, dual
meaning and word-splitting *(nôṭārîqôn)* to reveal the hidden
meaning of the text.[183]

More recently E. Slomovic has tentatively discussed the
use of rabbinic exegetical techniques in the Qumran writings.[184]
Although he warns that no techniques of exegesis are explicitly
named in Qumran literature, he amasses sufficient evidence to
make the use of *gĕzērâ šāwâ, zēker lĕdābār* and *'asmaktā* seem
very probable at Qumran.

Alongside these scholars, and the list could be augmented,
several have concentrated more on an analysis of the content
of the Qumran biblical interpretation than on precise discussion of methods whereby that content was reached. Among
those seeing Qumran exegesis as lying close to the mainstream
of midrashic development in the intertestamental period is,
above all, G. Vermes.[185] R. Bloch also understood the pesharim
within the context of the early midrashim,[186] but she noted
that where they come close to apocalyptic literature ("revelation")
then they diverge generically from the more reflective rabbinic
midrashim. It is in fact this apocalyptic or revelatory
characteristic of the pesharim in particular, but also of some
of the other Qumran scrolls (e.g. 1QM), that has been the cause
of considerable difficulty in the second approach to the use
of scripture in the Qumran literature, for, of its very nature,
revelation eludes those who desire a complete systematic
explanation of scriptural usage at Qumran.

Shortly after Brownlee's initial treatment of the exegetical

methods used in 1QpHab, K. Elliger published an extensive
commentary on the scroll[187] with some lengthy remarks about
the "Methode der Auslegung"[188] of which the last section is
a critique of Brownlee's thirteen Hermeneutic Principles.
Elliger's own understanding of the exegetical method used in
1QpHab is based on the order of priorities that he saw the
interpreter to have: primarily the interpreter wished to use
the text of Habakkuk word for word or slightly paraphrased,
secondarily he would resort to atomization of the text to
convey the desired interpretation, and only if there was no
other way would he use other modes of exegesis (allegory,
wordplay, rearrangement of the text, use of corruptions in
the text, etc.).[189] With the understanding that the prophets
were preaching about the endtime and that he was living in
that time, the interpreter, according to Elliger, revealed the
mysteries of the prophetic words in the same way as dreams and
visions are interpreted in the book of Daniel. Yet therein
lies the ambivalence of Elliger's presentation, for even in
the book of Daniel the interpretations are somewhat midrashic;[190]
also Elliger does not totally exclude midrashic exegetical
techniques from his explanations of the connection between
citation and commentary,[191] though he does minimize their role.

Both F. F. Bruce and O. Betz have developed understandings
of the use of scripture at Qumran that allow for the supposed
dichotomy between revealed interpretation and the deliberate
use of exegetical techniques, a dichotomy to which Elliger's
work bears witness. Bruce maintains assuredly that as
"principles" in the Qumran use of the prophets must be seen
the attitude that God's revelation to the prophets could only

be comprehended with the interpretation that He gave to the
Teacher of Righteousness through revelation, and the notion
that all the words of the prophets had reference to the time
of the end which was the present.[192] These principles were
put into operation through the atomization of the text, the
selection of variant readings, allegorization and the making
comtemporary of the prophets' words.[193]

O. Betz also recognizes the primary position that revelation
occupies as the correct perspective from which to view both the
prophetic oracle and the Qumran interpretation;[194] for Betz
the exegetical technique employed in the interpretation is
allegorical, and the authority of the interpretation depends
not upon any particular exegetical method but on the correct
reading of scripture itself from which can be calculated the
very imminence of the endtime.[195] That of itself vindicates
and justifies the claims of the interpreter, be he the Righteous
Teacher or anybody else.[196] Other scriptures too are to be
applied in various ways to the ordering of the sect because
of the belief of the members of the sect in the correctness
of their understanding of their own situation.

Beyond the suggestions of these scholars M. P. Miller has
noted that several factors need to be taken into account in
considering pesher: its use of midrashic methods and techniques,
its paraphrastic structure akin to the targums and its function
within an eschatological context - also the unique position of
the interpreter as one favoured by God to unlock the mysteries
of the prophets.[197] D. Patte has also pointed to the importance of the techniques used in the interpretation of the
prophets' visions,[198] yet he also stresses that the pesharim

are the fruit of "an inspired search of Scripture."[199]
M. P. Horgan offers a similar picture: whilst the pesharim
contain divine revelations, yet the various biblical texts
are interpreted in a variety of modes involving a number of
exegetical techniques.[200]

There would appear, therefore, to be an impasse in the
understanding of the use of the Bible at Qumran, particularly
as regards the pesharim. It seems as if all the ingredients
of the Qumran use of scripture have been described more than
adequately but that the description is not entirely satisfying
as an explanation of the whole. From the next two chapters
it should become clear that in all of the Qumran documents
that cite or allude to biblical texts one should expect the
use of certain and various exegetical techniques that are more
or less close to those used and accepted later by the rabbis;
at the least there is an exegetical tradition represented which
in some instances goes back to scripture itself and which rests
upon certain valid inherited interpretations of scripture.
Furthermore, it is also noteworthy that no one technique is
the prerogative of any particular kind of literature, pesher,
targum, sectarian halakah or whatever. Thus the use of exegetical
techniques is not solely constitutive of the genre, if that it
be, of pesher;[201] neither for that matter is its eschatological
outlook.

These observations will receive their complete significance
when the genre of material in 4QFlor is discussed. Suffice
it to say for the moment that the use of exegetical techniques
abounds in all the scrolls that in any way refer to scripture.
Inspiration, if any, does not lie in the result of the exegesis

as such, in its content, but rather in the ability of any
member of the community and especially the Teacher of
Righteousness to interpret scripture through the correct
application of exegetical techniques. If the techniques
had not been used, then there would have been no objective
means whereby the Qumran audience could have judged the
validity or otherwise of the "inspired" interpretation.

NOTES

[1]For the purposes of this study the sectarian Qumran
writings are taken as from the centuries immediately preceding
the destruction of the second temple. For a summary statement
to this effect and bibliographical support, see, e.g.,
R. N. Longenecker, *Biblical Exegesis in the Apostolic Period*
(Grand Rapids: W. B. Eerdmans, 1975), 26 and n.19.

[2]It is to be regretted that the method of comparative
midrash is of little use for the study of 2 Samuel 7 and
Psalms 1 and 2 in intertestamental literature. Philo, Josephus
and the various works of the Apocrypha and Pseudepigrapha
hardly allude to either text. Similarly there is no messianism
present in the targum of 2 Samuel 7; see S. H. Levey, *The
Messiah: An Aramaic Interpretation, The Messianic Exegesis
of the Targum* (MHUC 2; Cincinnati: Hebrew Union College), 37.

[3]E.g., that is the very assumption of the essay by
O. Eissfeldt expressed in its title, "Die kleinste literarische
Einheit in den Erzählungsbüchern des Alten Testaments" (*TBl*
6 1927 , 333-37). More recently, the first aspect of the
methodology outlined by W. Richter (*Exegese als Literatur-
wissenschaft*, Göttingen: Vandenhoeck & Ruprecht, 1971, 49-69)
is entitled "Einheit oder Zusammengesetztheit des Textes."
Also, R. Knierim ("Old Testament Form Criticism Reconsidered,"
Int 27 1973 , 459) in describing "a programmatic unfolding of
the method of structural interpretation" writes: "Assuming
that texts are entities, we are concerned with the factors
which constitute such entities."

[4]*Early Jewish Hermeneutic in Palestine*, SBLDS 22;
Missoula: Scholars Press, 1975, 63-81.

[5]*Early Jewish Hermeneutic,* 6.

[6]*Early Jewish Hermeneutic,* 7; this is to overemphasize
the contrariness between the language and the speaker. Cf.
J. M. Robinson's assessment of Bultmann: "Thus Bultmann's
program of demythologizing is embedded in a specific view of
language as the objectification of understanding, an objectification that is itself contrary to the understanding seeking
expression in it" ("Hermeneutic Since Barth," *The New
Hermeneutic*, NFT 2, eds. J. M. Robinson & John B. Cobb Jr.;
New York: Harper & Row, 1964, 37).

[7]*Early Jewish Hermeneutic,* 7.

[8]In fact, as Patte (*Early Jewish Hermeneutic,* 4) concludes
from M. Noth's essay, "The 'Re-presentation' of the Old
Testament in Proclamation" (*Essays on Old Testament Hermeneutics,*
ed. C. Westermann: Richmond: J. Knox, 1963, 80), there is no
choice between different kinds of hermeneutic once a specific
exegesis of the text has been accepted.

[9]Hence Patte's discussion of certain texts as revelation
alone is incorrect.

[10]"Biblical Interpretation among the Sectaries of the
Dead Sea Scrolls," *BA* 14 (1951), 54-76.

[11]*Studien zum Habakuk-Kommentar vom Totem Meer,* BHT 15;
Tübingen: J.C.B. Mohr, 1953.

[12]"Unriddling the Riddle. A Study in the Structure and
Language of the Habakkuk Pesher (1QpHab)," *RQ* 3 (1961-62), 323.

[13]"Targum, Midrash and the Use of the Old Testament in
the New Testament," *JSJ* 2 (1971), 53.

[14]Later these were derived from scripture itself; e.g.,
for the use of *nôṭārîqôn* as derivable from Gen 17:5, see
Gen. Rab. 46:7. Study of wherein lies the authority of these
principles or techniques is the subject of a dissertation in
itself; see the preliminary remarks of I. L. Seeligmann in
his paper "Voraussetzungen der Midrashexegese" (*Congress
Volume, Copenhagen 1953*, VTSup 1; Leiden: E. J. Brill, 1953,
150-81). Recognition of the use of these principles is
sufficient for our present purpose.

[15]*Paul and Rabbinic Judaism*, (London: SPCK, 1948, 1955[2]), 8.
For a recent exposition of Jewish education, particularly that
of the scribe, in the first century, see M. Goulder, *Midrash
and Lection in Matthew*, 10-13; he portrays a traditional rabbinic
picture and omits mention of Hellenistic influences: see
below n. 60.

[16]*Judentum und Hellenismus*, WUNT 10; Tubingen: J.C.B. Mohr,
1969, 1973[2]; ET, *Judaism and Hellenism*, 2 Vols., London: SCM,
Philadelphia: Fortress, 1974.

[17]*Judentum und Hellenismus*, 31.

[18]*Judentum und Hellenismus*, 49-50.

[19]MT reads: "Is not this the fast that I choose . . . .
to undo the thongs of the yoke and to let the oppressed go free
and for you (s.) to break every yoke."

[20]*Judentum und Hellenismus*, 99 - a bit of an overstatement.

[21]*Judentum und Hellenismus*, 112-114; though admittedly some

Jewish writings of the period appear deliberately purified
of Greek loanwords: yet, that in itself, shows the
pervasiveness of Greek.

[22]*Judentum und Hellenismus,* 125-52.

[23]*Judentum und Hellenismus,* 138-39. The polemics of
Ben Sira and the predilection for Greek names in the upper
class of Jerusalem from the end of the third century B.C.
point in this direction.

[24]*Judentum und Hellenismus,* 148-49.

[25]For those less privileged the local *bēt hamidrāš* and
the family were the sources of education.

[26]*Judentum und Hellenismus,* 451.

[27]*Judentum und Hellenismus,* 452, n. 809.

[28]*A Wandering Aramean: Collected Aramaic Essays,* SBLMS 25;
Missoula: Scholars Press, 1979, 49, n. 23. Fitzmyer also cites
other evidence of the Hellenization of Palestine at the time
of Jesus.

[29]E. Schürer, *The History of the Jewish People in the Age
of Jesus Christ* (175 B.C. - A.D. 135), revised and edited by
G. Vermes, F. Millar, M. Black, Vol. 2, Edinburgh: T. and T.
Clark, 1979, especially 417-22. This section on education in
the late Second Temple period acknowledges (422, n. 41) that
"although Jewish education founded on the Torah was intended
to be exclusive, it had to compete with the influence of
Hellenistic civilization." "The Cultural Setting," Section 22
in the same volume, similarly testifies to the extent of the
influence of Graeco-Roman culture though it argues also that

Judaism defended itself successfully against pagan religions;
it may be that the distinction is not altogether tenable.

[30] *Bridge Between the Testaments: A Reappraisal of
Judaism from the Exile to the Birth of Christianity*, PTMS 14;
Pittsburgh: Pickwick, 1976, 69-72, 91-95, and generally
throughout Part One.

[31] *Scriptures, Sects and Visions: A Profile of Judaism
from Ezra to the Jewish Revolts*, Philadelphia: Fortress, 1980,
especially chapters 4 and 9.

[32] E.g., Hengel (*Judentum und Hellenismus*, 183) points out
that from the sources that survive, it appears that whereas the
interest in Alexandrian Judaism was in philosophy, that in
Palestine seems to have been in history-writing. Indeed, Hengel
understands (356-57) that it is in the apocalyptic understanding
of history that there is "eine Frucht des jüdischen Kampfes um
die geistig-religiöse Selbstbehauptung gegenüber dem Einbruch
des hellenistischen Geistes in Jerusalem."

[33] *Judentum und Hellenismus*, 314-15.

[34] "Rabbinic Methods of Interpretation and Hellenistic
Rhetoric," *HUCA* 22 (1949), 239-64. Cf. Daube's article
"Alexandrian Methods of Interpretation and the Rabbis"
(*Festschrift Hans Lewald*, Basel: Helbing und Lichtenhahn,
1953, 27-44) for a discussion of the Hellenistic basis of
certain exegetical methods used by the rabbis but not included
in any list of *middôt*.

[35] "Rabbinic Methods of Interpretation," 252.

[36] "On the Third Chapter of the Lex Aquila," *LQR* 52 (1936),

265. In this Daube follows among others W. Bacher ("Hillel,"
The Jewish Encyclopedia, 6; New York: Funk and Wagnalls, 1904,
400). *The Encyclopedia Judaica* ("Hillel," *EncJud*, 8, col. 482)
presents the predominant current opinion (shared e.g. by
J. Goldin, "Hillel the Elder," *JR* 26 1946, 268): "It is not
to be assumed that Hillel was the first to formulate these seven
hermeneutical rules, but it does seem that he was one of the
first to apply them for the determination of practical *halakhah*."
This hardly advances the treatment of the rabbinic sources
beyond that of Bacher. Vermes, Millar and Black (Schürer,
The History of the Jewish People, Vol. 2, 333-34) understandably
do not attempt to analyze the history of the traditions
concerning Hillel and the *middôt*; presumably such analysis does
not fall within the scope of their work.

[37]The same citicism can be made of Chapter II of Bonsirven's
work *Exégèse rabbinique*, 77-115). However, Bonsirven provides
many useful examples of the various rabbinic exegetical principles
from rabbinic literature. Bonsirven's conclusion of the great
difference between Pauline and rabbinic exegesis lies not in
his critical treatment of his rabbinic sources as much as in
his conception of the nature of the Gospel that Paul was
preaching. It is that aspect of the kerygma that has led to
the exclusion of the NT from consideration in this study.

[38]Most clearly stated in "The Meaning of Oral Torah,"
Early Rabbinic Judaism,(SJLA 13; Leiden: E. J. Brill, 1975),
3-33. A typical statement that the Mishnah is the heir of
oral halakic midrashim since the time of Ezra is made by
B. M. Casper (*An Introduction to Jewish Bible Commentary*, New

York: T. Yoseloff, 1960, 30-31). One very important
corollary of Neusner's view of "oral" law is the suggestion
that the reliability of the oral preservation of the law is
a rabbinic device to ensure the supremacy of pharisaic-
rabbinic halakic traditions. There is no firm evidence that
material was not written down before the second century - in
fact, the opposite is most likely the case; e.g. Gamaliel and
the written Targum of Job (*Šabb.* 115a). D. Patte (*Early Jewish
Hermeneutic,* 13-15) is among the most recent to accept somewhat
uncritically the rabbinic assertions.

[39]E.g., Neusner would justifiably deny the usefulness for
critical study of the *middôt* of work such as that done by
S. Zeitlin ("Hillel and the Hermeneutic Rules," *JQR* 54 1963-64 ,
161-73). It is an approach to rabbinic materials similar to
that of Neusner that has negated the usefulness of most of the
rabbinic writings for this study - hence their omission from
this section on comparative material.

[40]שבעה דברים דרש הילל הזקן לפני זקני פתירא קל וחומר וגזירה
שוה ובינייו אב וכחוב אחד ושני כתובין וכלל ופרט ופרט וכלל וכיוצא
בו ממקום אחר ודבר הלמד מעניינו אליו שבע מידות דרש הילל הזקן
לפני בני פתירא (*Tosephta,* ed. M. S. Zuckermandel, Paserwalk,
Trier: Lintz, 1880-82 , Jerusalem: Wahrmann Books, 1963, 427;
ET for this passage: H. Danby, Tractate Sanhedrin, London: SPCK
1919, 76-77; J. Neusner, *The Rabbinic Traditions about the
Pharisees before 70* Part 1; Leiden: E. J. Brill, 1971, 240).
These principles are commented upon by H. L. Strack, *Einleitung
in Talmud und Midrasch* (München: C. H. Beck, 1976[6]), 96-99.
The list in *'Abot R. Nat.* A 37 is almost certainly dependent
upon that preserved earlier in this Tosefta passage (*'Abot R. Nat.*

A 37: Hebrew text: S. Schechter, אבות דרבי נתן, Vienna:
Lippe, 1887, 110; ET: J. Goldin, *The Fathers According to
Rabbi Nathan*, New Haven: Yale University, 1955, 154).

[41] *Rabbinic Traditions*, Part 1, 241.

[42] In fact, Hillel is credited with use of *gĕzērâ šāwâ*,
qal wāḥōmēr, and *hiqqiš*, this last not even being one of the
seven *middôt* (*y. Pesaḥ*. 6:1; French tr., M. Schwab, *Le Talmud
de Jerusalem*, Vol. 3, *Pesaḥim*, Paris: Imprimerie Nationale, 1874,
81-82; ET, Neusner, *Rabbinic Traditions*, Part 1, 246-48).   The
earlier version of the encounter in *t. Pesaḥ*. 4:13 (text ed.
S. Lieberman, *The Tosefta*, New York: The Jewish Theological
Seminary of America, 1962, *Moᶜed*, 165-66, 11.   80-94; ET, Neusner,
Rabbinic Traditions, Part 1, 231-32) does not cite the exegetical
principle by name, though it contains the same exegeses as
y. Pesaḥ. 6:1.

[43] *y. Pesaḥ*. 6:1 is composite too, but more clearly
emphasizes in its parts the subordination of Hillel to his·
masters.

[44] Neusner's sound conclusion based on form analysis on
t. Pesaḥ. 4:13 (*Rabbinic Traditions*, Part 1, 235) runs:
"That a shred of historically usable information is before
us seems to be unlikely."

[45] See F. Maass, "Von den Ursprüngen der rabbinischen
Schriftauslegung," *ZTK* 52 (1955), 156 for further literature
on this aspect of the use of exegetical *middôt*; also R. Loewe,
"The 'Plain' Meaning of Scripture in Early Jewish Exegesis,"

Papers of the Institute of Jewish Studies London (Vol. 1,
ed. J. G. Weiss; Jerusalem: Magnes, 1964), 152-53. Loewe
stresses the legal and therefore conservative setting mentioned
by Daube in relation to the origin of the list of *middôt*.

[46] *Hellenism in Jewish Palestine,* New York: Jewish
Theological Seminary of America, 1962^2.

[47] E.g., for Lieberman, *gĕzērâ šāwâ* = σύγκρισις προς ἴσον,
which term he sees used technically by Hermogenes (*Progymnasmata,*
8) amongst other 2nd century A.D. authors (*Hellenism in Jewish
Palestine,* 59); Daube ("Rabbinic Interpretation," 259) discusses
the Greek equivalents of some of the Hebrew terms, citing
Aristotle (*Rhetoric* 1:2:19).

[48] Citing material quoted in Liddell and Scott(*A Greek-
English Lexicon,* revised ed. Jones-McKenzie; Oxford: Clarendon,
1968^9, 1667) under σύγκρισις II.

[49] *Hellenism in Jewish Palestine,* 68-82. Lieberman relies
heavily upon Artemidorus' *Oniroeriticon* for comparative
material (2nd century A.D.).

[50] *Hellenism in Jewish Palestine,* 62.

[51] Thus some such presentation as that of F. Maass ("Von
den Ursprüngen der rabbischen Schriftauslegung") can arguably
be seen to describe the origin of much of the content of
rabbinic literature adequately in relation to certain determinative events in the times after Ezra, but its form and
terminology remain that of the tannaitic rabbis.

[52] Hebrew text: תורת כהנים (ed. J. H. Weiss, Vienna, 1862;
reprinted, New York: Om, 1946) 1-3; *Sifra or Torat Kohanim*

according to Codex Assemani LXVI (ed. L. Finkelstein; New
York: The Jewish Theological Seminary of America, 1956),
1-3: German Tr., J. Winter, *Sifra*, Breslau: S. Münz, 1938,
1-2. See Strack, *Einleitung in Talmud und Midrasch*, 99-100.

[53]Strack (*Einleitung in Talmud und Midrasch*, 199)
describes the rivalries of the rabbis of the 2nd century
A.D. Further straightforward description of R. Ishmael and
the thirteen *middôt* can be found in Schürer, *The History of
the Jewish People*, Vol. 2, revised and edited by Vermes, Millar
and Black, 376-77.

[54]Or *The Midrash of Thirty-Two Hermeneutic Rules*, New
York: Bloch, 1933. Formerly the text was known only from
the introduction to *Midrash Ha-Gadol* and in *Midrash Ha-Ḥefeṣ*:
German tr., Strack, *Einleitung in Talmud und Midrasch*, 100-108.

[55]On the actual number, see Lieberman, *Hellenism in
Jewish Palestine*, 68, n. 168.

[56]E.g., none of them mentions the principle of *'al tiqrē'* .
The most complete list of exegetical terms in rabbinic literature
is that of W. Bacher, *Die exegetische Terminologie der Jüdischen
Traditionsliteratur* (I, *Die bibelexegetische Terminologie der
Tannaiten*, Leipzig: J. C. Hinrichs, 1899; II *Die Bibel- und
traditionsexegetische Terminologie der Amoräer*, Leipzig:
J. C. Hinrichs, 1905). Furthermore, we must deny that the *middôt*
developed from 7 to 13 to 32 in an evolutionary way (e.g., as
understood by R. N. Longenecker, *Biblical Exegesis*, 33); rather,
the increase in *middôt* represents a relaxation of an earlier
rigidity in Pharisaic interpretation.

[57] *Hellenism in Jewish Palestine,* 68-82.

[58] Except perhaps portions of James and Jude. For an
exposition of James as a midrash on Psalm 12 see M. Gertner,
"Midrashim in the New Testament," *JSS* 7 (1962), 283-91.

[59] H. M. Shires (*Finding the Old Testament in the New,*
Philadelphia: Westminster, 1974, 29) expresses this well:
"Scripture was only one authority for early Christianity.
Another was Jesus Christ, and he alone is the key to the
Christian understanding of all scripture."

[60] E.g., K. Stendahl, *The School of St. Matthew* (Lund:
C.W.K. Gleerup, 1954); and more recently, R. H. Gundry, *The
Use of the Old Testament in St. Matthew's Gospel* (NovTSup 18;
Leiden: E. J. Brill, 1967; with a full bibliography, pp. 235-40),
W. Rothfuchs, *Die Erfüllungszitate des Matthäus-Evangeliums*
(BWANT 88; Stuttgart: W. Kohlhammer, 1969), M. Goulder,
Midrash and Lection in Matthew (London: SPCK, 1974) and
B. Gerhardsson, "The Hermeneutic Program in Matthew 22:37-40,"
Jews, Greeks and Christians (eds. R. Hammerton-Kelly and
R. Scroggs, SJLA 21; Leiden: E. J. Brill, 1976), 129-50.

[61] E.g., J. Bonsirven, *Exégèse rabbinique et exégèse
paulinienne* (Paris: Beauchesne, 1939), W. D. Davies, *Paul
and Rabbinic Judaism* (London: SPCK, 1948, 1955[2]), E. E. Ellis,
Paul's Use of the Old Testament (Grand Rapids: W. B. Eerdmans,
1957) and A. T. Hanson, *Studies in Paul's Technique and Theology*
(London: SPCK, 1974).

[62] *The New Testament and Rabbinic Judaism,* London: Athlone,
1956.

[63] *Kommentar zum Neuen Testament aus Talmud und Midrasch,*
München: C. H. Beck, 1924-28. As often pointed out, its
major weakness is its naive methodological appreciation of
the rabbinic sources such that it is really a 'Commentary on
the Talmud and Midrash from the NT'. Noteworthy for the
present observations is that the volume on Matthew contains
1055 pages whereas that on the rest of the Gospels and Acts
has only just over 800. Cf. a similar predominance of Matthew
in M. Smith's *Tannaitic Parallels to the Gospels* (SBLMS 6;
Philadelphia: SBL, 1951).

[64] *Hellenism in Jewish Palestine,* 78.

[65] Even if the form of an exegetical tradition appears
peculiarly rabbinic, the content of the exegesis is more often
than not expressed in an Hellenistic way. E.g., S. Towner
(*The Rabbinic 'Enumeration of Scriptural Examples'*, SPB 22;
Leiden: E. J. Brill, 1973, 95-117) has identified a peculiarly
rabbinic form, but he fails to see beyond the overall pattern
that the parts are related in a very Hellenistic fashion (118-
213). For an opposing presentation, see the study of H. A.
Fischel, *Rabbinic Literature and Greco-Roman Philosophy* (SPB
21; Leiden: E. J. Brill, 1973), in which are shown, from
tannaitic literature, many parallels to Graeco-Roman orations
basically intact as to structure and stylistic interpretative
devices.

[66] E.g., R. Williamson, *Philo and the Epistle to the Hebrews*
(ALGHJ 4, ed. K. H. Rengstorff, Leiden: E. J. Brill, 1970),
520: "The method of interpretation which Philo used to get
beneath the superficial, literal level of meaning to the under-

lying truth of the OT was the allegorical method."

[67]*Praem* 61, *Som* i, 120. This point is made strongly by
R. Longenecker (*Biblical Exegesis*, 29); cf. *b. Yebam.* 11b.
All references to Philo's works are to the Loeb Classical
Library edition (tr. F. H. Colson & G. H. Witaker, Cambridge,
Mass.: Harvard University, 10 vols., 1929-62) and the titles
of Philo's works are abbreviated according to the Loeb system
provided on pp. xxiii-xxiv of volume 1.

[68]*Mig* 89-94, as discussed by S. Belkin, *Philo and the
Oral Law* (Cambridge, Mass.: Harvard University, 1940), 11-13.

[69]The phrase is that of S. G. Sowers, *The Hermeneutics
of Philo and Hebrews* (Richmond: John Knox, 1965), 28-34. For
a clear exposition of the way one level may fairly compromise
but not deny the other see S. Sandmel, "Philo's Environment,"
249-50.

[70]E.g., "Broadly speaking, all or most of the law-book is
an allegory," *Jos* 28; "Let us not, then, be misled by the
actual words, but look at the allegorical meaning that lies
beneath them," *Cong* 172.

[71]Homeric Allegories 5:2.   ὃ γὰρ ἄλλα μὲν ἀγορεύων τρόπος,
ἕτερα δε ὧν λέγει σημαίνων, ἐπωνύμως ἀλληγορία καλεῖται (Text:
Héraclite: Allégories d'Homère, ed. F. Buffière, Paris:
Société d'Edition Les Belles Lettres, 1962 , 4).

[72]E.g., I. Christiansen, *Die Technik der allegorischen
Auslegungswissenschaft bei Philon von Alexandrien* (Tubingen:
J.C.B. Mohr, 1969), 132-33 and 150-51.

[73]As most often proposed by S. Belkin (see n.68, n.87).

[74]C. Siegfried (*Philo von Alexandria als Ausleger des Alten Testaments*, Jena: H. Dufft, 1875) long ago suggested that Philo's allegorical exegesis was something *sui generis* as a whole but sharing in certain elements with other interpretations of scripture; he outlined 24 rules which he discerned Philo followed, albeit unconsciously at times, in his exegetical method (pp. 168-97) - at least one of these is not really a rule (No. 24: "Gattungen der Allegorie"), but for several Siegfried enumerates rabbinic parallels (Nos. 1, 2, 3, 5 and 6) without, however, any mention of technical rabbinic terminology for the particular items. Something akin to Siegfried's opinion is now becoming the general majority approach: even Belkin might not hesitate to adopt it. It is the view most recently of R. G. Hammerton-Kelly, "Some Techniques of Composition in Philo's Allegorical Commentary with Special Reference to *De Agricultura* - A Study in the Hellenistic Midrash," (*Jews, Greeks and Christians,* ed. R. G. Hammerton-Kelly and R. Scroggs, SJLA 21, Leiden: E. J. Brill, 1976, 45-56).

[75]As does Sowers, *The Hermeneutics of Philo,* 11ff.

[76]B. J. Bamberger, "Philo and the Aggadah," *HUCA* 48 (1977), 153-85, argues that Philo had a modest knowledge of Palestinian haggadic tradition.

[77]"Aspects de l'exégèse philonienne," *Exégèse biblique et Judaisme,* ed. J. E. Ménard, Strasbourg: Université des Sciences Humaines, 1973, 108-15.

[78]"L'exégèse de Philon d'Alexandrie," *RHPR* 53 (1973), 309-29; e.g., p. 309: "Les idées philosophiques sont entièrement mises au service de l'interpretation du passage étudié."

[79]"Exegetical Traditions in Alexandrian Judaism: A
Program for the Analysis of the Philonic Corpus," *SP* 3 (1974-75),
75. In all this Mack argues for the appropriateness of
comparing Philo's exegesis with other exegetical traditions
of the Hellenistic period: Midrash, Halachah, Homer Exegesis,
etc., ("Exegetical Traditions in Alexandrian Judaism," 103-6).
Indeed, through his succinct description of Philo's individuality
within its setting S. Sandmel ("Philo's Environment and Philo's
Exegesis," *JBR* 22 1954 , 251) implied nearly 30 years ago
that study of Philo might take this approach.

In relation to Philo's scriptural exegesis and its
importance for the Jewishness of Philo, see H. A. Wolfson,
Philo (Cambridge, Mass: Harvard University, 1947) 1, 95-96.

[80]"Preliminary Issues in the Analysis of Philo's *De
Specialibus Legibus,*" *SP* 5 (1978), 1-55.

[81]"Moses and Pythagoras: Arithmology as an Exegetical Tool
in Philo," *Studia Biblica 1978: Papers on Old Testament and
Related Themes,* ed. E. A. Livingstone, JSOTSup 11; Sheffield:
JSOT, 1979, 205-8; "Arithmology as an Exegetical Tool in the
Writings of Philo of Alexandria," *SBL Seminar Papers 1*, Missoula:
Scholars Press, 1978, 191-227. On the work of the Philo Project
at Claremont, California with which Mack, Hecht and Moehring
are all connected see "The Philo Project," *The Institute for
Antiquity and Christianity Report 1972-80*, ed. M. W. Meyer,
Claremont: The Institute for Antiquity and Christianity, 1981,
15-18.

[82]Loeb Vol. 5, 125.

[83]A. Hanson, "Philo's Etymologies," *JTS* N.S. 18 (1967), 130.

[84] Notwithstanding the evidence inferred by J. -G. Kahn
("Did Philo Know Hebrew? The Testimony of the Etymologies,"
Tarbiz 34 1964-65 , 337-45, Eng. Summ. iv-v) that Philo
copied his etymologies from a Greek model in which Hebrew
names were already transliterated and explained.

[85] Loeb Vol. 5, 125.

[86] Nowhere in his long treatment of Abraham in Philo's
writings does S. Sandmel discuss the etymology of the name;
rather, for Sandmel, the change in name is solely significant
for the change in character that God gives Abraham (*Philo's
Place in Judaism,* Cincinatti: Hebrew Union College, 1956,
168-69, 172, 184-85).

[87] "Philo's Etymologies," 136. E. Stein (*Die allegorische
Exegese des Philo aus Alexandria,* BZAW 51; Giessen: A. Töpelmann,
1929, 58) had selected the first two of these, אב and בר, but
for the third suggested that רתם was understood by Philo as
a variation of רעם "to thunder." S. Belkin ("Some Obscure
Traditions Mutually Clarified in Philo and Rabbinic Literature,"
Studies in Judaica, ed. L. D. Stitskin, New York: Ktav, 1974,
22) adequately dismissed Stein's proposal: "According to Philo,
sound here stands for "the uttered word, for in living creatures
the instrument of sound is the vocal power." It would be
unwarranted, therefore, to convert this vocal power into a
power of the elements, a metamorphosis which Philo did not intend."

[88] One reason for this somewhat forced though possible
etymology is that in discussing the character of Abraham, Philo
appears interested to stress the faculty of speech, whereas
with Jacob/Israel he stresses sight (ראה). In relation to

Abr 61-84 this is the observation of J. Cazeaux ("Interpréter Philon d'Alexandrie," *REG* 84 1972 , 352).

[89]*Gen. Rab.* 46:7 (Text: *Midrash Rabbah*, ed. H. Freedman; London: Soncino, Vol. 1, 1939, 393). The phrase is associated with third century Babylonian Amoraim. On the other hand *b. Šabb.* 105a claims that the use of *nôṭārîqôn* belongs to the interpretation of אב המון: *"If one writes a letter as an abbreviation, R. Joshua b. Bathyra holds him liable, whilst the sages exempt him.* R. Johanan said in R. Jose b. Zimra's name; How do we know (that) abbreviated forms (are recognized) by the Torah? Because it is written, *for AB (the father of) HaMWN (a multitude of) nations have I made thee:* a father *(Ab)* of nations have I made thee; a chosen one *(Baḥur)* among nations have I made thee. *HaMWN:* beloved *(Ḥabib)* have I made thee among nations; a king *(Melek)* have I appointed thee for the nations; distinguished *(Wathiḳ)* have I made thee among the nations; faithful *(Ne'eman)* have I made thee to the nations" (Edition: *The Babylonian Talmud*, ed. H. Freedman, London: Soncino, Vol. 8, 1938, 505).

S. Belkin maintains because of *Šabb.* 105a that בחר and not בר served Philo as a pattern and that the rest of the exposition of המון was dropped because of the possible political misunderstandings that might have arisen from the use of "king" ("Obscure Traditions," 23-24). Yet Belkin's treatment is inadequate: he fails to suggest an alternative way in which Philo came to use ἠχοῦς and he fails to remember that Philo is not expounding אב המון but the name Abraham.

[90] *Gen. Rab.* 47:1. R. Aḥa was a 4th century Palestinian Amora.

[91] *B. Ber.* 13a. The targums do not help towards an
understanding of the interpretation of the name Abraham,
though, interestingly, Neofiti renders כי אב המון גוים by
the elaborate phrase קהל כנשת אומין זדיקין which is exactly
repeated at Gen 28:3, 35:11 and 48:4. Against the tradition
represented in *Ber.* 13a Neofiti thus clearly limits the
blessing of Abraham to the tribes of Israel and relates it
to Abraham's acquisition of life in the world to come (*Neof.*
Gen 15:1).

[92] A further example of a possible interpretation of the
name can be seen in the extracts of an anonymous historiographer
wrongly named Eupolemus among the Jewish fragments of the
collective work of Alexander Polyhistor preserved in Eusebius'
Praeparatio Evangelica 9, 17. There Abraham is the universal
bringer of culture, not so much the father of many nations as
their teacher. This text is most recently discussed by
M. Hengel (*Judentum und Hellenismus,* 162-69). Sir 44:19a
and Jubilees both remain very close to the LXX.

[93] *Mut* 61-63.

[94] There is much literature on this subject. Among those
for Philo knowing Hebrew are C. Siegfried (*Philo von Alexandria
als Ausleger,* 144: "Er verstand hebräisch - nicht im modernen
Sinne, aber nach den Ueberlieferungen über Gesetze und Wort-
schatz der heiligen Sprache, die nach Alexandria von den
Palästinen überbracht und daselbst seit lange einheimisch waren"),
S. Belkin (*Philo and the Oral Law,* 35) and H. Wolfson (*Philo,*
1, 88-90). Ascribing Philo some elementary knowledge of
Hebrew are S. Sandmel (*Philo's Place in Judaism,* 12-13; "Philo's

Knowledge of Hebrew," *Studia Philonica* 5 1978 , 107-111) and
A. Hanson ("Philo's Etymologies," 138-39). Denying Philo any
knowledge of Hebrew are E. Stein (*Die allegorische Exegese,*
20-21), E. R. Goodenough (*An Introduction to Philo Judaeus,*
Oxford: B. Blackwell, 1962^2, 9, 11) and J. -G. Kahn ("Did Philo
Know Hebrew?" iv-v). Stein's argument is most comprehensive,
but his denial is largely on the basis that the etymologies are
often far from literal translations; yet the list Stein gives
(53-61) demonstrates the necessity of an initial explanation of
a majority of the etymologies in terms of Hebrew not Greek -
though whether this was Philo's or somebody else's is still
open to debate; Stein, of course, proposes that Philo had a
Greek source for these and other haggadic materials (*Philo
und der Midrasch,* BZAW 57; Giessen: A. Töpelmann, 1931, 15).

In fact both those for and against Philo's knowing Hebrew
agree in varying degrees that he was most likely acquainted with
Palestinian rabbinic traditions: e.g., Siegfried lists instances
of traditions which Philo may have used (145-56) as well as
those he may have influenced (281-88); and, on the other hand,
Stein (*Philo und der Midrasch,* 50-51) concludes that the
Palestinian haggadah may have played some part in the history
of the traditions which Philo uses. D. Rokeah ("A New
Onomasticon Fragment from Oxyrynchus and Philo's Etymologies,"
JTS N.S.19 1968 , 70-82) denies Philo knowledge of Hebrew and
proposes the existence of a first redaction of a list of
etymologies in Greek in the second century B.C.; Rokeah's
treatment of an onomasticon fragment thus supports one proposal
for a Hellenistic dating for such etymologies as occur in Philo's
writings. More recently J. T. Milik (*The Books of Enoch.*

Aramaic Fragments of Qumrân Cave 4, Oxford: Clarendon, 1976,
213-16) in discussing 4QEn^c 5 ii 22-24 (*1 Enoch* 106:18) has
supported Rokeah by noting that the etymologies in 4QEn more
often play on the Hebrew than the Aramaic meaning, suggesting
that the author of *1 Enoch* used a secondary Hebrew source for
his etymologies.

[95]1 Kgs 14:9, Ps 41(2):4, Amos 5:23, Joel 3(4): 14,
Jer 28:16, 42, 29:3.

[96]As noted by G. B. Caird ("Homoeophony in the Septuagint,"
Jews, Greeks and Christians, ed. R. G. Hammerton-Kelly and
R. Scroggs, SJLA 21, Leiden: E. J. Brill, 1976, 84) who
classifies it simply as a mistranslation.

[97]Cf. Philo's treatment of Israel as based on the Hebrew
איש ראה אל; the same etymology may be the basis of the wordplay
in John 1:46-51.

[98] *Die Technik,* 99-131.

[99]"Philo's Allegorical Commentary," 55-56.

[100]Hammerton-Kelly ignores the opening section of the unit
and so his structural interpretation is slightly out of balance.

[101]"Philo's Allegorical Commentary," 55.

[102]Loeb Vol. 2, 95.

[103]LXX has προσετέθη.

[104] *Sac* 5; Loeb Vol. 2, 99.

[105] *Sac* 6; Loeb Vol. 2, 99.   Gen 35:29 (LXX) reads: καὶ
κατέπαυσεν Ιακωβ ... καὶ προσετέθη πρὸς τὸν λαὸν αὐτοῦ.

[106] *Sac* 10; Loeb Vol. 2, 101.

[107] *Philo and the Oral Law,* 32. Philo exegetes Num 27:7-11 by means of *qal wāḥōmer* in *Spec* 2, 132; this is the same as the method employed in *Sifre* Num 134.

[108] *Philo and the Oral Law,* 33-34. The rabbis have a similar exegesis of Deut 22:23-27 in *Sifre* Deut 243. Clearly the reservations of R. D. Hecht, "Preliminary Issue in the Analysis of Philo's *De Specialibus Legibus,*' 2, must be taken into account in any use of Belkin's conclusions.

[109] *Cong* 73 reads: "Now it is worth considering carefully why in this place Moses again calls Sarah the wife of Abraham, when he has already stated the fact several times; for Moses did not practise the worst form of prolixity, namely tautology." Siegfried (*Philo von Alexandria als Ausleger,* 168) names this as the first rule of Philo's method of allegorization.

[110] *Philo and the Oral Law,* 35; a list criticized justifiably for its very brevity by D. Daube (*BO* 5 1948 , 65).

[111] Hammerton-Kelly, "Philo's Allegorical Commentary," 56.

[112] For exegetical techniques other than those discussed here (*gēzērâ šāwâ, nôtārîqôn, 'al tiqrē'*) see the work of scholars involved in the Claremont Philo Project (above, n.81).

[113] For bibliographies of recent and important works see: J. Bowker, *The Targums and Rabbinic Literature* (Cambridge: Cambridge University, 1969), 327-48; M. P. Miller, "Targum, Midrash and the Use of the Old Testament in the New Testament," *JSJ* 2 (1971), 29-82; and the works of B. Grossfeld: *Bibliography of Targum Literature* (New York: Ktav, 1972) and his continuing bibliographies in the *Newsletter for Targumic and Cognate*

Studies (ed. W. E. Aufrecht; Toronto: Victoria College).

[114]*Masoreten des Westens II*, BWANT 14; Stuttgart:
W. Kohlhammer, 1930.

[115]Ms. Neofiti 1 of the Vatican Library. The volumes used
in this section are editions by A. Díez Macho: *Neophyti 1,*
Madrid: Consejo Superior de Investigaciones Científicas,
Tomo 1: Génesis, 1968; Tomo II: Exodo, 1970.

[116]4QtgLev, 4QtgJob, 11QtgJob.

[117]E.g., G. Vermes, "Haggadah in the Onqelos Targum,"
JSS 8 (1963), 154-69 and J. Bowker, "Haggadah in the Targum
Onqelos," *JSS* 12 (1967), 51-65.

[118]For a brief outline of the interrelationship of the
targum recensions see R. Le Déaut, "Les études targumiques.
État de la recherche et perspectives pour l'éxègese de l'ancien
testament," *De Mari à Qumran* (ed. H. Cazelles; BETL 24; Gembloux:
J. Duculot, 1969), 302-31 - especially the diagram and its
explication, 314-19.

[119]"The Recently Discovered Palestinian Targum: Its
Antiquity and Relationship with the Other Targums," *Congress
Volume: Oxford* (VTSup 7; Leiden: E. J. Brill, 1960), 222-45.
This was countered (on the basis of lack of evidence) by
P. Wernberg-Møller, "An Inquiry into the Validity of the Text-
critical Argument for an Early Dating of the Recently Discovered
Palestinian Targum," *VT* 12 (1962), 312-31.

[120]*The Genesis Apocryphon of Qumran Cave 1* (BibOr 18A; Rome:
Biblical Institute, 1971[2]), 193-227. This is more completely
worked out, with consideration of Díez Macho's work, in

A Wandering Aramean, Chapter 3.

[121]Thus, in reviewing M. Black's *An Aramaic Approach to the Gospels and Acts* (Oxford: Clarendon, 1967[3]), Fitzmyer remarks that "any discussion of the Aramaic substratum of the NT must begin with local and contemporary Aramaic." The Aramaic of Qumran and of first century inscriptions "must be the latest Aramaic that should be used for *philological* comparisons of the Aramaic substratum of the Gospels and Acts" (*CBQ* 30 1968 , 420); see also, *A Wandering Aramean,* Chapter 1.

[122]*Urschrift und Übersetzungen der Bibel,* Frankfurt, 1928[2]. In his second excursus he studied more than 100 passages which appear to him to contain an interpretation of the Hebrew text. He fails, however, to outline the exegetical technique of the targumist.

[123]See especially the work of R. Le Déaut ("Targumic Literature and New Testament Interpretation," *BTB* 4 1974 , 243-89), of M. McNamara (*Targum and Testament,* Grand Rapids: W. B. Eerdmans, 1968) and of G. Vermes (*Scripture and Tradition in Judaism,* SPB 4; Leiden: E. J. Brill, 1973[2]; *Post-Biblical Jewish Studies,* SJLA 8; Leiden: E. J. Brill, 1975) for studies of particular exegetical traditions that appear in the targums and for reference to other works; also see the bibliographical sources listed on p. 65, n.113, especially *Bibliography of Targum Literature,* 79-84.

[124]E.g., L. H. Brockington ("Septuagint and Targum," *ZAW* 66 1954 , 80-85) has concluded that there are numerous parallels, especially in the stress on salvation in Isaiah, between the LXX and the Targum, but that there is no evidence

for outright borrowing either way. Cf. P. Churgin's
proposition ("The Targum and the Septuagint," *AJSL* 50
1933-34 , 41-65) that particular word-use in the LXX reveals
that its text has been emended shortly after composition to
bring it into line with targumic interpretations: Churgin
views the LXX as a Greek targum. For further bibliography
see S. P. Brock, C. T. Fritsch, S. Jellicoe, *A Classified
Bibliography of the Septuagint* (ALGHJ 6; Leiden: E. J. Brill,
1973), 52.

[125]The substitution of each letter by its counterpart in
sequence counting either from the beginning or from the end
of the alphabet as required, e.g. א ⟨=⟩ ת, ב ⟨=⟩ ש, etc.

[126]A. Díez Macho, "Le Targum palestinien," 47.

[127]*La Nuit pascale,* AnBib 22; Rome: Institut Biblique
Pontifical, 1963, 58-62.

[128]*La Nuit pascale,* 59.

[129]Although all translation is interpretative, the
targumim deserve their categorization as interpretative
translation because they fulfilled more than just a trans-
lational role in their setting in the synagogue; see D. Patte,
Early Jewish Hermeneutic, 49-86. Patte does not, however, give
a single example of a targumic text the form and content of
which could almost certainly go back to the period which he
discusses (first centuries B.C. and A.D.); all his remarks are,
therefore, somewhat inconclusive for his thesis, though there
may be some value in them. Indeed, A. Paul (*RSR* 64 1976 543)
criticizes Patte's work in that it "lacks historical perspective."

^{130}For a summary of these various rabbinic interpretations
see B. Grossfeld, "Targum Onkelos and Rabbinic Interpretation
to Genesis 2:1, 2," *JJS* 24 (1973), 176.

^{131}As also at Gen 17:22, Gen 49:33, Exod 34:33 and Deut 32:45
("Targum Onkelos and Rabbinic Interpretation to Genesis 2:1, 2,"
177).

^{132}Trans. of J. W. Bowker, *The Targums and Rabbinic
Literature,* 112.

^{133}E.g., 2 Sam 13:39, Ps 84:3, 119:81, 82, 123, 143:7,
Isa 38:14. It may be that the targumist knew that to achieve
his interpretation he would be implying כלה + ל in the Hebrew
text but that he justified that to himself by considering the
preposition ל simply as designating a direct object as
Aramaic grammar allows.

^{134}Complutensis 1516/17.

^{135}As are allusions in *Jub.* 4:15, 22, 5:1; *T. Reub.* 5:6, 7;
2 Apoc. Bar. 56:11-14; Philo, *Gig.* 2:6ff. For other references
see Charles, *APOT 2,* 191, J. Morgenstern, "The Mythological
Background of Psalm 82," *HUCA* 14 (1939), 86-95, and P. Alexander,
"The Targumim and Early Exegesis of 'Sons of God' in Genesis 6,"
JJS 23 (1972), 61, n.5.   11QtgJob 30:5 renders בני אלהים (MT)
as מלאכי אלהא.

^{136}According to *Gen. Rab.* 26:5; trans. in J. W. Bowker, *The
Targums and Rabbinic Literature,* 153.

^{137}E.g., *b. Yoma* 67b, *Nid.* 61a. In the non-authoritative
Pirqe R. El. 22 angels are mentioned once more. Alexander
attributes the change in the Jewish understanding of בני אלהים

to the reassertion of Torah Judaism against Gnosticism and
its like after the second Jewish war ("The Targumim and Early
Exegesis," 68-71).

[138]Rendering אלהים as earthly judges or nobles, the same
phrase as that used by R. Simeon b. Joḥai: בני דייניה.

[139]1 Enoch presupposes this *'al tiqrē'*. On the fall of the
Angels see especially A. Lods, "La chute des anges," (*RHPR* 7
1927, 295-315) who wishes to see a predominantly Babylonian
influence behind the creation of the myth; also J. Morgenstern
"The Mythological Background of Psalm 82," 40-70.

[140]Namely: 1) Angels descend on a good errand but fall
victim to the charms of the daughters of men (*Jub.* 4:15, *2
Apoc. Bar.* 56:11-14); 2) Angels disparage man and so are sent
to earth to be tested - and fail (*Ps.-Clem. Homilies* 8:11-15);
3) Angels are simply seduced from heaven by the daughters of
men (*1 Enoch* 6-11, *Pirqe R. El.* 22). This third tradition is
the one to which *Ps.-Jonathan* comes closest ("The Targumim and
Early Exegesis," 70-71).

[141]On this term see J. Bowker, *The Targums and Rabbinic
Literature,* 318, and W. Bacher, *Die exegetische Terminologie
der jüdischen Traditionsliteratur* II, Leipzig: J. C. Hinrichs,
1905, 65-66.

[142]*Tg. Ps.-Jonathan* and Cairo Genizah Fragment C give no
proper name but refer to "an angel" and to "the angel in the
likeness of a man" מלאך עמיה בדמות גבר respectively. *Midr.
Rabbah* has the guardian angel of Esau wrestle with Jacob.

[143]*Tg. Onqelos* has only "let me go for the dawn has risen;"

Tg. Ps.-Jonathan Gen 32:27 adds, "I am one of the praising
angels. Since the day that the world was created, my time
to praise has never arrived until this moment." The *Fragmentary
Targum* and *Fragment C* of the Cairo Genizah are nearly identical
with *Tg. Neofiti*.

[144]"Iacob . . . cum luctaretur in pulvere cum angelo qui
stabat super (h)ymnos . . ." (Text: G. Kisch, *Pseudo-Philo's
Liber Antiquitatum Biblicarum,* Indiana: Notre Dame University,
1949, 159); cf. M. R. James' translation, *The Biblical Antiquities
of Philo* (New York: Ktav, 1971), 124: "Jacob also, when he
wrestled in the dust with the angel that was over the praises,..."

[145]Sariel also appears at 4QEn[a] 1 iv 6 but the angels are
in a different order there from that of 1QM 9:12-15.
Unfortunately not enough of the text of Gen 32:25 is preserved
in 4QBibParaph (4Q158) to determine whether Sariel is mentioned.

[146]"The Archangel Sariel. A Targumic Parallel to the Dead
Sea Scrolls," *Christianity, Judaism and Other Greco-Roman Cults*
(SJLA 12:3; Leiden: E. J. Brill, 1975) 159f. Vermes notes
that Sariel (Σαριελ) of *1 Enoch* 20:6, who is rendered as
sǎ-rā-qā-ē-l(ě) in the Ethiopic text, belongs to a group of
seven in which the four archangels already occur, Uriel
supplanting Sariel in 1QM 9:15. A third Sariel features at
1 Enoch 6:8, 8:3; he does indeed derive his name from the
Aramaic שהרה, "moon," as proposed by R. H. Charles (*APOT 2* ,
191) as his name in 4QEn[a] 1 iii 11 is שהריאל (J. T. Milik,
The Books of Enoch, 154).

This short study on Gen 32:29 is largely dependent on
Vermes' work. Some additional comments by Vermes are available

in his article "The Impact of the Dead Sea Scrolls on Jewish
Studies during the last Twenty-Five Years," *JJS* 26 (1975),
1-14, reprinted in *Approaches to Ancient Judaism: Theory
and Practice*, ed. W. S. Green, BJS 1; Missoula: Scholars
Press, 1978, 201-14, especially 211-13.

[147]Gen 32:29, Hos 12:4-5; BDB, KB: "to struggle, persist,
exert oneself, persevere." Cf. R. Coote's conclusion ("The
Meaning of the Name *Israel*," *HTR* 65 (1972), 137-40): "The
meaning of the name Israel is probably 'El judges', from the
verb *śry* or *yśr* meaning 'to govern by rendering judgment or
decree'."

[148]LXX ἐνισχύειν, "to be strong," implies an understanding
of the root שרר and this is reflected in the Peshitta's אשתרר.

[149]"The Archangel Sariel," 165. Vermes supports this
understanding with reference to the various treatments of שרר
in Num 16:13. *Tg. Onqelos*, *Tg. Ps.-Jonathan* and *Tg. Neofiti*
translate it by אתרברב and this time the LXX agrees with them
(κατάρχεις and ἀρχων) as does the Peshitta: אתרברב.

[150]"The Archangel Sariel," 162.

[151]As Vermes ("The Archangel Sariel," 165) suggests.

[152]R. H. Charles, *The Ethiopic Version of the Book of
Enoch* (Oxford: Clarendon, 1906), lists the variants of the
name on p. 24: B-f have *ă-rĕ-sĕ-yă-lā-lĕ-yē-r(ĕ)*, m has
ă-sū-rĕ-yē-ū-lĕ-yē-r(ĕ), q has *ă-să-rē-yē-lă-lĕ-yē-r(ĕ)*,
t has *ă-sĕ-rĕ-ē-lĕ-yē-r(ĕ)*, and u has *ă-sĕ-rĕ-yē-lĕ-yē-l(ĕ)*
(For the Ms sigla see Charles, *Ethiopic Enoch*, xvii-xxi).
According to A. Lods (*Le Livre d'Hénoch*, Paris: E. Leroux,

1892, 112) the combination of "Arsial = Sariel et de
Aliour = Ourial."

[153]"A Targum on Exod. xv 7-21 from the Cairo Geniza,"
VT 11 (1961), 340.

[154]This is, however, the targum recension that comes closest
to the Peshitta (איך דבזקא רדיא) according to the comparison of
all the recensions at this point by A. Voöbus (*Peschitta und
Targumim des Pentateuchs*, Stockholm: Etse, 1958, 41). M. Black
(*A Christian Palestinian Syriac Horologion,* Texts and Studies, N.S. 1;
Cambridge: Cambridge University, 1954, 24) translates the
phrase of the Syriac as "like gravel the streams."

[155]As pointed out most recently by E. Levine, " *Neofiti 1:
A Study of Exodus 15,*" *Bib* 54 (1973), 311. BDB translates נד
as "dam, barrier;" KB as "dam or wall" citing Arabic *nadd.*
Cross and Freedman, ("The Song of Miriam," *JNES* 14 1955 , 246,
n. 21), comment: "This is a rare word apparently meaning 'hill'
or 'heap'. The other occurrences of the word are related to
this passage and are probably dependent on it. Cf. Josh. 3:13,
16; Ps. 78:13. The other references are obscure and perhaps
corrupt." Cross continues to support this in his *Canaanite
Myth and Hebrew Epic,* Cambridge, Mass.: Harvard, 1973, 128,
n. 58; presumably there is nothing in 4QExod[c] to call into
question the antiquity of the MT at this point. The suscept-
ibility of *'āleph* to the method of *'al tiqrē'* may be further
represented in 1QIsa[a] 40:15 which reads מזנים over against
מאזנים of the MT; this variant is not mentioned by J. R. Rosen-
bloom, *The Dead Sea Isaiah Scroll: A Literary Analysis,* Grand
Rapids: W. B. Eerdmans, 1970, 49, but it is recognized in *BHS.*

[156]LXX reads: ἐπάγη ὡσεὶ τεῖχος τὰ ὕδατα

[157]E.g., *Mek.* Exod 15:8, *'Abot R. Nat.* 33; the ten miracles
at the sea are not extrapolated in *'Abot R. Nat.* B 36 or
Pirqe 'Abot 5:5.

[158]"*Neofiti 1:* A Study of Exodus 15," 312.

[159]Trans. of E. Cashdan in *The Babylonian Talmud* (translated
under the editorship of I. Epstein, London: Soncino, 1935-52);
b. Menaḥ 36b-37a is in the Vol. published in 1948, p. 227.

[160]*The Cairo Geniza,* (London: Oxford University, 1959²), 123.
The complete text of Exod 22:4 in Cairo Geniza Fragment A
(Cambridge: T.-S. 20.155) reads: כי יבער איש/ארום יבקר גבר
הקל או כרם וישלח ית יקידתה ויוכל בחקלה דאחרן (Ed. P. Kahle,
Masoreten des Westens II, 3).

[161]As *RSV.* In 4Q *158,* frgs. 10-12, בעה is substituted for
the initial בער of v 4 and appears to be a deliberate alteration
of the sense, by the Qumran scribe or in his Vorlage, to avoid
the difficulty of understanding the verse in the sense of the
targum whilst not denying something akin to the mishnaic ruling.

[162]"A Sixth Century Fragment of the Palestinian Targum?"
VT 1 (1951), 125-29.

[163]Oxford: B. Blackwell/New York: Praegar and Sons, 1959,
205-8.

[164]Probably largely because of the vindication of his thesis
which *Tg. Neofiti* now provides.

[165]"Exodus xxii 4 im *Palästinischen Targum,*" *VT* 8 (1958),
253-63.

[166]"Exodus xxii 4 im *Palästinischen Targum,*" 255.

[167]"Exodus xxii im *Palästinischen Targum*," 258.

[168]As does the Samaritan text. 4QBibParaph 10-12 lacks
the phrase at issue though other parts of Exod 22 that are
present suggest an understanding similar to that of the
LXX and Samaritan versions.

[169]As pointed out by Schelbert, 262. *Mekilta Nez.* 6, 11.
15-16 reads השולח את הבערה (ed. J. Z. Lauterbach, 52) "The
one that kindled the fire shall make restitution" (Exod 22:4 5).
But *Mekilta Nez.* 14 carries the standard mishnaic interpretation
of the text (ed. J. Z. Lauterbach, 108-13).

[170]"The *Targum* of Ex. xxii, 4 and the Ancient *Halakha*,"
Tarbiz 38 (1969), V; Heinemann writes largely against D. Reider
("On the Targum Yerushalmi MS Neofiti 1," *Tarbiz* 38 1968, 81-86)
who maintains that the Geniza Targum Fragment A contains a
simple scribal error in reading יקידתה for בעירה in Exod 22:4
and that the rendering of *Tg. Neofiti* is a case of mistranslation. In a later article ("Early Halakhah in the
Palestinian Targumim," *JJS* 25 1974, 114-22) Heinemann maintains
his position on Exod 22:4; he cites a wealth of bibliographical
material on the subject.

[171]As phrased by A. Díez Macho, *Neophyti 1*, Tomo II: Éxodo,
Introducción, 43*.

[172]See the summary of M. P. Miller, "Targum, Midrash and
the Use of the Old Testament in the New Testament," *JSJ* 2
(1971), 49-55. Not to be excluded, though more elusive, are
interpretative variants within biblical manuscripts at Qumran;
see, among others, J. V. Chamberlain, *An Ancient Sectarian*

Interpretation of the Old Testament Prophets, Dissertation:
Duke University, 1955, 138-202; S. Talmon, "DSIa as a Witness
to Ancient Exegesis of the Book of Isaiah," *ASTI* 1 (1962),
62-72; W. H. Brownlee, *The Meaning of the Qumran Scrolls for
the Bible,* New York: Oxford University, 1964, 155-259.

[173]G. Vermes, "The Qumran Interpretation of Scripture in
its Historical Setting" (*Dead Sea Scroll Studies 1969,* ALUOS
6; Leiden: E. J. Brill, 1969), 86.

[174]CD 16:2 speaks of the Torah as that wherein "all things
are strictly defined," and 1QS 1:1-3 outlines that it is the
aim of the members of the community "to seek God with a whole
heart and soul, and to do what is good and right before him,
as he commanded by the hand of Moses and all his servants
the Prophets."

[175]Broadly defined as including all the prophetic books
and any other visionary material in scripture; maybe better
defined as the former and latter prophets of Tanak. 1QpHab
7:4-5 tells how the Teacher of Righteousness can interpret
all the words of the prophets.

[176]As has been done by L. H. Schiffman, *The Halakhah at
Qumran* (SJLA 16; Leiden: E. J. Brill, 1975), 22-76.

[177]That these techniques are more than literary devices
is clear from study of 4Q *186* which is devised cryptically
being written backwards in square Hebrew, proto-Hebrew, Greek
and other secret alphabets (DJD V, 88-91).

[178]See especially, "Biblical Interpretation among the
Sectaries of the Dead Sea Scrolls," *BA* 14 (1951), 54-76 (this

is discussed and adjusted in the comments on 1QpHab in
Chapter 3) and more recently, *The Midrash Pesher of Habakkuk*,
SBLMS 24; Missoula, Scholars Press, 1979. I have already
acknowledged Brownlee's influence on this study in the Preface.

[179]"Unriddling the Riddle. A Study in the Structure and
Language of the Habakkuk Pesher (1QpHab)," *RQ* 3 (1961-62),
323-64.

[180]"Unriddling the Riddle," 327.

[181]"The Pesher of Dreams and Scriptures," *RQ* 4 (1963-64),
357-70.

[182]Which itself is dependent on the use of scripture:
e.g., Finkel notes that in interpreting the dream in 1QapGen
19:14-21 the symbolic elements are a cedar and a palm, taken
most certainly from Ps 92:13: "The righteous (=Abraham; Gen
15:6) shall flourish like a palm tree, He shall grow like a
cedar (=Sarah; ארז could be an anagram and pun on שרה in
Lebanon."

[183]Assignation of technical terms mine.

[184]"Toward an Understanding of the Exegesis in the Dead
Sea Scrolls," *RQ* 7 (1969-71), 3-15.

[185]See especially his collected essays in *Scripture and
Tradition in Judaism*, SPB 4; Leiden: E. J. Brill, 1961,
1973[2] and in *Post-Biblical Jewish Studies*, SJLA 8; Leiden:
E. J. Brill, 1975, and his article "Interpretation (History
of) at Qumran and in the Targums," *IDBSup* (1976), 438-43.

[186]"Le *Commentaire d'Habacuc*, qui est une paraphrase
actualisante des deux premiers chapitres d'Habacuc, met en

oeuvre tous les procédés midrashiques connus" (*DBSup* 5, 1277).

[187] *Studien zum Habakuk-Kommentar vom Totem Meer,* BHT 15;
Tübingen: J.C.B. Mohr, 1953.

[188] Title of chapter six, pp. 118-164.

[189] These three categories are outlined on pp. 127-39,
139-42 and 142-49 respectively.

[190] E.g., the interpretation of the writing on the wall:
Dan 5:24-8.

[191] As pointed out by J. V. Chamberlain, *An Ancient
Sectarian Interpretation,* 109 n. 57.

[192] *Biblical Exegesis in the Qumran Texts,* Grand Rapids:
W. B. Eerdmans, 1959, 9.

[193] *Biblical Exegesis,* 16.

[194] *Offenbarung und Schriftforschung in der Qumransekte,*
WUNT 6, Tübingen: J.C.B. Mohr, 1960, 75-77.

[195] *Offenbarung,* 78; CD 1:5-10, 20:14.

[196] Bruce shares this understanding that the new situation
understood from a scriptural perspective is the basis for
the authority of the Qumran interpretation (*Biblical Exegesis,*
18-27, 59-65).

[197] "The Use of the OT in the NT," 51-52.

[198] *Early Jewish Hermeneutic,* 303-8. Patte cites uncritically
the conclusions of Brownlee and Silberman; see, however, below,
pp. 283-288, 291-292.

[199] *Early Jewish Hermeneutic,* 299.

[200] *Pesharim: Qumran Interpretations of Biblical Books,*
CBQMS 8; Washington: The Catholic Biblical Association of
America, 1979, 244-59.

[201]See my article "Qumran Pesher: Towards the Redefinition
of a Genre," *RQ* 10 (1979-81), 483-503.

Chapter II

4Q FLORILEGIUM

A. Description

The material of Chapter I has enabled us to establish
the boundaries within which a first century Jew used scripture
and to suggest that, between the scriptural text cited and
the hermeneutical result achieved, there was the use of certain
principles of exegesis: correctly carried out, such
principles went some way to demonstrating the validity of
the hermeneutical result. 4QFlor can be placed within these
same boundaries.

Because 4QFlor is a genuine fragment, a work known only
in this one instance, it is worth beginning its detailed study
with a complete description. The Florilegium is part of the
large group of scroll fragments which were found by the
Ta[c]amireh Bedouin in the summer of 1952, and which were
eventually purchased by the Palestine Archaeology Museum.[1]
In 1967 the scroll pieces passed into Israeli hands and came
under the authority of the Shrine of the Book, Jerusalem.[2]

M. Burrows has described the find as

the climax of the whole extraordinary series of
discoveries . . . at an out-of-the-way spot in the
plateau on which Khirbet Qumran stands. This plateau
is cut by a ravine, and at the point where the ravine

joins the Wady Qumran the Bedouins found a chamber,
hollowed out of the soft marl, containing many
fragments of manuscripts. This is the cave now
known as 4Q.[3]

J. Allegro, then of Manchester University, was the scholar
assigned the task of editing and sorting some of the 4Q
material including the text that is the subject of this study.
He has also described the events surrounding the discovery of
the 4Q cave with its entrance "in the precipitous edge of the
plateau,"[4] very near to the site of Khirbet Qumran.

In his first publication solely concerned with 4QFlor,
Allegro gives it the following description:

The skin of the fragments is fairly coarse, in
colour a rather striking reddish-brown. It is
clear from the nature of the edges that at some
time in antiquity the scroll was brutally torn
apart. One result has been that the fragments
have suffered differently from the ravages of
time, so that pieces which should fit together
often differ in coloring and warping, or in the
state of preservation of the writing. Margins:
bottom 2.5cm., top 2cm., right-hand side 1.4cm.,
left-hand side 1.8cm. The ruling is regular at .8cm.[5]

Earlier Allegro had mentioned that column 1 is made up
of some 21 fragments and he published a photograph of some of
them.[6] On the basis of study of that photograph J. L. Teicher
challenged Allegro and argued that column 1 was not a continuous
text.[7] If he had kept solely to description of the

photograph, he might have been forgiven, for the cut-off
nature of the reproduction is indeed deceptive, and Allegro
provided no explanation of it. Teicher continued his
argument, however, by saying that the contents of the text
made no sense, and that all the evidence, including the
context, pointed to the fact that the text was "spurious."
Allegro was allowed to reply to Teicher and did so as politely
as he could.[8] The best refutation came with publication of
the whole passage in "Fragments".[9]

All twenty-one fragments of column 1 were again reproduced
in Allegro's *Qumran Cave 4, I (4Q 158-4Q 186)*,[10] classified as
No. 174, 1 and 2, along with 24 other fragments which he had
identified as part of the scroll. The description of the scroll
may be completed by noting that, if all the fragment pieces
are accepted, it contains at least five columns: column 1, in
fact, starts in the middle of a passage and is thus a second
or later column, column 2 is evidenced in the same fragment as
column 1, and furthermore fragments 9 and 13 both contain the
top right hand corner of a column.

Allegro provisionally named the scroll Florilegium in
1956[11] and this was confirmed in his later publications of the
text: in his article "Fragments" and in the volume DJD V.
Other titles have been suggested. A. M. Habermann entitles it
מדרש על אחרית הימים,[12] which G. Vermes parallels in his "A
Midrash on the Last Days."[13] Y. Yadin is more precise: "A
Midrash on 2 Sam. vii and Ps. i-ii (4QFlorilegium)."[14]
W. H. Brownlee notes that to be in keeping with the general
preference of finding an appropriate Semitic name for each
book the title of Allegro's article "Fragments" might seem to

suggest the name 4Q Midrashim.[15]   T. H. Gaster, qualifying
Allegro's title, proposes "A 'Messianic' Florilegium."[16]

The title Florilegium, the latinized form of the Greek-
rooted 'anthology', will be retained throughout this study
because it has become the convenient label that the great
majority of scholars use, and because, even though it suggests
a certain randomness in the selection of passages and that all
the biblical passages are equally important, it is less
restrictive as a title than any other.

Allegro describes the script as a "neat bookhand,"[17] and
comments about 4QOrdinances that "the writing is in a beautifully
shaped and proportioned bookhand, bearing a marked resemblance,
if not identical with that of 4 Q Florilegium."[18]   J. Strugnell
also notes the resemblance of the script of the two scrolls
but adds that "cette main hérodienne ancienne formelle (avec
des elements du semiformel rustique, voir le *shin* et l'*aleph*)
est assez largement représentée dans la quatrième grotte."[19]

A suggested date for this "Herodian" script can be deduced
from palaeographical studies. N. Avigad classes 1QIsa[b], 1QM,
1QpHab and 1QH as Herodian, distinguished by its "strict formal
hand" and proposes that the date for this class of scrolls is
roughly 50 B.C. to A.D. 70.[20] Further detailed comparative
material can be found in S. A. Birnbaum's work on the Hebrew
scripts.[21] This expands other evidence he has provided in
relation to the Dead Sea Scrolls[22] and from the arguments and
diagrams presented concerning the evolution of the Hebrew script,
it is clear that for him 4QFlor would belong at the very end
of the first century B.C. or in the first century A.D.[23]
F. M. Cross also offers a table of scripts in relation to which

4QFlor most nearly belongs to line 6 which he describes as
"a late hand belonging to a Deuteronomy manuscript (4QDeutj).
The script is to be dated ca. A.D. 50; it is the immediate
typological forbear of the standard hand of the second century
A.D. and later."[24]

Palaeography provides a rough date; yet a sufficient
terminus ante quem for 4QFlor is given by the archaeological
date of the discovery itself. R. de Vaux has concluded thus:
"Aucun des manuscrits de la communauté n'est plus récent que
la ruine de Khirbet Qumran en 68 ap. J.-C."[25] Remarks will be
made throughout this study concerning the relation of 4QFlor
to the various manuscripts at Qumran with the hope that it can
be put in the context of its own tradition. Thereby its date
will be made more precise; yet this can only be done after a
detailed discussion and analysis of the text of 4QFlor.

B. Text and Translation

1. *Introductory Remarks*

In establishing as certainly as possible the textual content
(not necessarily the same thing as the meaning content) of the
fragments the following steps have been taken:

1. An accurate reading of the fragments was carried out.
This is not always as easy as it sounds; for example, גו in
4QFlor 1:4 is situated on a crease in the manuscript and may yet
prove to have defied a precise reading. Also, for instance,
there is an often confusing similarity in Herodian script between
a *wāw* and a *yôd*. W. H. Brownlee has provided additional evidence
at several points from unpublished photographs in the Palestine
Archaeology (Rockefeller) Museum.

2. Where partially extant letters and words have to
be read, it is hoped that all the possibilities have been
admitted. For example, in 4QFlor 1:17 every scholar has read
עצ as the initial letters of עצתו, a good Qumran word, to be
sure, but not necessarily what is required by the context.
Thus arises the question as to what are valid criteria for
the textual restoration of words and letters. For word
restoration, the letters that are wholly extant or are beyond
doubt must be recognized as such. For example, Y. Yadin
reads a *tāw* in 1:17 for his phrase באחרית הימים [26] but the
letter is clearly a *hē'*, as all other scholars have correctly
recognized. For word and letter restoration where there is a
multiple choice, other considerations must be taken into account:
grammar, syntax, context, the presupposition of known vocabulary
(in this case Hebrew with possible Aramaisms), and comparative
literature. No restoration that might affect the apparent
structure of the passage has been made, unless it is demonstrably
the best option,[27] all known alternative possibilities being
clearly excluded.

3. Measurement of the length of the proposed restoration
has been done when necessary. The discussion concerning 1:19
provides an example of the use of this simple method.

4. Special treatment has been given to the restoration of
quotations from the Hebrew Bible. This has taken account of
the style of the author and of his general intention; for
example, in 1:10-11 the author only cites those parts of the
scriptural verses that suit his purposes, and the possibility
has been recognized that that may be the case elsewhere. In
4QFlor the writer is consistently accurate in citing Biblical

texts when he announces his intention to do so with some
introductory formula, or when he is quoting the text of the
midrash, even though it is abbreviated. Restorations have been
made, therefore, according to our best understanding of the
version(s) the author had available or knew, even if his
subsequent comments and expositions seem to require some
different reading of the text. For example, Yadin's reading
of משחיו in 1:19 (Ps 2:2) is unacceptable as it is only
required because of his restoration of the pesher.

5. More often than not one has to admit that the
restoration can never be known - unless a second copy of the
fragments is found.

2. *The Text*

ที   = partial letter; if a letter is included, it is the
         surest reading.

[ ]   = restoration.

[....] = restoration impossible, text probably continues.

Fragments 1 and 2 (1:1-19)

1   ....ע]וֹד אויבֿ]יו ולוא יוסי]ף בן עולֿה [לענות]וֹ כאשר
     בראישונה ולמן הֿיום אשר

     צויתי שופטים] עֿל עמי ישראל הואה הבית אשר [יבנה] לֿ[ו וא]
     בֿאֿחרית הימים כאשר כתוב בספר

     מושה מקדש אדוני כ]וֹננו ידיכה יהוה ימלוך עולֿםֿ וֹעֿד הואה
     הבית אשר לוא יבוא שמה

     נם דור עשירי ועד עֿ]ולם ועֿמֿוני ומואבי וממזר ובן נכר ונר
     עד עולם כיא קדושו שם

יג[ל]ה [כבודו ל]ע[ו]לם תמיד עליו יראה ולוא ישמועהו עוד   5
זרים כאשר השמו בראישונה

את מקד[ש י]שראל בחטאתמה וייאמר לבנות לוא מקדש אדם להיות
מקטירים בוא לוא

לפניו מ[ע]שי תודה ואשר אמר לדויד ו[הניחו]תי לכה מכול
אויביכה אשר יניח להמה מכ[ו]ל

בני בליעל המכשילים אותמה לכלותמ[ה במשגת]מה כאשר באו
במחשבת [ב]ל[י]על להכשיל ב[נ]י

א[ו]ר] ולחשוב עליהמה מחשבות און למ[ען ית]פשר לבליעל
במשגת א[ו]נ]מה

והג[י]ד לכה יהוה כיא בית יבנה לכה והקימותי את זרעכה   10
אחריכה והכינותי את כסא ממלכתו

לעו[לם אני א]ה[י]ה לוא לאב והוא יהיה לי לבן הואה צמח דויד
העומד עם דורש התורה אשר

ימשול] בצי[ו]ן ב[א]חרית הימים כאשר כתוב והקימותי את סוכת
דויד הנופלת הואה סוכת

דויד הנופל[ת א]ש[ר יעמוד להושיע את ישראל

מדרש מאשרי [ה]איש אשר לוא הת[ה]ל[ך בעצת רשעים פשר הדב]ר
על] סרי מדר[ך [חטאים על

אשר כתוב בספר ישעיה הנביא לאחרית ה[י]מים ויהי כחזקה [יד   15
יסירני מלכת בדרך

הע[ם הזה והמה אשר כתוב עליהמ[ה בספר יחזקאל הנביא אשר לו[א
יטמאו עוד בכול

ג[ל]ו[ל]יהמה המה בני צדוק וא[נ]ש[י עצ]תמ[ה רוח]קים מרע
....]ו[א]חריהמ[ה [....] יחד

למה רג[ש]ו גויים ולאומים יהג[ו ריק ית]יצבו [מלכי ארץ
ו]רוזנים נוסדו ביחד על יהוה ועל

משיחו פ]שר הדבר [אשר הגויים המה הכ]יים וח[ו]סי בוא המה]
בחירי ישראל באחרית הימים

Fragments 1 and 3 (2:1-6)

1   היאה עת המצרף הב[אה על בית יה]ודה לתחם [....

2   בליעל ונשאר שאׄ֗ר [הע]ם [ישר]אׄל ועשו את כול התורה֗ [....

3   מושה היאה ה[ו]עת כאש[ו]ר כתוב בספר דניאל הנביא להרשיׄע

        [רשעים ולוא יבינו

4a   וצדיקים יׄ[תבררו יתלב]נו ויצטרפו ועם יודעי אלוה יהזיקו

        הׄמֹ]ה

4   הׄ[משכילים יבינו ....]אחרי הׄ[....] אשר אליהמה יו[....

5   [.... ברדתו מ]ו[....

6   [....] אׄ [....]

Fragment 4

1   [....הׄמבלעים את צאצאיׄ

2   [נ]וׄטרים להמה בקנאתמה

3   [....היאה העת אשר יפתח בליעל

4   [....לבית יהודה קשות לשוטמם

5   [....וׄבקש בכול כוחו לבזרמה

6   [....וׄ֗ הביאמה להיות

7   [....יה]ודה ואל ישׄר֗אׄל יו[....

Fragment 5

1   [....] ˙ [....]

2   [....ה כאשר ה]ו[....

3   [....י]שׄ֗ראל ואהרון[....

4   [....י]דׄע כיא הואה מ[....

5   [....הׄ] בכול החוזים[....

6   [....] לׄ [....]

Fragments 6 and 7 (Deut 33:8-11 and interpretation)

2

....[ל להאביד את קרן]....

3   וללוי אמר תומיכה ואוריכה לאיש חסידכה אשר נסיתו במס]ה
ותר]י]בהו על מי מריבה ה]א]ומר

4   לאביו ולאמו לוא ידעתיכה ואת אחיו לוא הכיר ואת בניו לוא
י]דע כיא [שמרו אמר]ת]כה] וברי]ת]כה

5   ינצורו ויאירו משפטיכה ליעקוב ותורתכה לישראל ישימו קטורה]
באפכה וכליל על מזבחכה]

6   ברך יהוה חילו ופועל ידיו תרצה מחץ מתנים קמיו ומשנאיו מן
י]קומון

7

....]הא]ו]רים והתומים לאיש]....

8

....]ל]....

Fragment 8 (Deut 33:12)

1   ....[אשר]....

2   ....[א]רץ כיא ה]....

3   ....[לבנימן אמ]ר]]ד]יד]]הוה....

Fragments 9 and 10 (Deut 33:19-21 + pesher)

1   וההיד]ד.... ....]ה זבח הצד]ק....

2   ....טוב הא]רץ.

3   ....ולגד א]מ]ר

4   ....]מחקק]

5   ....]על שב]י]

6   ....]לה]צ]י]ל]

Fragment 11 (Deut 33:19?)

....[הספון ע̇ו]....

...[כ̇ול אשר צונו עשו את כולן]....

Fragment 12

1   ....] [....

2   ....] כול [....

3   ....]אמ̇ם̇[....

4   ....] לוא[....

5   ....]בספ̇ו̇ר[....

Fragment 13   Fragment 14

1   ....] ר̇ו̇ו̇[....   1   ....]ב̇ה לק[....

2   ....הקש]ת̇   2   ....]ל̇אחרית ה[....

3   ....]הדבר[....   3   ....]ב̇יא המה[....

Fragments 15 and 19

1   ....כתוב בספר יש]ע̇יה הנ]ביא....

2   ....כ]ימי עץ [ימי עמי]ו̇א ומעשה ידיהמה יבלו בחי]ר̇י ל]וא יגעז לריק

3   ....המה[.... .... ברך יהוה המ]ה כיא זרע [ולוא ילדו לבהל]ה̇ ....

Fragment 16   Fragment 17

1   ....] ̇[....   1   ....]ג̇ורל[....

2   ....] יקים ̇[....   2   ....]מ̇ה את פ̇ו[....

3   ....]ו̇ברקי[....   3   ....]ב̇חו עליה̇[....

4   ....]א̇[....   4   ....]ל̇[....

Fragment 18   Fragment 20

    ....]° [.... 1   ....]את כל[.... 1

    ....]א ה[.... 2

    ....]בֵטۡ[.... 3

Fragment 21   Fragment 22

    ....] יהוה לۡ[.... 1   ....]ס 1

    ....] [.... 2   ....]ה יחד 2

Fragment 23   Fragment 24

    ....]דורשۡ[° 1   ....]° [.... 1

                     ....]מۡצרף [.... 2

              .   ....]° [.... 3

Fragment 25   Fragment 26

    ....]שۡ[.... 1   ....]° [.... 1

    ....]לשמۡו[.... 2   ....]° צ ° [.... 2

    ....]° [.... 3

Unpublished Fragment

                     ....]יۡשראל הוא[.... 1

                     ....]פדוכה[.... 2

3. *Translation* [28]

Fragments 1, 2 and 3

    (1:1) . . . "and his enemies [will not disturb him] any
more; neither will a son of wickedness afflict him anymore as
formerly and as from the day that (2) I commanded judges to be
over my people Israel." That is the house which [he will build]
for him in the latter days, as it is written in the book of

(3) [Moses], "The sanctuary of the Lord which thy hands have
established; The Lord will reign for ever and ever:" that is
the house to which shall not come (4) [even to the tenth
generation and for] ever, Ammonite nor Moabite nor bastard
nor stranger nor proselyte for ever, for his holy ones are
there. (5) [His glory shall] be revealed for ever; continually
it shall be seen over it. And foreigners shall not make it
desolate again, as they desolated formerly (6) the sanctuary
of Israel because of their sin. And he promised to build for
himself a sanctuary of men, for there to be in it for him
smoking offerings (7) before him, works of thanksgiving. And
that he said to David, "And I will give you rest from all your
enemies," that means that he will give rest to them for all
(8) the sons of Belial who cause them to stumble in order to
destroy them [through their errors], just as they came with
the plots of Belial to cause to stumble the sons of (9) light,
and in order to devise against them plots of wickedness so that
they [might be caught] by Belial through their [wicked] error.

(10) "And the Lord declares to you that he will build you
a house. And I will raise up your seed after you, and I will
establish the throne of his kingdom (11) for ever. I will be
to him as a father, and he will be to me as a son:" he is the
shoot of David who will stand with the Interpreter of the Law,
who (12) [will rule] in Zion in the latter days as it is written,
"And I will raise up the booth of David which is fallen:" he is
the booth (or, branch) of (13) David which was fallen, who will
take office to save Israel.

(14) Midrash of "Happy is the man who does not walk in
the counsel of the wicked;" the real interpretation of the

matter concerns those who turn aside from the way of [sinners concerning] (15) whom it is written in the book of Isaiah the prophet for the latter days, "And it will be that as with a strong [hand he will cause us to turn away from walking in the way] (16) of this people;" and they are those concerning whom it is written in the book of Ezekiel the prophet that "they shall not [defile themselves any more] (17) with their idols." They are the Sons of Zadok and the m[e]n of their cou[nc]il who keep fa[r from evil....] and after them [....] a community (or, together).

(18) "Why do the nations rage and the peoples meditate on a vain thing, the kings of the earth set themselves and the rulers take counsel together (or, against the community) against the Lord and against (19) his anointed;" the real interpretation of the matter [is that "the nations" are the Kitt]im and those who take [refuge in Him" are] the chosen ones of Israel in the latter days; (2:1) that is the time of refining which is coming [upon the house of] Judah to complete [....] (2) of Belial and a remnant of [the people] Israel will be left, and they will do all the Law [....] (3) Moses; that is [the time as] it is written in the book of Daniel the prophet, "For the wicked to act wickedly but they do not understand" - (4a) "but the righteous [shall purify themselves] and make themselves white and refine themselves, and a people knowing God will be strong," - they are - (4) the wise will understand" [....] after the [....] to whom [....] (5) [....] in his descent [....].

Fragment 4
(1) ....] those who consume the offspring of
(2) ....an]gry towards them in their zeal
(3) ....] that is the time when Belial shall open

(4) ....] to the house of Judah severe things to cherish
    emnity against them

(5) ....] and shall seek with all his strength to scatter
    them

(6) ....] brought them to be

(7) ....Ju]dah and to Israel [....

Fragment 5

(1) ....] when [....

(2) ....I]srael and Aaron [....

(3) ....k]now that he [....

(4) ....] among all the seers [....

Fragments 6-7 (Deut 33:8-11 and pesher)

        (3) "And to Levi, he said, your Tummim, and your Urim
to your pious one whom you tested at Massah] and with whom you
quarreled at the waters of Meribah; who said (4) [to his father
and to his mother, I do not know you, and who did not acknowledge
his brother, and his sons he did not] know, for [they observed
your word and your] covenant (5) [they will keep. They shall
cause your laws to shine before Jacob and your Law before Israel.
They shall cause incense to rise] into your nostrils and a burnt
offering on your altar. (6) [Bless his power, O Lord, and
accept the work of his hands. Smite his adversaries on the loins
and his enemies so that they will not] rise." (7) ....] Urim
and Tummim to a man [....

Fragment 8 (Deut 33:12 [?] and pesher)

(1) ....] which [....

(2) ....] land, for [....

(3) .... of Benjamin he sa]id "The beloved of the [LORD....

Fragments 9-10 (Deut 33:19-21 and pesher)

(1) "And the shou[t....] "right sacrif[ice"....

(2) good of the la[nd ....

(3) "and to God he sa[id....

(4) a commander [....."

(5) concerns the penitents of [....

(6) to deliver [....

Fragment 11 (Deut 33:19, 21?)

(1) ....] hidden [....

(2) ....] all that he commanded us, they have done all [....

Fragment 12

(1) ....] all [....

(2) ....]   [....

(3) ....] to him [....

Fragment 13

(1) ? [....

(2) the bo[w....

(3) the matter [....

Fragment 14

(1) ....] ? [....

(2) ....] for the latter d[ays ....

(3) ....] for they are [....

Fragments 15 and 19 (Isa 65:22-3)

(1) ...in the book of] Isaiah the prophet [....(2)
.... "like the days of a tree shall] the days of my people
be [and the works of their hands] my chosen [will enjoy; they

shall not weary themselves in vain, (3) or bear children in]
terror, for the seed [of the blessed of the Lord are they....]"
they are [....

Fragment 16
(1) ....] ? [....
(2) ....] he will raise up [....
(3) ....] and lightnin[gs ....
(4) ....] ? [....

Fragment 17
(1) ....] lot[....
(2) ....] with [....
(3) ....] ? upon her [....

Fragment 21
(1) ....] the Lord [....

Fragment 22
(1) ....]
(2) ....] together

Fragment 23
(1) ....] Interpreter of [....

Fragment 24
(1) ....] [....
(2) ....] refining [....

Fragments 18, 20, 25 and 26 contain only a few letters
and are not translatable.

Unpublished Fragment 27

(1) ....] Israel, he [....

(2) ....] [....

4. *Textual Notes*

Fragments 1, 2 and 3

Column 1

    Line 1

    The reading]אויב וד[comes from an examination of the
original manuscript and of photograph 41.807 in the Rockefeller
Museum which confirms beyond doubt the *bêt* of אויב   Also, at
least part of the *wāw* of וד[ע appears probable under magnification.[29] These readings show that Yadin's proposal of ע[ו ד
או]תו is incorrect.[30]

    Yet the problem remains as to how the text is to be
construed. Are these two words near the beginning of 4QFlor 1:1
part of a previous interpretation or part of a text of 2 Samuel 7?
No known text-type of 2 Samuel 7:10 includes אויב or its
translation at this point. This has led several scholars to
suggest that אויב in 4QFlor 1:1 is part of an earlier interpretation. Habermann's presentation suggests that nothing was
written after אוי]ב save the quotation from 2 Sam 7:10b.[31] That
requires there to be a considerable gap after אוי]ב. Though
there is a large space at the end of line 9 before the biblical
quotation in line 10, it is unusual to find such a space in
the middle of a line. A. Dupont-Sommer[32] and E. Lohse[33] in
their translations have argued explicitly that the words at
the start of line 1 belong to a previous interpretation.

Two considerations, however, argue against their proposal.

The first consideration is that textually in quoting
2 Samuel 7 4QFlor follows no single known text-type slavishly.
The text of 2 Samuel 7 represented in 4QFlor is neither that
of the MT, LXX nor Syr, yet it is not far from any of them.
For example, 4QFlor and the LXX read the singular בן עולה, the
MT and Syr have the plural; again, at the end of line 1 4QFlor
has the singular היום in agreement with the MT and Syr whereas
the LXX (and 1 Chr 17:10) has the plural.[34] Furthermore אויב
occurs several times in 2 Samuel 7[35] and it would not be unlikely
from the contextual influence, if not from Psalm 89:23,[36] that
it would be included as the subject of רגז at this point.

The second consideration is that two structural points
argue for construing עוד אויב as part of the text of 2 Sam 7:10a.
In the first place the commentary for the text of 2 Sam 7:11aᵝ
is cited in a structurally subordinate position that requires
that it is linked somehow with the main quotation: the joint
occurrence of אויב in both would provide a sufficient link.
Secondly from such an understanding that the commentary, and
particularly the biblical texts within the commentary, are
related intricately to this quotation of 2 Samuel by means of
an exegetical technique, one can argue that because of the
later use of Exod 15:17-18, the author of 4QFlor presupposes
2 Sam 7:10a in his interpretation.[37] מקום of 2 Sam 7:10a is
the most apt referent for "the house" in 4QFlor 1:2.

On these grounds it is preferable to combine the reading
of עוד אויב with the text of 2 Samuel 7. Vermes has proposed
"[I will appoint a place for my people Israel that they may dwell
there and be troubled no more by their] enemies."[38] Yet since

no *hoph^al* is attested for רגז, Vermes' passive may be seen
as a translation from a *hiph^îl* that might be reconstructed
as ולוא ירגיז עוד אויביו. This is better translated actively:
"and their (Israel's) enemies will not disturb them any more."

In sum, more precise readings in connection with a
structural understanding that takes account of the method of
the Qumran interpreter lead us to say that at the beginning of
4QFlor 1:1 we are dealing with a direct or indirect quotation
of 2 Samuel 7:10 (possibly as reflected in the textual tradition
of Psalm 89). Thus הואה הבית of line 2 refers back to מקום
of 2 Sam 7:10 and אויב can be restored with a suffix to make
the correct length for the lacuna: עֹ[וֹד אויב [יו ולוא יוסי]ף
בֹּ[ן] עוֹלֹה [לענות] וֹ

Line 2

All scholars agree upon restoring צויתי שופטים at the
beginning of the line; plene spelling is used throughout the
manuscript.[39] As to the second lacuna in the line neither
Allegro in "Fragments" nor Habermann has identified the top
of the *lāmed*; while Allegro made no attempt at a restoration,
Habermann restored as יבנה יהוה.[40] That correctly derived the
sense from the following supportive Biblical quotation, yet
Yadin managed to include the *lāmed* too: [יעשה] ל[ך בא] חרית.
This he did with reference to the end of 2 Sam 7:10.[41] Strugnell
corrects Yadin's לך to לכה but would rather read לו or preserve
the *lāmed* by using some form of the verb as if from Exod 15:17.

W. H. Brownlee has suggested[42] reading יתן or יתננו which
is used of God's "putting" the future sanctuary in the midst
of Israel (Ezek 37:26); נתן would thus be a synonym for שים of
2 Sam 7:10. But the prepositional phrase is to be construed

differently in Ezekiel from the most likely idiom in 4QFlor,
and due to the frequency of בנה in the rest of 4QFlor and
particularly its occurrence in line 10 where the corresponding
section of the MT has יעשה, it seems best to use that root with
Habermann[43] and to render the *lāmed* with the preposition. There
is also room enough for the third person singular suffix to have
a final *'āleph* as in lines 6 and 11.[44]

The more complete reading of בָּאָחרית (over against ב[אחרית
of DJD V) is made possible by close examination of photograph
41.308 of the Rockefeller Museum; there are faint dots of the
first two letters.

Line 3

All scholars agree upon restoring the quotation of Exod
15:17 back as far as מקדש,[45] but there is some dissension as
to what, if anything, was the first word of the line. By reconstructing the Exodus quotation from letters in the fragment
one can certainly say, against Habermann, that there was a space
before מקדש. It is, however, barely large enough for מושה and
it therefore seems unlikely that התורה of five letters be
restored (as Gaster).

For the version of Exod 15:18 it is worth comparing the
LXX   κύριος βασιλεύων τον αιῶνα καὶ ἐπ'αιῶνα καὶ ἔτι   with the
MT: יהוה ימלך לעלם ועד. As with the quotation of Amos 9:11
in line 12, 4QFlor diverges from both LXX and MT.[46]

Allegro's reading of כ[וננו is borne out by photograph
41.308.

Lines 4 and 5

Allegro in DJD V compares the words at the end of line 3

with Deut 23:3-4 and Ezek 44:9. Strugnell takes up the latter
to suggest a restoration consisting of [ערל לב וערל בשר עד .
Vermes proposes "[the unclean shall] never [enter, nor the
uncircumcised,] nor . . . ", which seems to be a free allusion
to the Ezekiel verse. Dupont-Sommer's "(ni l'impie ni l'impur
à) jamais," is yet another step further away.[47] Yadin, supported
by Slomovic and the translations of Maier and Tocci, refers to
1QM 7:4-5 as the basis for his restoration: "(איש אשר בשרו מום),
Anyone in whose flesh there is a permanent blemish." Maybe
the permanent blemish is a euphemism for the phrases in Deut 23:2.

Because of the occurrence of three of the excluded classes
of people in Deut 23:3-4, it certainly is preferable to make
proposals for restorations from study of those verses.[48] It is
noteworthy in this respect that the ממזר and the עמוני ומאבי
share the same qualification in the phraseology of Deuteronomy;
none of them shall enter even to "the tenth generation." Thus
the restoration could read גם דור עשירי ועד עולם and this then
stresses neatly the analogical phrase, עולם ועד, of the Exodus
quotation.[49] No restoration at this place can be made
definitively, but one that contains a direct verbal link to
Exod 15:17-18 is perhaps to be preferred on the basis of our
understanding of the exegetical principles involved; at least,
the text is most likely concerned somehow with those that are
to be excluded.

Three views exist in relation to the correct reading of
the middle of line 4. Firstly there is the proposal by Allegro,
"Fragments" and DJD V (supported by Strugnell, Lohse and the
translations of Tocci, Carmignac, Dupont-Sommer, Moraldi and
Vermes) to read וגר in the middle of the line. Secondly there

is the suggestion by Yadin to read וֹעַד, based on וֹעַד עַד עוֹלָם
in Isa 30:8 (suggested also by Habermann and supported by Maier
and Slomovic). Thirdly, Strugnell has hinted that instead of
וֹגֵר it is possible to read יֵגַד, "être séparé." While photograph
42.605 shows that what Yadin takes to be the left arm of an
^c*ayin* is in fact a crack, photographs 41.308 and 41.807 show
that וֹגֵר and יֵגַד are equally possible.

The recent work of J. M. Baumgarten has helped decide the
issue.[50] In support of the reading גֵר, which seems most likely
from the context, he has offered evidence from rabbinic tradition.
This is derived especially from *b. Qidd.* 4:1 where גֵר is
associated with מַמְזֵר and the נְתִינִים (= בֶן נֵכָר according to the
arguments of Baumgarten). Thereby Baumgarten considerably
reduces the contextual objections raised by Yadin and others
based on a comparison of this section of 4QFlor with CD 14:4
where the גֵר is given a definite rank in the congregation (עֵדָה)
for public meetings.

Baumgarten suggests, however, that the barrier of
significance for the author of 4QFlor was entry to the assembly
of the Lord (קְהַל יְהוָה), which is the context of Deuteronomy 23,
and not simply participation in some of the activities of the
congregation (עֵדָה). He also lists a similar distinction in
1QSa where "those with bodily afflictions were included in the
general congregation and were granted the right to present
inquiries (2:9-10); they were, however, ineligible to enter the
exclusive *qahal* (2:4) of those 'called to the council of the
yahad'."[51]

Thus, if Yadin's emendation for the beginning of the line
is correct (see above), then there is even less reason for him

to describe וגר as "impossible," a direct association being
made between the blemished and the גר in 1QSa. A problem
with Baumgarten's proposals is that neither קהל nor עדה is
specifically used in 4QFlor, so the exact referent must remain
obscure.

The problem with the final phrase of line 4, כיא קדושי
שם, is threefold. Firstly, as Strugnell has pointed out, the
last letter of קדושי could equally well be a *wāw*; secondly, the
question needs to be answered whether or not the end of line 4
is the end of the sentence, and, if not, then what might the
restoration be at the beginning of line 5; and thirdly, שם can
be read as either "there" or "name" and that may have some
influence on any proposal for the start of the next line.

To start with the beginning of line 5, we can see that a
yôd and part of what is almost certainly a *gimel*[52] are the first
two letters of the line; after a lacuna the length of one or,
at the most, two letters, two cut-off vertical strokes most
probably represent a *hē'*. A further lacuna is followed by the
words עולם תמיד עליו יראה. Since it is unlikely that תמיד and
עולם belong to the same phrase, we may conclude that the words
after עולם are a unit in themselves. It can be taken in one
of three ways: "always he (it) will be seen above it,"[53] or,
"always he (it) will appear upon it,"[54] or, "always he (it)
will protect it."[55]

For the phrase at the start of the line several alternatives
have been suggested but none has taken into account the *gimel*
in the second letter position. Because of the considerable
length of the lacunae most scholars do not restore anything at
the opening of the line. Yet, if the first word of the line

should be יגלה, as proposed by W. H. Brownlee,[56] then it can
be taken either as *qal* or as *pi^{c}el* or as *niph^{c}al*. Whichever
the case, the subject or object of the verb, the most probable
content of the second and major lacuna of the line, needs to
be one that might also be used as the subject of ראה in the
phrase already treated.

The restoration that seems most probable[57] derives from
the use of כבוד with גלה in Isa 40:5, "and the glory of the
Lord shall be revealed," a phrase that is contextually close
to the verse concerned with the preparation of a way in the
wilderness (Isa 40:3) which was so important for the self-
understanding of the Qumran community.[58] Of those scholars
who have not recognized the verb גלה at the start of line 5
Vermes has come the closest to perceiving such an understanding
in the lacuna. His translation reads: "[Its glory shall endure]
forever; it shall appear above it perpetually."[59] Our restoration may be translated either as, "He will reveal his glory
for ever, always it will appear upon it," or as, "His glory will
be revealed for ever, continually it will be seen over it." It
is the second of these that comes closer to Isa 40:5, "And the
glory of the Lord shall be revealed, and all flesh shall see it
together." Ezek 43:2-5 describes how the glory of God filled
the temple and some such image is surely the referent here,
since 4QFlor is discussing who may enter the sanctuary.[60]
Further support for restoring כבוד in 4QFlor comes from a
similar sentence in 11QTemple 29:8-10 which reads ואקדשה] קֹדשי
בכבודי אשר אשכן/ עליו את כבודי עד יום הברכה אשר אברא אני את
מקֹדשי/ להכינו לי כול הֹימים.[61] D. R. Schwartz has offered an
acceptable translation of these lines, "I will sanctify My temple

with My glory which I will cause to dwell upon it, until
the day of blessing when I will create My temple to establish
it for Me forever."[62]

Having determined how line 5 most likely began, we can
treat the final phrase of line 4. Here there is no lacuna
but ambiguity in the suffix of קדוש and in how שם is best
understood. Before dealing with the various understandings of
קדושו שם, the suggestions of scholars which use line 5 can be
dismissed. Habermann proposes קְדוֹשֵׁי שֵׁם /יהוה ימלוך and
Gaster translates, "but where (only) those shall be that are
God's saints." These two suggestions are only produced after
straining the Hebrew grammatically, the former with an unusual
appositional construction, the latter with a complex compound
sentence. Neither can Yadin's rendering be correct: "for His
holy ones there will be for ever."[63]

Most scholars read a *yôd* on קדוש and conclude the sentence
at the end of line 4, taking שם as "there." Thus Allegro
(DJD V) translates, "for my holy ones are there," commenting
that this refers to angels as in the MT of Deut 33:3 and elsewhere. Similarly Vermes renders the phrase, "for there shall
My Holy Ones be." Unless this phrase is an actual scriptural
citation, it is difficult to justify the occurrence of the 1st
person suffix.

Dupont-Sommer and Lohse take קדושי as a participle, read
"name" and conclude line 4 respectively: "mais ceux qui portent
le nom de saints"[64] and "sondern diejenigen, die den Namen
Heilige tragen." But this is an exceptional construction that
it is difficult for the Hebrew to carry without some recourse
to the following line.

It is also possible to end the sentence at the end of
the line but to read a *wāw*, considering that these cannot be
the words of God and that therefore they require the third
person suffix: "for His holy ones are there," or, as Carmignac
suggests, the somewhat awkward phrase: "Son Saint (est) là."
Carmignac explains: "c'est à dire: Dieu, le Saint d'Israel,
y réside." It has already been noted that several scholars
read the suffix as a *wāw* while continuing into line 5. The only
difficulty with such a reading is that the orthography of 4QFlor
is consistently *plene*, and although there are no third singular
suffixes for plural nouns present in the manuscript with which
comparison could be made, the reading of such a defective form
can only be justified on the basis of comparison with 1QpHab
where such a form occurs in both scriptural citation (1QpHab
3:6-7; Hab 1:8) and in the commentary (e.g., 1QpHab 5:13).

If the third singular suffix is for a singular noun, then
קודש must refer either to God himself, as Carmignac suggests,
or to God's Holy One, the Messiah. Since the eschatological
figures are described later in 4QFlor, we take the suffix as a
plural written defectively and read the phrase: "for his holy
ones are there."[65] Such is to exclude the possibility of
reading שם as "name,"[66] even though in 4QFlor 1:3 the adverb
is spelled with a *hē'*. שם is the normal Qumran spelling of the
adverb and may simply be spelled differently in 4QFlor 1:3
because of the verb of motion.[67]

From all this it is not surprising that many scholars
refrain from filling the lacuna at the start of line 5; yet,
some matters can be settled. Structurally line 5 is a continuation of the reasons for the exclusion of certain groups from

the house; in providing further reasons, there is also further
description of the house. It thus seems more advisable to
read this section as three phrases than to try to link line 4
with line 5 in some closer way.

For the first phrase at the end of line 4, קדושו שם is
preferable, as proposed by Yadin; to read a *yôd* would make the
phrase into some direct speech of God. The phrase "My holy
ones" never occurs in Qumran literature or in the MT. "His
holy ones are there" is further supported by 1QM 7:6: כיא
מלאכי קדוש עם צבאותם "For the holy angels shall be with their
hosts." שם is the most frequently used form of the adverb at
Qumran and the use of שמה in line 3 is to be considered in
relation to בוא as the directional "thither."

For the second phrase it thus remains only to decide upon
something that could be revealed for ever and that might fit
the context. The use of כבודו in that capacity reflects the
thought of Ezekiel[68] which the whole of Qumran literature echoes;
its suffix refers to the Lord. Then, for the third phrase, by
reading a *niphᶜal* with Allegro and Gaster, one avoids any awkward
break in the flow of the sense of the three phrases.[69]

In sum, therefore, a workable text is:

כיא קדושו שם/ יג [ל] ה [כבודו ל] עֹ[וֹ]לם תמיד עליו יראה

For his holy ones are there. His glory will be revealed
for ever, continually it will be seen over it.

Line 6

All scholars rightly agree upon restoring מקדש ישראל. לוא
in this line could be either the negative particle or the preposition with the third masculine singular suffix - the appearance
of לו and בו with *'āleph* is frequent at Qumran.[70]

Line 7

All scholars restore מעשי. Strugnell correctly mentions
the reading of תודה for the second word which is indeed
confirmed from the original manuscript and earliest photographs.
This is surprising in view of the excellent sense that מעשי
תורה would make in the context of the Qumran stress on obedience
to the Law.[71] Yet, the "deeds of thanksgiving" as appositional
to מקטירים shows that the author's intention is more inclusive
than the traditional thankoffering alone. In the middle of the
line והניחותי is restored *plene* from the MT. Interestingly the
certain restoration at the end of the line produces a phrase
that is unique in extant Qumran literature.[72] Yadin suggests
that 2 Sam 7:11 may also be alluded to in 11QT 3:3 which
passage shares certain similar concerns with 4QFlor 1:4-7.[73]

Line 8

In the centre of the line, which Allegro does not restore
beyond the suggestion that it may contain another infinitive,
Yadin proposes לכלותמ[ה בעוננותי] מה and he makes reference to
1QM 13:11 and CD 8:2 for this restoration.[74] The relevant
section of 1QM reads, "and his (Belial's) purpose is to bring
about wickedness and perversity," (Vermes), ובעצתו להרשיע ולהאשים;
that of CD, "they shall be visited for destruction by the hand
of Satan," לפוקדם לכלה בעד בליעל. Both these texts suggest that
Belial is to cause destruction through his scheming. Habermann
on the other hand follows Allegro's idea and provides a parallel
infinitive: ולהשחית] מה. It is impossible to declare which is
correct, but because of the large number of infinitives in this
part of the sentence, it seems preferable to restore with an
instrument of the destruction, as Yadin, which then parallels

the instrumental *bêt* at the end of line 9. Yet, Yadin's
choice of word may be too long for the lacuna. It is preferable
to restore, therefore, the shorter במשגחמה, which is then
explained in the following phrases.

In the middle of the line Yadin proposes to read כאשר תעו
in place of Allegro's כאשר באו, but Strugnell disagrees with
him in favour of Allegro's original reading which certainly
appears more likely from the photograph and is confirmed by an
examination of the original manuscript. It also makes better
contextual sense in relation to the subsequent infinitival phrase.[75]
Near the end of the line the phrase מחשבת בליעל can be restored
with certainty; it also occurs at 1QH 4:12-13 which is, therefore,
a guarantee to a restoration that all scholars agree in making.

Line 9

Most scholars follow Allegro in restoring בני אור as the
necessary object of the infinitive of line 8. Certainly the
suggestion of Yadin, followed by Maier and Slomovic, of להכשיל
ולחשוב [ ] ב[ה] can be excluded as this provides only an indirect
object for the *hiphᶜil* of כשל; nowhere in the MT or Qumran
literature is this attested as either a grammatical or idiomatic
possibility. Furthermore Yadin's suggestion does not fully
account for the space at the start of line 9 where an *'āleph* can
be restored with reasonable certainty. In fact the phrase
להכשיל בני אור actually occurs at 1QS 3:24 and seems preferable
to anything else.

Concerning the lacuna at the centre of the line, if פשו
is taken as the end of a verbal form, then the most satisfactory
root to restore is תפש. In CD 4:16ff. the discussion similarly
concerns how men are ensnared by Belial and there the root תפש

is used three times. Thus למען יחפשו of Yadin and Habermann
is accepted here;[76] this phrase also occurs at 1QH 4:19.
Mention should also be made of the reading נפשו, the noun with
the third masculine singular suffix. Because the subject and
object of this explanation are clearly in the plural this reading
is unlikely unless one sees that נפש is being used collectively,
as suggested by Allegro, with reference either to the sons of
light or, cryptically, to the Teacher of Righteousness, with
Belial as the wicked Priest or Man of Lies.[77]

    For the end of the line it is worth noting that the one use
of משגה in the MT occurs at Gen 43:12 in the Joseph story.[78]
Jacob reluctantly tells his sons to return to Egypt with
Benjamin and that, as they are going, they must also take back
the first payment that Joseph had ordered to be put in the top
of their sacks, since, in Jacob's mind, perhaps there was an
"error." Nowhere is it described as a sin to return money to
people or to give them grain when in need. When used in 4QFlor,
therefore, the term would require some qualification, as it is
there implied that the mistake is wrong. That fact together
with a close study of the photograph (DJD V, Plate 19) excludes
Yadin's restoration, for from the shape of the edges of the
fragment it is not at all certain that it could be joined so
closely as to enable the reading במשגתימה; also much of the *yôd*
would have had to have faded. Rather it is more certain, because
the last preserved letter before the text breaks off preserves
most of the head of what is most probably an *'āleph*.[79]

    Those who make a restoration all supply or understand
אונמה except Strugnell who proposes אשמה and translates "guilty
error". However, although Strugnell's proposal gives a stronger

sense and a more clarificatory reading, the מה of the word
to be restored is better read as the suffix from a syntactical
point of view, and that is the reading followed here. The scroll
is very damaged at this point and it is impossible to measure
the resulting lacuna accurately: it could possibly hold some
such reconstruction as א[שמח]מה, "through their guilty error".[80]

Lines 10-13

These four lines were first published by Allegro in 1956.[81]

Line 10

The restoration at the beginning of the line is agreed
upon by all scholars on the basis of the MT of 2 Sam 7:11b,
though one should not forget that the text tradition of the
Samuel quotations in 4QFlor is in many respects closer to the
LXX.[82] The text of 2 Samuel 7 cited at this point omits three
phrases found in the MT: יהוה כי ימלאו ימיך ושכבת את אבתיך,
את ממלכתו הוא יבנה בית לשמי וכננתי and אשר יצא ממעיך. As
Carmignac observes, all three omissions are explicable in
relation to the MT on the basis of homoeoteleuton.

Yet, if the text of 2 Samuel 7 that the author of 4QFlor
had was approximately the same as that of the MT (or LXX for that
matter), then it would seem to be a more remarkable coincidence
that three times in two verses, he should make the same mistake
and leave it uncorrected. Certainly the scribe was not beyond
making corrections in his manuscript; see, for example, his
insertion at 4QFlor 2:4a. We are thus pushed to the conclusion
that the text of 2 Samuel 7 has received some deliberate editing
at this juncture; and this is tantamount to saying that omission
through homoeoteleuton may be correctly considered as a correct
exegetical principle used here by the author deliberately!

From the context of the interpretation, certain reasons
can be advanced for the omissions. To begin with the third,
"he will build a house for my name": this goes against the
main intent of the passage which is trying to suggest that the
future house (sanctuary) is not to be made with human hands
but to have its origin from God. Secondly, "who will come
forth from your body" introduces the delicate subject of the
origin of the messianic kingly figure. That this person is
coming is repeated often in the Qumran texts but nowhere is
his origin described - it was either not an issue or, as this
second omission perhaps suggests, it was a matter to be avoided.[83]
The first phrase, "when your days are fulfilled and you lie
down with your father," may simply have been excluded because
of its temporal content.

Further support for the deliberate use of homoeoteleuton
comes from the fact that, if the second and third phrases were
to be omitted for some such reasons as those given above, then
the only way in which both phrases could be left out by means
of this technique is that used by the author of 4QFlor: he
could not jump directly from אחריכה to וכננתי, but through the
use of והכינתי which is "conveniently" preceded by ממעיר (ממעיכה)
he could proceed directly to the last half of verse 13. What
was formerly in scholarship described as a scribal error is now
to be seen as the correct use of a valid exegetical technique.

Line 11

In his first publication of this line Allegro tentatively
proposed at its start עד עול[ם, referring to 2 Sam 7:13; in his
later article, "Fragments," he restored לעויל[ם?, and in DJD V
he became more definite: לעו[לם. This last reading is endorsed

by Strugnell[84] against Yadin's לע[ד, proposed on the basis of
lack of space for לעולם . The MT reads עד עולם but the LXX text
type, that seems to be followed here, has ἔως εἰς τὸν αἰῶνα
which would corroborate the MT, or even suggest a Hebrew of
עד לעולם.[85] The author then abbreviated that to the much more
common לעולם that is the most likely reading here.

Line 12

Again the beginning of the line is missing in part from the
manuscript. Allegro has omitted a first word restoration from
all his publications but has proposed בצי[און בא[חרית for the
lacuna that follows, with which all scholars agree; yet, traces
of the *'āleph* occur in photograph 41.807, hence that letter may
be partially restored. Van der Woude, Dupont-Sommer and Vermes
all render the whole lacuna alike; Vermes translates: "with the
Interpreter of the Law [to rule] in Zion [at the end] of time."
These three scholars have correctly understood the grammatical
structure of the passage. It is similar to that in line 13
where both the participle with the article and the relative
clause[86] clearly refer back to סוכת דויד.

The restoration of Yadin and Habermann, יקום, seems to be
an attempt to make the action of the דורש התורה parallel to the
העומד of the צמח דויד; Strugnell, who also adopts יקום, certainly
interprets it so. In fact, he makes the whole of lines 12 and
13 refer to the דורש התורה, reading the penultimate word of
line 12 as הואה , of common gender, and translating that phrase,
"He (i.e. the דורש התורה) is the tent of David which is fallen,
who will arise etc." But this not only misunderstands the
earlier use of the extended dependent relative clause in Hebrew,
expressed with the article prefixed to the participle, but also

misinterprets the long citation of 2 Sam 7:11b-14, especially
edited by the author of 4QFlor, of which lines 11-12 are all
explanatory. What at first appears to be an ambiguous construction at the end of line 11 and the beginning of line 12,[87]
is clear. Furthermore the sequence משל + עמד occurs also at
Dan 11:3 and 1QpHab 8:9.[88] Thus the restorations of van der
Woude, Dupont-Sommer and Vermes are followed here - grammar and
context being used to decipher the structure and proper content
of the passage.

     As for the text of Amos 9:11 that is quoted in 4QFlor,
J. de Waard has pointed out that its text is identical in
Acts 15:16 and 4QFlor 1:12.[89] Both differ from the LXX and
from the MT. Even the introductory formula in Acts, καθὼς
γέγραπται, has its Hebrew equivalent in 4QFlor, כאשר כתוב, over
against the כאשר אמר introducing the same verse in CD 7:16.
De Waard, therefore, postulates a common text tradition for
4QFlor and Acts, which to him is much preferable to other
theories of the text tradition of Amos 9:11 in the Book of Acts.[90]

     At the end of the line הואה is read rather than היאה because
of the gender of the verb. The author appears to be playing
on the varied meanings of סוכה.

     Line 13

     All scholars correctly agree upon restoring הנופל [ח א] שׁר
in the lacuna near the beginning of this line.

     Line 14

     The middle of the line is warped and it is clear from the
original manuscript that הח [ה] לּיֹ should be read instead of הלי.
No adjustment in the sense is required.

     The difficulty at the end of this line is chiefly derived

from the crumpled state of the fragment which allows neither
precise readings nor the exact measurement of the lacuna.
With that, it is clear that any decision must be tentative.

Of the three alternatives פשר הדבר אשר, פשר הדבר אשר and פשר
הדבר על, the first is very infrequent in Qumran literature,
occurring with certainty only at 4QpIsa[b] 2:1, and although that
should not necessarily exclude it as a restoration, it does make
the other two more likely. It also seems that any attempt to
restore the letter preceding סרי as a *hē'* or a *rēš* is asking
too much of the fragment, for, although there are traces of ink
there, they occur partly at a much greater height than the
letters that follow, so that the only letter, if any, that could
be restored is a *lāmed*.[91] Concerning סרי, the head of the third
letter, the distinguishing feature of the *yôd* is even larger
than that of the normal *yôd*; thus the *yôd* of Allegro, Habermann
and Lohse is to be preferred to the *wāw* suggested by Yadin.

Strugnell, in the light of the subsequent quotation of
Isa 8:11, restores the whole of the end of the line either as
פשר דב[ר אש]ר סרו מדרך or as דב[ר המ]ה סרי מדרך [העם (הרשעים?)
(הרשעים?) העם] but apart from what has been said about reading
אש[ר and המ[ה it is rare for a pesher preceding a supportive
biblical quotation to contain a large amount of that quotation;[92]
rather, it is more likely that it would contain words from the
text of which it is the pesher, in this case רשעים.[93] Or, if
the first lines of the psalms are quoted with the intention that
the rest of them is to be understood, then the restoration would
be better as חטאים from Ps 1:2,[94] used there in a phrase with
דרך, the linkword, by *gĕzērâ šāwâ* to the Isaiah quotation. Once
again an understanding of the exegetical principle involved

enables a particular restoration to appear much more likely
than any other. על is added at the end of the line to complete
the formula אשר כתוב of line 15; for such a restoration it is
worth comparing line 16: אשר כתוב עליהמה.[95]

Line 15

The restoration of the phrase לאחרית הימים[96] is agreed
upon by all scholars, and is confirmed in its present more
definite reading from photograph 41.807.

Since the reading כחזקת agrees with 1QIsa[a] and many Mss.,
the rest of the cited verse is restored from 1QIsa[a] and not
from the MT. Thus, whereas most scholars restore the MT היד
but translate it indefinitely, 1QIsa[a] has יד. Similarly יסירנו
of 1QIsa[a] is to be preferred to the MT's ויסרני.[97]
F. du T. Laubscher has proposed reading ויסירני here[98] but it
seems unnecessary to preserve the initial *wāw* as if the MT text-
type was normative. Indeed to omit that *wāw* because it is not
in 1QIsa[a] renders Laubscher's proposed future translation of
the whole phrase more likely. With Laubscher the initial ויהי
is taken as an imperfect with *wāw* copulative[99] and the second
verb is read as a *hiphᶜil* form of סור,[100] not יסר as in the MT,[101]
but with a first person plural suffix which gives greater sense
to the plural identification in the pesher that follows.

Line 16

When Allegro first published the text of this line in 1958,
he provided no restoration for the end of the line but suggested
that it might contain a paraphrase of Ezek 44:10;[102] but by the
time of the publication of DJD V he had come to give preference
to the reading of Yadin and Habermann who restored the quotation
as if from Ezek 37:23.[103] Although it is impossible to fit both

a *bêt* and a *gimel* before the *lāmed* at the beginning of line 17,[104]
there are several good reasons for following Yadin here, but
in the version of Strugnell.

    1. Of all the thirty-nine occurrences of גלול in Ezekiel,
11 of which are in the plural with the third plural masculine
suffix, only Ezek 37:23 can account clearly for the לו at the
end of line 16 as it stands in the fragment.[105]

    2. To restore the text as if from Ezek 37:23 requires
that there be only very slight editing of the biblical quotation.
The author has announced his intention to quote from Ezekiel
as support for his pesher and such an introductory formula is
usually followed by an exact quotation - or else it is no support -
even if later that quotation receives some radical treatment
in exegesis.

    3. Ezek 44:10 is clearly concerned with the Levites,
whereas almost the only thing of which we can be certain in the
ensuing clarification in 4QFlor is that the concern in the
quotation from Ezekiel should fit the Sons of Zadok. Vermes,
for one, has wondered if the Levites are included under the
title "Sons of Zadok."[106] However, 1QSa 1:2 and 9 describe the
Sons of Zadok as the "Priests who keep the Covenant," and again
in 1QSa 1:2 and 24 the Sons of Zadok are the "priests;" also
it is clear in 1QSa 2:3 that the Levites are summoned prior to
the "Sons of Zadok the priests." While there remains some
confusion as to who exactly the Sons of Zadok in 4QFlor are,
even if they are the whole community, the context of the pesher
fits more precisely with Ezek 37:23,[107] as will be discussed
below in the remarks on line 17.

    4. When the phrase from Ezek 37:23 is recalled in full,

there is a linkword with Psalm 1 to enable the *gĕzērâ šāwâ*.[108]

5. In the last case, Ezek 37:23 fits very well with certain passages from CD with which 4QFlor seems to be closely associated.[109]

Line 17

The context of the quotation from Ezekiel 37 concerns the future unity of Judah and Israel (Ezek 37:15-28), that God will gather the divided and scattered people under one king,[110] and that "they shall not defile themselves any more with their idols." The matter concerns two groups of people.[111] That the sect called itself the "House of Judah" on occasion is well known;[112] it would not be unlikely, therefore, that one of the groups mentioned should be the Sons of Zadok. At the end of the line there appears with reasonable certainty the sometime designation of the whole community, יחד.

Between the בני צדוק and the phrase leading up to the final יחד, there was probably mention of a second group. Indeed it is possible to see that the word following צדוק begins with a *wāw*, introducing the second subject of the commentary on Ezek 37:23. Study of the passages in which בני צדוק הכוהנים is used[113] shows that more often than not the group is mentioned alone; but in 1QSa 1:2 they are associated with the אנושי בריתם, "the men of their covenant," who are further defined as אנושי עצתו, "the men of his council."[114] So, rather than giving this second group some negative role such as ודורשי עצתמה,[115] the suggestion of several scholars[116] is adopted here, but in plene spelling which none has proposed: ואֹ[נו]שי עצ[חמ]ֹה.

Any restoration at the centre of the line is highly

tentative. After ה[תמ]עצ occur the two letters *rēš* and *wāw*
at the beginning of a word; they are followed by a stroke
that could be either a *dālet* or a *bêt*. Using a *dālet*, some
scholars have suggested phrases beginning with a word from
the root רדף, "to pursue."[117] But רדף is primarily a military
term in the Qumran writings, only occurring once in a nonmilitary sense (1QS 18; poetry) and from the nonmilitary
context of 4QFlor it is perhaps advisable to read a participle
from a verb of which the first two root letters are *rēš* and
ḥēt: רחק appears most suitable.[118] In partial fulfilment of
1QS 1:4 the Sons of Zadok and the men of their counsel have
kept far from all evil.

As for the end of the line, there is complete agreement
among scholars that יחד should be read as the last word. In
the lacuna before that, the remaining letters require the
reading of אׁחריהמֹה.[119] Habermann's הׁבריהמֹה is difficult to
fit into the context unless one follows his other less certain
readings for the line,[120] and anyway, photograph 41.802 shows
most of the word's initial *'āleph*.

Remembering the context of the Ezekiel passage in which
two parties will be united (אחד) and expecting the comment to
describe those two parties as they are part of the eschatological
community (יחד) it is best to restrict any restoration to the
following:[121] המה בני צדוק וא[נו]שי עצ [תמ]ה רוח[קי מרע....]
יחד [....] וׁ[אׁחריהמֹה....

> They are the Sons of Zadok and the men of their counsel
> who keep far from evil . . . after them . . . community
> (or, together).

Line 18

All agree in restoring Psalm 2:1 in full from the
beginning of the line, and make recourse to the MT to do so.
However, traces of ink appear at the edge of a small hole in
the manuscript and it would seem that these belong to a *bêt*
prefixed to יחד. Although נוסדו is clearly written in 4QFlor,
this would bring the text of Ps 2:2 closer to the LXX (συνήχθησαν
ἐπὶ τὸ αὐτὸ); that does not negate the common scholarly opinion
that the LXX verb represents a Hebrew *Vorlage* of נועדו. The
phrase is thus ambiguous and can be rendered either "take
counsel together (lit. in a gathering)" or "take counsel
against the community."

Line 19

Referring to CD 4:3-4, "the Sons of Zadok are the Chosen
of Israel," Yadin wishes to read the content of the pesher as
concerning the "chosen of Israel" whom he relates to the
quotation of Psalm 2 by reading משיחו as the plural משיחיו.
But nowhere in QL are the Qumran Covenanters as a body called
"anointed" nor is the title בחירי ישראל restricted solely to
the expected messianic figures.[122] Indeed, to take משיחו as
a plural in the interpretation based on a collective understanding of the word in the Psalm or to restore a plural in
the text of the Psalm itself is to risk too much.

Furthermore, if attention is paid to the positioning of
Fragment 2 with regard to line 18 (where restoration is certain),
it can be seen that it should be further to the right than
either of Allegro's photographic reproductions depict. Thus
Yadin's restoration for line 19[123] (נים [על בני צדוק הכוה),
(וה[מה] בחירי ישראל), apart from having debatable content, is

too long before the portion of Fragment 2, and too short
after it.

On the other hand, Habermann's ייm פ[שר הדבר [על הגו] is
too short before Fragment 2,[124] though he suggests the
interesting restoration of יה[גו ריק על] for the centre of
the line, staying close to the vocabulary of the Psalm citation.
Strugnell adopts a similar policy and suggests the following
alternative restorations: פ[שר הדבר [אשר ירגשי מלכי הגו]ייm
וה[גו, הגויים or, for the space after וה[תיצבו על] בחירי ישראל
ריק על]. Although it is most uncharacteristic of Qumran
pesharim to start with such a long adapted requotation of the
original biblical citation, Strugnell's work does point to the
way in which restoration can be made in both lacunae.

The suggestion that the lacunae contain close references
to Psalm 2 is to be considered seriously since there needs to
be some logical connection between the interpretation and the
biblical text; and yet the uneasiness that identification of
the "chosen ones of Israel" with the "anointed" makes must
imply that the chosen ones are to be seen in relation to some
other characters in the Psalm. The remarks made on the
restoration for line 14 show that, to provide the best text for
the lacuna at the end of that line, reference must be made to
a later section of Psalm 1.

Similarly it is Psalm 2:12 that provides the best vocabulary
and most sensible reading for the last lacuna of 4QFlor 1:19.
Extant in the text are a *wāw* and what must be either a *hē'* or
a *ḥēt*. With regard to Psalm 2:12 either is possible. If the
text of the Psalm is adhered to then a *ḥēt* is to be read with
the result of וח[וסי בו המה] בחירי ישראל; if a *hē'*, perhaps

less preferable, then the Psalm text can be adjusted
accordingly: וה[חוסים בו המה] בחירי ישראל [125] Once again, an
understanding of the methodological presuppositions of the
writer has enabled us to decide upon a particular restoration.

For the second lacuna of the line, there is preserved on
Fragment 2 the end of a word, most likely correctly read as
gentilic. At least Yadin's הכוה[נים is most unlikely for his
nūn (though blurred) would then be touching the following *yôd*;
in 4QFlor the *nūn* is consistently written upright. In taking
account of the gentilic ending several scholars have suggested
restorations using גויים from Psalm 2:1;[126] yet all require some
forced readjustment of the text of the Psalm to result in
reading גו[יים in that place. If none of them is right, then
it could be that as there is an identification from Psalm 2:12
in the second half of the line, so also in the first half some
party from the psalm is being identified in a gentilic way:[127]
the options are several, but it is כתיים , suggested by
W. H. Brownlee,[128] that would best suit an identification of
the גוים of Psalm 2:1.

Concerning this restoration 1QpHab 2:11-12 identifies
the Chaldeans, "that bitter and hasty nation" (גוי ; Hab 1:6),
as the Kittim and 1QpHab 3:4-5 has the Kittim inspire with fear
all the nations (גואים ; i.e. other nations). Indeed, just as
the Kittim laugh at the kings and people (Hab 1:10a, 1QpHab 4:1-3)
so in turn the Lord laughs at the kings of the earth and the
rulers in Psalm 2:4. Furthermore 4QpIsa[a] clearly describes the
Kittim in terms of the eschatological foe,[129] whose demise
occurs at the same time as the appearance of the shoot of David
(צמח דויד ; 4QpIsa[a] frgs. 8-10, 4QFlor 1:11, 4QPBless 3-4).

So a substantially justified restoration of the whole
line might read:

משיחו פ[שר הדבר ‎130 ‎[אשר הגויים המה הכת]יים וח[וסי בו המה]
בחירי ישראל באחרית הימים

Column 2

Apart from quoting the beginning of lines 1-4a as
published by Allegro, "Fragments," few scholars have made
much attempt at making sense out of what remains of Column 2 -
indeed, largely because Allegro did not publish the whole of
4QFlor until the appearance of DJD V. Just as for Psalm 1
there are supportive biblical texts for the pesher, so these
few lines in Column 2 contain at least one introduced quotation,
as well as what appears to be an indirect quotation from a
nearby passage. Assuming that the lines of Column 2 are of
similar length to those of Column 1,[131] then the most important
question becomes that of ascertaining how far or near Fragment 3
should be placed to Fragment 1. It is quite possible that they
are not so very far from each other, as the restoration here
intends to demonstrate.

Line 1

The restoration of בית יהודה is to be preferred to פתאי
יהודה considering the concern of 4QFlor with houses and because
the phrase actually occurs in Fragment 4, line 4.[132] בליעל
of line 2 might be preceded in line 1 by a phrase such as כול
מחשבת [133]

Line 2

The original manuscript is the basis of the reading
ונשאר שאֹר over against Allegro's ונשאר ש]. It is worth

comparing this line with CD 1:14: השאיר שארית ישראל, "he
left a remnant to Israel."[134] The line is to be completed
with something that might fit between התורה and מושה of
line 3. For the phrase כול התורה cf. 1QS 5:16, 8:2.

Lines 3 and 4

From the repetition of היאה and from the fact that the
context of the Daniel quotation is very concerned with the
"time," it seems that, as in line 1, there is to be an
explanation of עת.[135] The proximity of Fragment 3 to Fragment 1,
according to the above restoration of lines 1 and 2, enables
a short restoration to be made utilizing the clearly visible
rêš at the start of line 3 in Fragment 3. Because of the very
likely reading of המשכילים in line 4, it is possible to identify
the quotation as from Dan 12:10; but it is also necessary to
admit that, according to the MT, this requires alteration of
the *hiph^{c}îl* perfect to the infinitive to fit the evidence of the
Fragment. The existence of a different text tradition cannot
be ruled out. Dan 12:10 and 11:35 are both connected to Psalm 2
through their common use of the root שכל: again understanding
of exegetical presuppositions enables a more certain restoration to be proposed. At the end of line 3 magnification of
the original manuscript reveals vestiges of an ^{c}*ayin* Allegro
(DJD V) reads להרשי]ע.

Line 4a

This insertion is clearly by the same hand as the rest of
4QFlor. It seems to contain a quotation of Dan 11:32b,[136] ועם
ידעי אלהיו יחזקו ועשו and the phrase before that seems to be
drawn from verbs used in Dan 11:35 concerning the action of
the משכילים which is the link back to Dan 12:10 in lines 4 and 5.

The restoration proposed used the three roots צרף, ברר and
לבן from Dan 11:35, one of which is definitely in Fragment 3,
and one of which is partially represented.[137]

Lines 5 and 6

Strugnell wonders whether these lines may contain a
quotation of Psalm 3:1-2. However, none of the remaining
words are the same.[138] If ברדתו is part of a biblical verse
it can only be from Exod 34:29 where the context discusses
Moses after his descent from Mount Sinai where he had talked
with God. Psalm 2 does indeed contain an actual speech of the
Lord to the king - which may be the connection between the
passages, if indeed Exod 34:29 is being cited.[139]

If ברדתו is not part of a direct quotation of scripture
then the descent mentioned could be that of Yahweh in a
theophany. Isa 63:19 (Eng. 64:1) calls on God to come down
(ירד) and intervene. Ps 18:10 (Eng. 18:9) uses ירד with Yahweh
as subject; indeed in verse 12 the thick clouds dark with water
are described as his *sukkāh* (סכתו) which might suggest how
4QFlor 2:5 is to be linked with the earlier interpretation
(4QFlor 1:12). Zechariah 14 associates Yahweh's theophany with
the feast of Tabernacles (14:16); the defeat of the nations
(Zech 14:2) echoes the language of Ps 2. Similarly Joel 4
proclaims a theophany in battle; the description of Yahweh as
the refuge (מחסה) of his people (Joel 4:16; Eng. 3:16) echoes
Ps 2:11, used above to restore 4QFlor 1:19.[140]

Fragment 4

The content of this fits well with that of Fragments 1-3.
There is mention of the "time," (Col. 2:1, 3?), of Belial (Col.
1:8), and, most likely, of Judah and Israel which is the context

of the Ezekiel quotation in the pesher of Psalm 1,
(Col. 1:16-17). Also צאצא appears frequently in 1QM and
1QH. Careful reading of photograph 41.810 shows יִשֹׁרֹאֹל more
fully preserved than Allegro allows (DJD V; יֹ[שׂר]אֹל).

It is impossible to say where this fragment might have
been within the context of the whole scroll.

Fragment 5

This fragment is interesting primarily because it may
contain a reference to the Messiah(s) in its having the same
phrase as occurs in 1QS 9:11, CD 12:23, 14:19, 19:10 and 20:1
but in the reverse order: אהרון וישראל. That the Messiah of
Israel should come before the one of Aaron may reflect a change
in attitude toward the messianic figures. This will be discussed
further below. A close reading of the original manuscript shows
the dot of an earlier line on this fragment's upper edge.

Fragment 6-11

These are all text and pesher of the blessings of
Deuteronomy 33. Because Fragments 9 and 10 are clearly at
the top of a column, one can presume that 6, 7 and 8 were in
a previous column. Strugnell has improved on Allegro's
suggestion for Fragments 6 and 7 by more carefully aligning
the fragments in relation to the text of Deuteronomy. Strugnell
also proposes using the text of 4QTest to restore the lacunae.
Allegro's text is cited here but it is emended according to
the suggestions of Strugnell.

For Fragment 10 Strugnell identifies an 'āleph at the
beginning of the fragment, from which he tentatively suggests
reading הואה.

Fragment 12

This is a piece of the right hand edge of a column.
For line 4 Strugnell reads בּסֹ and proposes בספר. This would
fit well with the frequent use of supportive biblical quotations
introduced by formulae containing such words in 4QFlor. In
fact, from photograph 42.608 the more complete בסֹפֹ]ר[can be
determined.

Fragments 13 and 14

These fragments can almost certainly be aligned to form
the third verse of Psalm 5, as Strugnell has pointed out. It
is also likely that these two fragments belong with those
Allegro lists under 4QCatena[a],[141] where there is material
concerned with psalm interpretation - Catena[a] is not to be
joined to 4QFlor: the hand is different and the column size
is smaller with only 16 lines.

The *bêt* in line 1 of Fragment 14 could equally well be
a *kaph*.

Fragment 15

Strugnell identifies this as being a quotation from
Isa 65:22-23, though, of course, the position of the text in
the column cannot be determined. The context of that section
of Isaiah speaks of the "chosen ones" which is certainly
relevant to 4QFlor. Strugnell mentions that it may also just
be possible to include Fragment 19 as part of this quotation,
though he admits of the difficulty in aligning the two texts.
Even if one follows the text of 1QIsa[a], the lines cannot be
fitted; in fact, the positioning is even less likely as there
is, as usual at Qumran, a *hē'* on ידיהמה and yet ברוכי of the MT

is shortened to ברך. Perhaps, however, the המה of Fragment 19
is part of the exposition, and not of the Isaiah quotation,
unless the Isaiah text has been edited at this point, as that
of 2 Samuel 7 was in Column 1:10-11.

Fragments 16-18 and 20-26

Little can be said concerning these fragments.

For Fragment 16 photograph 42.608 shows more of the letter
of the first line than is reconcilable with the vestiges of a
ʾāleph (Allegro, DJD V). Photograph 41.810 shows that the
letter preserved in line 1 of Fragment 18 is most probably a
bêt; for line 3 a final nûn is quite ascertainable.

For Fragment 21 Strugnell suggests that it could be
joined to Column 1 at line 3 to read there כ[ון יהוה מקדש].
The kaph fits well and יהוה for אדוני is attested in 86 Mss. and
the Samaritan text.

Fragment 23 may contain once again the title of the
figure who is to accompany the צמח דויד; Fragment 24 contains
מצרף which is found in 4QFlor 2:1.

Unpublished Fragment 27

W. H. Brownlee has observed that this fragment is preserved
in the Rockefeller Museum along with those depicted in Plate XX
of DJD V, although it was not published with the other fragments
of that plate. For the partial word of line 2 the wāw could
equally well be a yôd.

11QMelch

J. Carmignac suggests that 4QFlor and 11QMelch, because of
their similar "thematic" style and content, especially as both
contain a quotation of Isa 8:11, may originally have been two

pieces of the same work.[142] Yet, the column length, the
location of discovery and slight stylistic variations all
tell against this proposal.

C. Form-Critical Study

1. The Parts of the Text

a. 4QFlor 1:1-13

Extent of the Unit

      Any definition of the extent of a unit in this fragmentary
text is complicated through the lack of a clear beginning and
a clear end. The main body of the text (frgs. 1-3), however,
can be divided precisely at the end of 4QFlor 1:13: form and
content both show that 1:1-13 requires treatment apart from
1:14-2:6. In the former it is the text of 2 Samuel 7 that the
interpreter explains, in the latter it is Psalms 1 and 2 that are
expanded in a midrash. Formally, the explanation of 2 Samuel 7
is attached to the scriptural text in a different way from the
pēšer interpretations of Psalms 1 and 2 and their scriptural
citations. Since textual problems have already been dealt with,
consideration of the structure of the passage follows immediately.

Structure of the Text

      The main feature of the unit is the way in which the pun
on בית, "house," in 2 Samuel 7 is preserved in the two major
subdivisions: in the first place ביה is aptly taken to refer
to the sanctuary and secondly it is discussed in its metaphorical
significance in relation to the royal house of David. But within

the treatment of 2 Samuel 7:10-11a", the interpretation of
בית as מקדש is developed into an explanation of מקדש in terms
of קהל, "congregation" such that by the time 2 Sam 7:11aʾ is
introduced the discussion of the sanctuary has evolved solely
into a consideration of the community itself - that in itself
then forms the thematic link whereby discussion of the shoot
of David is seen in the perspective of saviour of the community
as well as in terms of ruler of Zion, the holy city.

Nathan's Oracle Interpreted   4QFlor 1:1-13

I. Concerning the Eschatological Sanctuary/Community 1:1-9

   A. Quotation of 2 Sam 7:10-11a"

   B. Interpretations

      1. Concerning the House   2-7

         a. Statement of identification (with explanation:
            relative cl. including temporal phrase)
            (הואה...הימים)

         b. Statement of explanation around Exod 15:17b-18
            1) Quotation of Exod 15:17b-18 with
               introduction (cKs)
               (כאשר...ועד)

            2) Interpretation of מקדש (הואה...תודה)
               a) Statement of identification
                  (הואה הבית)

               b) Statement of explanation (relative cl.)
                  (אשר...תודה)

                  (1) Conc. limited admission
                     (a) Allusion to Deut 23:3-4
                        (אשר...עולם)

        (b) 5 groups denied admission

          (ועמוני...עולם)

        (c) Threefold reason for exclusion

          (כיא...יראה)

      (2) Conc. non-desolation

        (a) Introductory statement

          (ולוא...זרים)

        (b) Comparative statement

          (כאשר...בחטאתמה)

      (3) Conc. promise and purpose of the Lord

        (a) Promise: to build

          (ויואמר...אדם)

        (b) Purpose: to offer

          (להיות...תודה)

2. Concerning the lack of enemies   7–9

  a. Quotation of 2 Sam 7:11aʹ with introduction

    1) Introductory formula (cA)

    2) 2 Sam 7:11aʹ

  b. Interpretation (relative cl.) (אשר...אונמה)

    1) Basic statement

      (אשר...במשגתימה)

    2) Comparative description of sons of Belial

      (כאשר...אונמה)

      a) Conc. their coming w. plots of Belial

        (כאשר...בליעל)

      b) Twofold purpose for coming with overall
        intention

        (1) To cause sons of light to stumble

          (להכשיל...אור)

(2) To devise against them plots of

wickedness

(ולהשוב...און)

(1) + (2) To catch them for Belial

(למען...אונמה)

II. Concerning the Eschatological Figures   10-13

    A. Quotations from 2 Samuel 7

        1. 2 Sam 7:11b

        2. 2 Sam 7:12aʼ

        3. 2 Sam 7:13b with verb from 12bᵃ

        4. 2 Sam 7:14a

    B. Interpretation

        1. Statement of identification (expanded)

(הואה...התורה)

           a. Demonstrative pronoun

(הואה)

           b. Subject of reference

(צמח...התורה)

              1) Name

(צמח דויד)

              2) Relative participial description

(העומד...התורה)

        2. Statement of explanation (relative cl.)

(אשר...ישראל)

           a. Basic statement with temporal phrase

(אשר...הימים)

           b. Comparative quotation w. interpretation

(כאשר...ישראל)

1) Quotation of Amos 9:11 w. introductory
   formula (cK)

   (כאשר...הנופלת)

2) Interpretation

   (הואה...ישראל)

   a) Statement of identification

      (הואה...הנופלת)

   b) Statement of explanation (relative cl.)

      (אשר...ישראל)

A detailed analysis of this kind is only justifiable in as
much as it arises from the text. In the case of the unit under
consideration one can see that the very layout of the text on
the scroll is itself informative. The second major subsection
of biblical text to which commentary is attached starts with
its first word at the margin and it may be presupposed on the
basis of this same feature in the second unit of the text (when
Psalm 1 and 2 are cited) that the material from 2 Sam 7:10-11a$^\alpha$
also began at the margin, possibly on the bottom line of the
previous column.

But apart from this physical clue certain formal characteristics support the analysis as outlined above. From the whole
of 4QFlor it appears that the major texts, which form the basis
for the various subsections of the two units so far identified,
are not themselves introduced with any formula. That alone
could lead to an understanding that the quotation of 2 Sam 7:11a$^\beta$
in line 7 is in some way subordinate; indeed the relative
significance of this quotation is central to a correct analysis
of the first subsection of the unit 4QFlor 1:1-13. The discovery
of two subsections within our first unit is further supported

on the basis of style: it is to be noted that each subsection
of 4QFlor contains the temporal phrase אחרית הימים (lines 2,
12, 15, 19) indicating for the first unit (4QFlor 1:1-13) that
there are two subsections which the author is insisting must
be seen in relation to the latter days - this already points
to one aspect of the purpose that the author had in his
interpretation.

Taking the first subsection (1:1-9) of this first unit
and remembering that certain exegetical principles were the
tools of the commentator of the first centuries B.C. and A.D.,
we can trace the treatment of one half of Nathan's pun, that
"house" is used of the temple. בית does not occur in 2 Sam
7:10-11aᵅ but is presupposed as the basis of the oracle of
Nathan from 2 Sam 7:5-6. In 2 Sam 7:10 it is מקום, "place,"
that is used: only in this verse is a place described concerning
which God takes the initiative, He is to appoint it for his
people Israel. It is the initiative of Yahweh that is the salient
characteristic of the first expanded demonstrative introductory
formula; coupled with such initiative is the thematic temporal
phrase באחרית הימים.

Then, immediately, the identification of מקום in this
introductory way is established through a comparative quotation
of Exod 15:17b-18 that is itself interpreted. Through the use
of the exegetical principle of *gĕzērâ šāwâ* in the association
of Exod 15:17b-18 and 2 Sam 7:10 through their analogical use
of the root נטע , the interpreter demonstrates that it is not the
Solomonic temple that is the referent of Nathan's oracle but
the eschatological sanctuary (מקדש). The circumstances of
that sanctuary are then expounded in lines 3-7 but not without

a second use of the demonstrative introductory formula, הואה
הבית, which highlights the tension of the interpretation: while
the sanctuary is to be expounded in terms of the congregation
the original reference is to the בית, "house."

4QFlor 1:3-7 is to be taken as interpretative of Exodus 15,
rather than of the "place" of 2 Sam 7:10. This can be seen
from the fact that this section of exegesis is not introduced
with the conjunction *wāw* as parallel pieces of exposition are
in lines 15 and 16; also, in line 12 the exposition that follows
Amos 9:11 without a *wāw* clearly directly corresponds to and
expounds the Amos quotation, and only indirectly the Samuel
verses. The structure reveals that for the content of lines
3-7 the tension within the ambiguity of understanding the
sanctuary is played out to the full. On the one hand it is a
heavenly building and on the other the eschatological community.
J. A. Fitzmyer has commented that the text of Exodus 15 is
modernized so as to refer to the Qumran community "which is
the new Israel, the new 'house'."[143] But a preferable way of
describing the development of the exposition on Exod 15:17b-18
would be in terms of the proleptic function of the Qumran
community in the age that is to be characterized by God's
initiative in establishing his sanctuary, from which he will
rule.

The interpretation of מקדש of Exodus 15 is carried out in
the consistent manner of our interpreter. Similar structures
of a statement of identification followed by a statement of
explanation occur overall for lines 2-7, 10-13, etc. Not only
is there a degree of formal consistency, but also, once again,
there is use of an exegetical principle in the statement of

explanation (relative clause). The first section of the
explanation concerns limited admission to the eschatological
sanctuary. It is introduced by an allusion to Deut 23:3-4
whereby it is made more clear that the author intends us to
understand one meaning of מקדש as referring most probably to
a group of people, הקהל. Since neither Deut 23:3-4 nor adjacent
texts refer to the "sanctuary" or the "house," it is reasonable
to suppose that the allusion is made through a parent text; an
example of the use of the principle of *binyan 'āb*. For such
purposes either Lev 16:33 or Num 19:20 would serve suitably;[144]
the latter reads ונכרתה הנפש ההוא מתוך הקהל כי את מקדש יהוה טמא
The two words מקדש and קהל are used in the one verse and the
author of 4QFlor could have treated them as synonymous.[145]

   Only in the third part of the explanation is the tension
fully played out in the description of the promise of the Lord
that he will build for himself a sanctuary of men. It is such
a statement that enables the interpreter to return to the text
of 2 Samuel 7. This he does not according to the consistent
pattern of starting fresh quotations of the main text at the
margin without introduction; rather, as the structure shows, the
quotation of 2 Sam 7:11aᵇ is subordinate to the longer quotation
that is already partly expounded in lines 3-7.

   The relation of 2 Sam 7:11aᵇ to the earlier Samuel citation
is problematical. The introductory phrase (line 7) ואשר אמר
must be considered in its entirety for the conjunction plays a
decisive role in enabling the correct identification of the
relative position of the two elements of the unit of 4QFlor 1:1-13.
In 1QpHab, where the same phrase occurs at least five times,[146]
it always introduces a requotation. The requoted text and its

interpretation are clearly in a subordinate position to the
main textual citation. In CD the same formula occurs three
times: CD 8:14, 9:2, 16:6. In each of these cases it introduces a fresh quotation in a position subordinate to the overall
theme but of a different content from that which immediately
precedes.

Since 2 Sam 7:11a$^\beta$ is not a requotation, although it is
a new and separate section of text awaiting interpretation, the
author has introduced it in a manner suggestive of its subordination to the overarching quotation of 2 Sam 7:10-11a$^\alpha$. That
subordination does not come in terms of the eschatological
sanctuary of which the quotation has nothing to say, and so
lines 7-9 cannot be subsumed in some way under the explanation
of the "house." The last and most reasonable option is to
consider it of equal weight structurally to the explanation of
the "house" as an explanation in its own right. Its following
after the interpretation of מקום (2 Sam 7:10) around Exodus
15:17b-18 consecutively links its content to that part of the
preceding interpretation which is speaking of the "sanctuary
of men."

Furthermore justification for the structural analysis
above is provided in the form of the most probable restoration
of the interpreter's citation of 2 Samuel 7:10: $y\ldots$ וֹד[
וי]בַיוא. The quotation of 2 Samuel 7:11a$^\beta$ is thus linked to
the earlier citation through their analogous use of אויב. The
interpretation of Nathan's oracle is thus continued by means of
a quotation from it and the discussion of the eschatalogical
sanctuary and community is superceded by an interpretation
concerning the removal of the enemies during the eschatological
age.

The structure of this second element in the interpretation
of 2 Sam 7:10-11a$^{\alpha}$ reveals clearly a lengthy description of
the enemy, the sons of Belial. The description mentions
firstly their coming and secondly outlines the reasons for their
coming. From this one can suppose that the prophecy of Nathan
as interpreted has evidently not yet happened: the enemy is
still present, the eschatological rest has not yet come.

The second subsection of the first unit of 4QFlor is of
four lines: 10-13. It contains quotations with interpretation.
Of great interest is that just as it is likely that 2 Samuel 7:10
has been adjusted through a particular exegetical technique so
that 2 Sam 7:11a$^{\beta}$ could be used as subordinate interpretation,
so also the quotation of 2 Samuel 7:11b-14a has been considerably
edited to provide the just text for the interpretation. And
such editing is done in a way that is far from random; rather,
as noted already, there is the deliberate use of an exegetical
principle whereby a text itself can be treated before it is
quoted, and in this way made suitable for purposes of commentary
upon those selected parts.

The structure of this subsection concerning the eschatological figures is very similar to that of the preceding
subsection. The quotation is followed by an interpretation
that has a statement of identification which leads into a
statement of explanation that contains a basic statement and
then a comparison. Of note is the recurrence within the basic
statement of the temporal phrase that is one of the unifying
factors between the two units of Fragments 1-3: אחרית הימים.

Within the comparison is a scriptural citation that is
again linked to the main quotation through use of an exegetical

principle. The analogous use of הקימותי in both biblical
verses is an example of *gĕzērâ šāwâ*. Furthermore the treatment
of Amos 9:11 witnesses a possible example of paronomasia: סוכה
could be taken to mean both "booth" and "branch" whereby the
identification of the צמח דויד is confirmed. Thus the quotation
of Amos 9:11 and its explanation are to be understood from their
place within 4QFlor; any imposition of the interpretation of
the same quotation in CD is inappropriate.[147] הקימותי refers
directly to 2 Sam 7:11aᵝ; the seed of David and the booth of
David are parallel phrases, and it is only the booth that
requires explanation. The requotation of part of Amos 9:11 in
its explanation is stylistic precision. The העומד of line 11
is balanced by הנופלת of line 12, and in inverted order the
הנופלת of line 13 is in turn balanced by יעמוד. The care with
which this is done is the best support for taking them as
expressing opposites of meaning, noting that עמד usually means
"take office" in Qumran Literature.[148]

So, in sum, 4QFlor 1:10-13 describes the royal family
aspect of בית as punned in 2 Samuel 7, and reflects the Qumran
expectation of the Davidic King-Messiah, accompanied by the
eschatological Interpreter of the Law, through whom God's proper
rule will be restored and who will save Israel.

Genre

In an article in *Revue de Qumrân*[149] I have argued that
three matters determine the classification of any genre:
"primary factors" (e.g., form, content, author, setting, function,
etc.), "secondary factors"[150] (largely a matter of method and
style), and the history of literary traditions. No one factor
alone is sufficient for the determination of a genre. For the

primary factors of this unit of 4QFlor the structural analysis
provides us with a generic clue: explicit scriptural quotations
are combined with interpretations which are a combination of
statements of identification and statements of explanation.
For the secondary factors of this text it would seem that the
use of certain exegetical techniques, especially *gĕzērâ šāwâ*,
has enabled the author to argue a particular theme within his
formal structural restraints. These two factors alone would
suggest that this unit is akin to rabbinic midrash, but such
an association has been complicated by scholars hastily labelling
the Qumran commentaries as pesharim and as a result it has often
been argued that these Qumran writings stand outside the literary
tradition of midrash.[151]

Detailed consideration of the literary tradition within
which the pesharim may stand will follow in the discussion of
the next unit of 4QFlor. In relation to 4QFlor 1:1-13, however,
it is necessary to say that an explicit association with pesher
is difficult, for nowhere in this unit of 4QFlor is the interpretation introduced formally by a phrase including the word
פשר as is familiar from other Qumran commentaries.[152] Given the
precision of the commentator in stylistic matters, this would
seem not to be accidental. Several explanations are possible.
Firstly, if Samuel was conceived *in toto* as being an historical
book, then it may be that such conception has made impossible
the use of the term פשר which in all other Qumran uses, including
its one occurrence in CD at 4:14, is reserved for prophetic
texts.[153] However, if the text of 2 Samuel 7 is considered by
itself then it is an oracle of the prophet Nathan, a prophetic
text of the first order.[154] Or, secondly, since the part played

by a particular speaker may be partly constitutive of genre,
it could be that this first unit of 4QFlor is not pesher because
it was not originally spoken by the Teacher of Righteousness.
From 1QpHab 7:3-5 we know that it was to him that God had "made
known all the mysteries of the words of His servants the Prophets."
Yet thirdly, 1QpHab 7:3-5 also implies that pesher was a genre
reserved for the *secrets* of the prophets as the Teacher interprets
them (correctly and once for all) for the Qumran community. So,
if the Teacher was believed to have or actually did pronounce
the interpretation upon the verses of Nathan's prophecy, then
one must suppose that Nathan's prophecy did *not* contain any
mystery (רז) that the Teacher had to unravel; rather, it was
clearly an eschatological prophecy and so only needed elucidation
and explanation as to its particulars.

In fact, the way in which the scriptural text has been
edited in both subsections suggests that the interpretation may
be precisely slanted towards their eschatological significance.
In other words the task of the פשר is carried out within the
editorial work done through valid exegetical principles upon
the scriptural text itself; pesher becomes, therefore, redundant
as a form of interpretation upon that text. Only in a somewhat
tenuous sense can 4QFlor 1:1-13 be classified generically as
פשר; otherwise it must be labelled solely as *Qumran midrash*.

Setting

If the lack of the פשר formula is attributable to the fact
that the Righteous Teacher was not considered to be the author
of this unit, then 4QFlor 1:1-13 may find its setting in any
one of the different communities that had their parenthood in
Qumran. The commentary, possibly in an oral form no longer

preserved, could thus have arisen out of some such group meeting
as described in 1QS 6:3-8 in which ten men and a priest form
a body sufficient for a community meal and uninterrupted study
of the Law.

On the other hand if we limit the unit under discussion to
Qumran itself then it can be seen against a background of what
we know to have been the place of study of the scriptures within
the community. Study of all the scriptures, but of the Law
especially, was an important part of the sectarian's life and
it was also assigned to certain people at certain times. As
mentioned, 1QS 6:3-8 contains information on scriptural study
that would have applied equally at Qumran itself: "and where
the ten are, there shall never lack a man among them who shall
study the Law continually, day and night" (1QS 6:6). And 1QS
8:11-12 states that the "Interpreter" was not "to conceal from
them . . . any of those things hidden from Israel which have
been discovered by him."[155]

It may be possible, by using material from Philo concerning
the Essenes, to identify the time in the daily life of the
sectarians when such exposition took place. In *De Vita
Contemplativa*, Philo describes how after the meal the head of
the community "discusses some question arising in the Holy
Scriptures or solves one that has been propounded by someone
else."[156] He does this in an allegorical fashion which enables
the audience "to discern the inward and hidden through the
outward and visible."[157] And so Bo Reicke concludes:

Qouique le supérieur, selon tout apparence, fasse
seulement un exposé oral, on peut facilement
admettre que des commentaires bibliques écrits

aient été composés dans ces milieux à partir de
tels exposés oraux. De cette façon on peut
comprendre un écrit tel que le commentaire
d'Habakkuk de Qumran comme le fixation par écrit
de recitations exégètiques.[158]

F. M. Cross similarly allows that such biblical exposition
may stem from the founder of the sect and that this was trans-
mitted and supplemented "in the regular study of scholars of
the community, and particularly in the regular sessions of the
sect mentioned in the sources, where Scripture was read and
systematically expounded by those who had become the experts
of the community."[159] However, Cross also points out that the
pesharim are autograph copies, as no duplicate copies have come
to light, and so they may not necessarily have had a large or
any oral tradition before being put into writing.[160]

Yet, as will be pointed out in relation to 4QFlor, it is
almost certain that a liturgical setting lies behind the
combination of scriptural texts in 4QFlor. Apart from such a
setting 1:1-13 remains primarily a written work and its not
being pesher may be a signal that the preaching of the Teacher
of Righteousness lies nowhere in its background.

Intention

Though it may be somewhat brash to suggest what may be
the intention of the unit, since it could be that the unit should
have been longer, preceding into the previous column, it seems
safe to suggest certain features that may come under this heading.
In 4QFlor 1:1-13 the author intends to provide a midrash on
Nathan's oracle from 2 Samuel 7, in which commentary is developed
the original oracle's pun on בית, "house," in terms of the

eschatological expectations of the Qumran sect. But the
midrash is far from arbitrary and throughout attempts to
demonstrate the correctness of its interpretation by using
generally accepted principles of exegesis.

The eschatological concern is emphasized through the
repeated use of the phrase אחרית הימים and is played upon in
the way in which the community is depicted as proleptically
representing the eschatological sanctuary. With such use of
Nathan's pun the commentator can discuss the Qumran community
and its expected messianic leaders while never negating the
idea of the eschatological sanctuary and of God's ultimate rule.
It is God's rule, indeed, that provides a secondary theme to the
commentary; it is expressed in Exod 15:17-18, in the expected
defeat of the enemies (a sign of kingly rule), and in the
representative rule of the shoot of David in Zion in the last
age. It is such motifs that provide links with the second unit
of 4QFlor, to be considered next.

b.   4QFlor 1:14-2:6

Extent of the Unit

The start of the unit is defined by the paragraphing of
the manuscript, by the formulary introduction and by the change
in content of the scriptural citations from 2 Samuel 7 to Psalm 1.
The introductory formula helps determine the extent of the unit.
It is not repeated before the quotation from Psalm 2 and so we
must suppose that it introduces the quotations and interpretations
of both Psalms 1 and 2. It could introduce more than that but
the text breaks off in column 2 so that we are left with a unit
that has no end. Enough is discernible from the subsections of

the unit that it is certainly valid to proceed with a form-
critical analysis, even though the unit remains incomplete.

Structure of the Text

　　The main feature of the unit is the very formal way in
which Psalms 1 and 2 are treated midrashically. The structure
of the unit is a long succession of two-part elements. The
strict consistency within the unit is suggestive of a uniform
literary composition.

Midrash on Psalms 1 & 2	4QFlor 1:14-2:6(?)
I. Introductory formula	1:14
II. Midrash proper	1:14-2-6(?)
A. Quotation of Ps 1:1aα with pesher	1:14-17

　　　　1. Ps 1:1aα

　　　　2. Pesher (פשר....יחד)

　　　　　a. Introductory formula (פשר...על)

　　　　　b. Pesher proper (סרי...יחד)

　　　　　　1) Statement of identification (abbreviated)

　　　　　　　(סרי...חטאים)

　　　　　　2) Two statements of explanation

　　　　　　　a) First explanation (relative cl.)

　　　　　　　　(על...העם)

　　　　　　　　(1) Introductory formula w. temporal

　　　　　　　　　phrase (cKsL) (על...הימים)

　　　　　　　　(2) Quotation of Isa 8:11 (=1QIsaa)

　　　　　　　　　(ויהי...העם)

　　　　　　　b) Second explanation (והמה...יחד)

　　　　　　　　(1) Reiteration of subject (demonstrative

　　　　　　　　　pronoun) (והמה)

            (2) Explanation proper (relative cl.)

                (אשר...יחד)

                (a) Quotation w. introductory

                    formula (אשר...גלוליהמה)

                    α. Introductory formula

                       (cKsL+A abbreviated)

                    β. Quotation of Ezek 37:23

                (b) Interpretation (המה...יחד)

                    α. Statement of identification

                    β. Statement of explanation

                       (mostly in lacunae)

B. Quotation of Ps 2:1-2 with pesher   1:18-2:6(?)

   1. Ps 2:1-2

   2. Pesher

      a. Introductory formula

      b. Pesher proper

         1) First statement of identification

           (הגויים...הכתיים)

         2) Second statement of identification with

           interpreted qualification (וחוסי...)

           a) Identification proper (וחוסי...ישראל)

           b) Adverbial qualification w. interpretation

               (באחרית...)

              (1) Adverbial qualification (temporal

                  phrase) (באחרית הימים)

              (2) Interpretation

                  (a) Statement of identification

                    (היאה...המצרף)

(b) Statement of explanation

   (relative cl.) (הבאה...)

   α. Description (הבאה...מושה)

   β. Further interpretation

      aa. Statement of identification

         (היאה העת)

      bb. Statement of explanation

         (relative cl.) (כאשר...)

         α. Introductory formula (cKs)

         β. Quotation of Dan 12:10

            w. insertion alluding to

            Dan 11:35 + quotation of

            Dan 11:32b

The material in 4QFlor 1:14ff is based upon citations of
the first verses of Psalms 1 and 2. The pesher following
Psalm 1:1a$^{\alpha}$ contains two supportive biblical quotations which
can be linked to the psalm by *gĕzērâ šāwâ* provided that it is
understood that in giving just part of the first verse of the
psalm the author assumes of his reader knowledge of the rest.
Such incipit verses appear in the MT, for example, at Exod 15:21
which implies that Miriam then sang the whole song of Moses in
Exod 15:1-18; Jer 33:11 also contains an incipit for either
Psalm 116 or 136.[161] This suggests also that, although Psalms
1 and 2 were known as belonging together, possibly in a certain
situation only, and although they require only one overall
introductory formula, they were considered at Qumran as two
distinct parts of a whole.[162]

For the first explanation Isa 8:11 is linked to Psalm 1
through their analogical use of דרך. This linkword does not

occur in the Psalm quotation but is implied from Ps 1:1a[*] by
its occurrence in the author's own words in the pesher. The
introductory formula to the quotation of Isa 8:11 is noteworthy
in that it is expanded with the temporal phrase that has
already featured twice in 4QFlor 1:1-13. The second explanation
is structured exactly like the first except that the quotation
has its own explanation. The citation of Ezek 37:23 is linked
to Psalm 1 through their analogical use of מושב. The secondary
explanation of Ezek 37:23 which follows after the quotation has
been discussed in detail under the textual notes.

The total effect of the structure of the passage is to
demonstrate how the Qumran community under its various designations, the converts, the Sons of Zadok and the men of their
Council, is illustrative of the type of Psalm 1 who "has not
walked in the counsel of the wicked." In fact because Isaiah 8
was talking of the last days, it is clear that, since valid
exegetical principles have been used, so also Psalm 1 must refer
to the Qumran community.

In line 18 the quotation from Psalm 2 begins at the margin
in the same way that the edited text of 2 Sam 7:11-14 had done
in line 10. The content of the pesher is formulated in two
statements of identification (according to the textual reconstruction that appears most likely). The first such statement
identifies one of the parties mentioned in the Psalm quotation,
גויים, with the Kittim (?); this first statement is then dropped
and is only significant in the background role that the Kittim
are bound to play in the guise of the sons of Belial.

The second identification is of those who take refuge in
the Lord as the chosen ones of Israel. Yet the chief concern

of the interpreter is with their situation in the latter days.
The key temporal phrase אחרית הימים is then explained in length
in a manner similar to that of the house in 1:2-6. The latter
days are to be a time of trial for the community, the "House
of Judah." The result is that just as 2 Sam 7:10-11a is treated
in terms of the ideal (Qumran) congregation proleptically
representing the heavenly sanctuary, and there is then discussion
of the enemies who no longer disturb God's rest, so the pesher
of Psalm 1 is a description of the present Qumran community and
it is followed by the pesher on Psalm 2 in which the time of
refining, of the domination of the sons of Belial, is described.
But the remnant of Israel will survive as they come to understand
the eschatological situation; Dan 12:10 and 11:35, both connected
with Psalm 2 through their analogical use of the root שכל, allude
to such understanding.

It is also just possible, if ברדתו represents a quotation
from Exodus 34:29, that it is connected with Psalm 2 through
their common use of הר, "mountain." In that way the interpreter
describes the eschatological age in terms of the identification
of the mountain on which the Law was given and the mountain,
Zion, on which the Lord will set his eternal king.[163] Thus,
once again the secondary theme of the kingship of God vicariously
carried out through the messianic king is represented as it was
in the treatment of the texts of 2 Samuel 7.

Genre

Like 4QFlor 1:1-13 4QFlor 1:14-2:6 must be considered
generically from three angles, those of "primary factors"
(structure, content, setting, author, purpose), of "secondary
factors" (style and method), and of the history of literary

traditions.[164] Since the basic structure of the unit is clear,
we may begin with consideration of primary factors. *Structurally*
this unit with its scriptural citations and interpretations made
up of statements of identification and explanation resembles the
other Qumran commentaries and the earlier unit of 4QFlor as well
as many sections of the other Qumran writings where there is
scriptural citation and interpretation.[165] This makes this unit
of 4QFlor akin to the rabbinic midrashim as defined in part by
such authors as H. L. Strack,[166] R. Bloch[167] and A. G. Wright.[168]
Indeed to the modern observer the structure of this unit is its
most obvious characteristic.

If midrash is the appropriate generic term for 4QFlor 1:14–
2:6, then the *content* of this unit would naturally be classified
as haggadah, given that all rabbinic midrash is categorized
either as halakah or haggadah.[169] The unit includes interpretation
of Psalms 1 and 2 treated as prophecy;[170] each interpretation is
introduced with a formula including the word פשר. Whilst all
that could be an aid to enable us to be clearer as to what kind
of haggadic midrash this unit is, several scholars would deny
this. For some careful study of the etymological associations
of פשר is sufficient for such a denial. For example, I. Rabinowitz
categorizes the pesharim firstly according to their form and
secondly according to how the content of the interpretation
relates as presage to the text receiving the pesher, yet he
states categorically: "neither in method nor in form is a Pesher
any kind of *midrash* as familiar to us from Rabbinic literature."[171]
M. P. Horgan in a careful treatment of the word פשר concludes
that it and the literature in which it occurs is to be considered
alongside the dream interpretations of Daniel;[172] from the

perspective of their respective historical contexts "the term
'midrash' is neither a useful nor an informative term by which
to characterize the pesharim."[173] For some the historical
concerns of the content of the pesharim speak decisively for
their being *sui generis*. For example, C. Roth argues that "we
are to assume therefore that a *pēšer* existed or at any rate was
communicated verbally, on all or most of the passages of the
Bible - about fifteen in all - in which the End of Days was
specifically mentioned."[174] Yet "the End of Days" cannot be the
exclusive criterion for defining pesher since אחרית הימים occurs
in 4QFlor 1:2, 12, CD 6:11 and 1QSa 1:1 but there is no mention
of pesher.

    For other scholars neither particular eschatological content
nor the presence of formulae containing the word פשר are sufficient
barriers against associating the pesharim with rabbinic midrashic
literature, especially when the most explicit criterion of
structure is remembered too. Pre-eminently L. H. Silberman has
noted that the structure of the rabbinic *Petirah* is the same as
that of 1QpHab: "It is immediately apparent that in structure
this midrash[175] is parallel to *Hab. Pesher*, with the Aramaic root
פתר standing in place of the Hebrew פשר. The term introduces
the specific point of reference from which the entire verse is
to be understood. This specification seems to be entirely
arbitrary, or rather it is not necessarily connected with any
word in the text."[176] Silberman continued by noting that the
actual word פשר is not structurally necessary since personal or
demonstrative pronouns can serve the same purpose; there can be
nothing that structurally distinguishes pesher from midrash.
Furthermore, in relation to content Silberman criticizes part

of W. R. Lane's conclusion[177] by saying "Pesher refers to
structure and not content. While Lane is correct in defining
4QFlor as a midrash, his suggestion that it be distinguished
from Rabbinic midrash because of its messianic, eschatological
orientation is irrelevant for the same intent is to be found in
some if not in all Rabbinic midrash."[178] Similarly W. H. Brownlee
describes the purpose of pesher as for the benefit of the whole
community by demonstrating from scripture the vindication of
the Righteous Teacher and his followers against their various
enemies and opponents and by instructing the community from an
eschatological perspective to endure persecution, to avoid
apostasy, to prepare the way of Yahweh and to be ready for the
future.[179] Yet none of this summary purpose deflects Brownlee
from stating that "one should not view midrashic exegesis and
eschatological interpretation as mutually exclusive categories,"[180]
nor from describing 1QpHab as *Midrash Pesher*.

One last but very important comment on the content of 4QFlor
1:14-2:6 is necessary. The whole unit is introduced with the
word מדרש.[181] Because of its positioning one must assume that
this is some kind of technical designation; its presence cannot
simply be sidestepped as an exception to the rule. Furthermore
the use of such a technical term is bound to influence how the
subordinate term פשר is to be translated. After a careful analysis
of the use of פתר and פשר in the Bible, I. Rabinowitz has concluded
that "the term pesher, in fine, never denotes just an explanation
or exposition, but always a presaged reality, either envisaged
as emergent or else observed as already actualized."[182] Yet, as
W. H. Brownlee has argued,[183] it is not necessarily the case that
this meaning was carried over unmodified at Qumran. For example,

while for 1QpHab 12:2-3 Brownlee concurs with Rabinowitz's
insight into the meaning of פשר by translating the relevant
formula as "the prophetic fulfillment,"[184] he points out that
in many cases "prophetic meaning" is more suitable especially
in equational statements.[185] The suggested translation of פשר
in 4QFlor 1:14 and 19 as "the real interpretation" is an attempt
to allow for the full range of meaning of phrases including פשר:
on the one hand the meaning of the text being interpreted will
be "realized" in the present or future (thus the dream actually
contains its interpretation [Gen 40], and Nebuchadnezzar expects
that whoever can tell him the interpretation of the dream must
also be able to tell him the dream) and on the other hand in the
explicit content of midrash the pesher provides a verifiable,
real, interpretation.[186] All in all while the content of pesher
may have certain distinct characteristics they are not sufficient
to prevent the association of pesher with midrash.

Further support for such an association comes from a
consideration of *setting*. Though it is far from clear precisely
in what setting the pesharim were created it is the suggestion of
this examination of 4QFlor that this kind of interpretation was
applied to texts that had some liturgical setting, within the
life of the community. R. Bloch included in her definition of
midrash that it is homiletical and largely originates from the
liturgical reading of the Torah.[187] Such once only interpretation
would go some way towards explaining why all the pesharim are
autographs; a sermon can only truly be delivered once.

The last primary factor to be considered is that of
authorship. Here there is a distinctive claim, arising from the
pesharim themselves, that the Teacher of Righteousness alone was

capable of making known the mysteries of the prophets.[188]
Because of the likely date of 4QFlor (and the continuous
pesharim) it is unlikely that it was composed by the Teacher
of Righteousness himself though it may well contain features
of interpretation that do go back to him.[189] The scroll's
authorship cannot determine for us in itself the nature of the
genre but it is a positive aid to our identifying the scroll and
the other pesharim with Qumran alone. Consideration of authorship
thus aids an understanding of this genre's setting. In light of
what has been said in chapter one and of what has already emerged
in this chapter in relation to 4QFlor any modern claim for the
divine inspiration of the interpreter, and hence the distinctiveness of the genre, must be balanced by the careful statement of
how we can see the interpreter going about his work and of how
his audience could see that his interpretation was valid: even
for the interpreter the pesharim do not reflect the direct intervention of God in any exclusive way.[190]

The secondary factors for determining the genre concern
style and method.[191] Nearly all the scholars who have investigated
these have associated the methodology of the author with that of
the rabbinic midrashim. Most notable amongst them are
W. H. Brownlee, who for many years has advocated identifying the
pesharim as *midrash pesher* because of what he early identified
as hermeneutic principles,[192] L. H. Silberman[193] and
E. Slomovic.[194] M. P. Horgan is an example of a scholar who
cites extensive examples of "modes of interpretation"[195] and yet
scrupulously avoids the word midrash in her discussion – that,
by implication, because she associates the pesharim with a
literary tradition that does not include rabbinic texts.

Indeed the third point to be considered in discussing the
genre of 4QFlor 1:14-2:6 is the history of literary traditions.
It might seem clear from what has been said that battle lines
are clearly drawn up. On one side there are those who associate
the pesharim with dream visions and their interpretations,
especially those of the book of Daniel.[196] For example, Horgan
has argued on the basis of the well-established observation that
פשר and רז are used in similar contexts in Qumran biblical
interpretations and in Daniel that it is the nearly contemporary
material in Daniel that provides the most suitable comparison
with the pesharim in formulae (Dan 5:26), method (e.g., Dan 5:
24-28) and interest in matters historical. Yet with all this
she merely hints at the end of her work that the apocalyptic
world of thought may provide a likely literary setting for the
pesharim.[197] On the other side there are those who argue with
determination that the pesharim are closer to the rabbinic
midrashim.[198] The work of Silberman needs restating as a position
that allows for these two schools of thought not to be mutually
exclusive. He concludes that the pesharim belong somewhere
between the contemporary dream interpretations and the later
rabbinic *Petirah* with all its midrashic features.[199]

In sum these three factors point to our labelling 4QFlor
1:14-2:6 as midrash but clearly not rabbinic midrash *simpliciter*.
The unit's structure, content, setting and method are all akin
to what is found in many definitions of midrash. Because the
term midrash may seem anachronistic to some it is best to define
the text as *Qumran midrash*;[200] and 4QFlor 1:14-2:6 is Qumran
midrash of a particular *haggadic* kind, that of *pesher*.[201] As
such some of its features echo those of contemporary dream visions

and their interpretations.

Setting

Little can be said as to the setting of this unit that
has not already been discussed in relation to the first unit
or in the debate over the generic definition of pesher. The
strict two-part structure, especially of the pesher on Ps 2:1-2,
might support an original oral form for the piece, and, since
the pesher form is used, that orality may have been considered
as going back to the Teacher of Righteousness himself. Yet, in
the final analysis, 4QFlor remains a written composition and
nothing certain can be said of the oral background of its two
parts or of the whole. The lack of first and second person
pronouns suggests that there is certainly no direct recording
of speech and that the passage was not composed to be read aloud.

Some further discussion on the setting will result from
the consideration of 4QFlor as a whole, from which certain
liturgical aspects of the setting of the scriptural texts in
combination may become apparent.

Intention

The unit provides the pesher to Psalms 1 and 2. The psalms
are treated together in the same unit under the same introductory
heading. Surprisingly the pesher does not develop the figure
of the king in Psalm 2 in terms of the messianic prince but,
rather, it is absorbed in seeing how the psalms presage the
condition of the community in the eschatological age. Because
of the fragmentary state of the text, its intention is not fully
discernible at this point.

The most probable understanding of the pesher that follows

Psalm 1:1a$^{\alpha}$ is that it is concerned with the members of the
community. Those who have walked in the counsel of the wicked,
in joining the community, have turned from the way of "this
people;"[202] and, in terms of the Ezekiel quotation, two groups
do not defile themselves any more with their idols, the Sons
of Zadok and the men of their council (if the restoration is
correct[203]). The Sons of Zadok are part of the house of Judah
(Ezek 37:16, 1QpHab 8:1).

   This would then bear out the research done upon the title
"Sons of Zadok" to determine that it is not a synonym for the
community. J. Liver has shown that, because of their particular
didactic function in 1QS, 1QSa and 1QSb, "'the sons of Zadok'
is not to be considered as a general sectarian appellation.
Rather it is to be regarded as the distinctive connotation of
a priestly hierarchy determining the sect's spiritual image
. . These very priests were the indubitable nucleus around which
the sect clustered."[204] In relation to 4QFlor, Liver notes that
the situation is far less clear, but, by following Yadin's
reading, based on 1QS 11:2-3, "they are the sons of Zadok and
the men of their counsel," he is able to explain the use of the
title in 4QFlor as correctly reflecting its use in the earlier
manuscripts, "the men of their counsel" being the community itself.

   In relation to the title in CD, Liver concludes that at
3:20-4:4 the sons of Zadok stand for the members of the sect
who are to serve as the latter-day Israel.[205] In other words,
the phrase has become a name for a particular part of the sect,
over against the priests and the Levites, the other groups
mentioned in the CD passage. But the title appears to have
undergone some change in its use; B. Gärtner has even suggested

that at this place in CD the whole community is referred to.[206]
It is noteworthy that the phrase has lost its qualificationary
"the priests;" also the sons of Zadok are identified as "the
chosen ones of Israel, the ones called by name who shall stand
in the latter days." The fact that 4QFlor also omits "the
priests" from the title of the sons of Zadok, connects them
with the latter days, and uses the phrase "the chosen ones of
Israel" as the sole reference to the community in the pesher to
Psalm 2, suggests that at the time of 4QFlor the phrase had
become a general appellative for the latter-days community, that
community which has been precisely delimited in the midrash on
2 Sam 7:10,[207] and of which a particular part is "the men of
their counsel."

The plural title "chosen ones" occurs three times in Mss.
contemporary with 4QFlor, at 1QpHab 10:13, 1QM 12:1 and 4, and
in all three cases refers to the whole community. If the
tradition history of the title "sons of Zadok" as suggested
above is correct, then there seem to be good grounds for maintaining that the sons of Zadok in 4QFlor refers to the whole
community; and it is thus the whole community that is the concern
of the pesher.

The pesher of Psalm 2 most likely continues in this vein
with a description of the testing of the chosen ones of Israel
in the latter days at the hands of the nations (the Kittim[?]).
It is in fact the latter days that receive the particular
exposition of the pesher. The latter days are a time of refining,
but a remnant, which we may suppose to be the community, will
survive, purified and refined - to use the terms of the quotations
from Daniel. It is just possible that "his anointed" (Ps 2:2)

is taken up in reference to a messianic figure who will reign
on the Lord's holy hill and that this is done in terms of
Exod 34:29, but nothing conclusive can be said on this score.

Thus the intention of the midrash on Psalms 1 and 2 is
to identify the good parties in those psalms with the community
and to suggest that it is the community who is the remnant that
is to survive the trial of the latter days, the period that
also looks beyond that testing to a time when the understanding
of the wise will be vindicated.

c. 4QFlor Fragments 6-11

These six fragments are text and commentary of the blessings
of Deuteronomy 33. Detailed structural treatment of the text
is impossible. Three things can be said. Firstly, as to genre,
none of these fragments contains the word פשר. Yet since there
is a small amount of non-scriptural material and since Frg. 9
line 5 begins with על, lines 1-4 having biblical text, Allegro
(DJD V) is probably correct in suggesting that the previous line
contained some such formula as פשרו or פשר הדבר. All these
fragments that deal with Deuteronomy might, therefore, be
considered as *Qumran midrash pesher*.

As to setting, it is noteworthy that a blessing should be
expounded. One wonders whether or not this chapter of
Deuteronomy might belong with 2 Samuel 7 and Psalms 1 and 2
in a particular liturgical setting. More will be said of this
when the text is treated as a whole.

As to intention, it could be that one of the functions
for provision of a pesher to Deuteronomy 33 is to expand upon
the figure of the messianic priest. In 4QTest 14-20 Deut 33:8-11

is used in such a way as to suggest its application to the
messiah of Aaron. Such discussion in 4QFlor would be very apt,
for in the exposition of 2 Sam 7:11b-14 the priestly messiah
is only mentioned in a secondary position, the emphasis there
being on the messianic king.

d. 4QFlor Fragments 4, 5, 12, 15-26

Once again detailed form critical treatment is impossible
for these fragments.

Fragment 4 concerns the struggle of the House of Judah in
the time (עת) when Belial will be the archenemy. The fragment's
vocabulary fits closely that of other Qumran literature. Of
interest, though very speculative, is on the one hand the
possible allusion to Gen 49:23-24 in line 4, the blessing of
Jacob, which in certain respects parallels Deuteronomy 33 and
may have had a liturgical use (cf. 4QPBless); on the other hand,
line 5 contains what may be some allusions to Daniel 11 (בזר
in Dan 11:24; כוח in Dan 11:15), which chapter has already
provided material to interpret Psalm 2 eschatologically.

Fragment 5 contains the phrase שראל ואחרון]ל the literary
order of which has already been discussed. That the reference
is to the two messiahs is most likely and the reversal of order
from that in all other of its Qumran occurrences except CD 1:7
might imply a predominant interest at the time of 4QFlor in the
kingly messiah, whereas at an earlier time the community with
its priestly background had primarily hoped for the leadership
of a priestly messiah. Also of note is the use of the root חזה
(line 4), perhaps an allusion to Num 24:16-17, part of Balaam's
oracle, which in 4Q Testimonia refers by implication to the two

messiahs (cf. CD 6:19-20). Could there be in Fragment 5 part
of a commentary on this messianic proof-text?

The significance, or rather, insignificance, of the
remaining fragments has already been pointed out under the
textual notes.

2. *The Composition of the Whole Midrash*

a. *As a whole*

From a form-critical standpoint the taking of 4QFlor as a
whole, inasmuch as we have it, must be justified. Such justification comes partly from palaeographical study which reveals
that the whole (extant) scroll was written in the same hand and,
therefore, almost certainly by the same person. The scribe must
have had some reason for writing the material in the order he
did, even if only because it was the order of the manuscript
from which he may have been copying. Unless such a manuscript
was a random composition by many scribes working independently
(an unlikely construction), then to isolate, say, two separate
literary units is to deny any and every possible connection
between them, and that is clearly untenable. Yet it is far
from certain how at least the first two units, 1:1-13 and 1:14-
2:6(?), are related to one another.

1. In the first place it could be suggested that the lack
of the word פשר in 1:1-13 implies that the section of 2 Samuel 7
that is treated there is not in fact the main text. Rather, by
analogy to 1:14ff., it is part of a pesher on some other text.
This argument is supported by the occurrence of statements of
identification in 1:2, 3 and 11 which therefore resembles the

subordinate parts of the pesharim in 1:14ff. Because the
midrash of 1:14ff. begins with the first verse of Psalm 1,
three possibilities are open. Firstly, if one wishes to see
4QFlor as a fragment of a complete commentary on a book of
Psalms,[208] then either the psalms are in a different order
from that in the MT, as in the case of 11QPss[a], or, secondly,
the material in 1:1-13 and presumably in the previous column
is all part of the pesher on an introductory title; and from
the content of 1:1-13 it might be safely guessed that that
title contained the name of David, to whom the composition of
many of the psalms is attributed.[209] Or thirdly, 1:1-13 is
part of a pesher on some other biblical book, the content of
which suggested to the scribe that he subsequently record the
midrash on the psalms.

However, these three possibilities depend on the initial
premise that 1:1-13 is only part of a pesher and not the whole
basis of the concern of the author. Nowhere in published Qumran
material is there a subsection or part of a pesher that is this
long and involved. On the contrary, the usual style of pesher
is very short and sometimes cryptic, and when it becomes more
involved, then the relevant section of the text upon which the
pesher is being made is quoted again.[210] The longest section
of pesher in 1QpHab, whose lines, however, are considerably
shorter than those in 4QFlor, is that of 10 lines at 2:1b-10a.
4QpNah and 4QpPs[a] both have lines of similar length to 4QFlor,
but in them the pesher is never longer than three lines.[211]
Also, nowhere is there any evidence, unless it is in the various
fragments of Deuteronomy in 4QFlor, that a supportive biblical
quotation of such length is used to expound a section of scriptur

such that it in turn is broken down and commented upon – rather
it is true that supporting quotations are short and clearly
relevant or easily made so by the addition of an explanatory
phrase.[212]

2.   When it is acknowledged that 1:1-13 is connected to
but different from 1:14ff., then some further observations can
be made from the structure. 2 Samuel 7 differs from Psalms 1
and 2 in that it has no pesher but rather is treated like the
supporting biblical quotations in 1:14ff. That suggests that
the difference between 1:1-13 and 1:14ff. lies in the nature of
the texts which are being expounded and not only in their
expositions. Thus 2 Samuel 7 and Psalms 1 and 2 need to be
generically defined, not from how they currently appear in the
MT, but as to how the author at Qumran saw them.

When the text of 2 Samuel 7 as the author of 4QFlor cites
it is set beside that in the MT, then it becomes clear that the
portions excluded from 4QFlor are the very ones that apply only
to the time immediately following David. The stress in 4QFlor,
however, is on the latter days as visible in the oracle of
Nathan, and no mention is made that David's immediate son will
build a house for the Lord – rather, the Lord builds a house
that is both the shoot of David and the sanctuary (of men) that
David himself wished to build for the Lord.[213] The parts of the
oracle of Nathan selected and quoted in 4QFlor require no pesher
as they already refer directly to the messianic age. Psalms 1
and 2, however, though containing the very word משיח, were
normally used in relation to the actual king of the moment (and
perhaps at a post-exilic enthronement festival[214]), and can only
be shown to talk of (presage, or have reality of) the messianic

age through the use of the form of pesher. Thus with the
diversity of form there is an overall unity of purpose that
can be seen as expressed in the consistent use of certain
exegetical principles.

   3. The decisive factor for considering 4QFlor as a whole
comes from a consideration of the setting as the Qumran author
knew it of the main biblical texts which the body of 4QFlor
comments upon: 2 Samuel 7 and Psalms 1 and 2 (and possibly
Deuteronomy 33 and Numbers 24). There is the thematic link of
messianism between the texts, particularly apparent in the royal
messiah being in a special sense Yahweh's son in both 2 Samuel 7
and Psalm 2. But, over and above such a theme, it is highly
probable that the scriptural texts used in 4QFlor were all known
from one particular liturgical setting. They were then adapted
through commentary for the intentions outlined above in relation
to the various units of text. Maybe the original orality of the
units of 4QFlor is best described in terms of their being
homilies on liturgical texts.

   Such thoughts on the unity of 4QFlor as being a "latter
days" midrash upon liturgical texts can be outlined structurally
according to the analysis that follows. Further discussion of
4QFlor as a whole will follow in terms of the genre of the whole
and in terms of the liturgical setting of the biblical texts
used in 4QFlor.

4QFlorilegium A Midrash on Festival Texts; for the Latter Days
   I. The Coronation Oracle explained   1:1-13
      A. Concerning the eschatological sanctuary/community 1-9
         1. Quotation of 2 Sam 7:10-11a[α]

            2. Interpretations

                a. Concerning the house

                b. Concerning the lack of enemies

        B. Concerning the eschatological figures   10-13

            1. Quotations from 2 Sam 7:11b-14a

            2. Interpretation

                a. Statement of identification

                b. Statement of explanation (relative cl.)

II. Midrash on the Coronation Psalm(s)   1:14-2:6(?)

    A. Introductory Formula

    B. Content of Midrash

        1. Ps 1:1a$^\alpha$ with pesher

        2. Ps 2:1-2 with pesher

III (?). Blessing of Moses explained

        The overall fragmentariness of the text enables only a
restricted description of 4QFlor as a whole. It has at least
3 major sections and probably many more. From the elements
within these three major sections, it can be seen that the
intention of the author or editor has been to provide midrash
on certain scriptural texts. The proposal below as to the
liturgical background of the combination of these texts provides
the reason for these particular scriptural texts being together
(and, most likely, for the order in which they are treated). In
providing the midrash the major concern has been to relate the
texts to the latter days. In Section 1 this is done partly
through treating the scriptural texts through certain principles
for midrashic purposes, and partly through accepting parts of

2 Samuel 7 as being eschatological prophecy. In Section II
the midrash is attained through pesher.

b. *The unity and consistency of the Midrash*

The difference in format between 4QFlor 1:1-13 and 1:14ff.
has already been pointed to and need not detain us further.
The unity of the various sections has also been alluded to, in
that midrash, as defined, accounts primarily for scriptural
citation followed by exposition; this is present throughout
4QFlor. Also present throughout are certain principles of
exegesis that are commonly associated with midrash[215] but which,
it has been shown, are not determinative of the genre midrash.

A minimal list of these principles for 4QFlor is as follows:

1. *Gězērâ šāwâ*[216] is used several times. Exod 15:17b-18
is linked to 2 Sam 7:10-11a[α] through the common occurrence of
the root נטע; Amos 9:11 is linked to 2 Sam 7:12 through והקימותי;
Isa 8:11 is attached to Ps 1:1 through דרך; Ezek 37:23 is linked
to Ps 1:1 through מושב; Dan 12:10 and 11:35 are linked to Psalm 2
through the root שכל; the possible quotation of Exod 34:29 would
be linked to Psalm 2 through הר .

2. Deliberate editing through homoeoteleuton is carried
out on the text of 2 Sam 7:11b-14a.

3. Through paronomasia, סוכת in 1:12 can be read in an
alternative way.[217]

4. Through a possible use of *binyan 'āb*, the parent text
being either Lev 16:33 or Num 19:20, מקדש in Exod 15:17 is
interpreted as קהל.

5. The principle of *sěmûkîn* may be present in 1:5, if it
is seen to come from Gen 22:14. In many other places there are

supportive scriptural allusions.

6. The double meaning intended in the biblical text is
kept and played upon as בית of 2 Samuel 7 is understood as the
sanctuary/community on the one hand, as the royal house on the
other.[218]

4QFlor thus evidences the use of various exegetical principles
that enhance its midrashic character and enforce the overall
generic designation for the extant parts of the scroll as
Qumran Midrash.

Furthermore, a consistent element within 4QFlor, and indeed
in all the pesharim, is that it only treats prophetic texts.
2 Samuel 7 not only contains the words of a prophet, but the
books of Samuel are part of the canon of the former prophets.
For Psalms 1 and 2, the books of Chronicles, in their description
of the Levitical guilds, reflect the attitude that psalmody was
considered prophecy. That tradition is almost certainly reflected
in the books of Samuel and Kings: indeed, one of David's
compositions is explicitly defined as an oracle (2 Sam 23:1-7)
and is to be found alongside the Psalms in 11QPss[a].[219]

Together with 2 Samuel 7 and Psalms 1 and 2, the fragmentary
parts of Deuteronomy 33 may form a third major unit of texts.
It is likely that it too was considered as prophecy, for 4QTest
includes a quotation of Deut 18:18-19 in which the Lord promises
Moses he will raise up a prophet like him. Whoever the new
prophet may be, that Moses was identified as a prophet, or even
as *the* prophet par excellence, is the assumption of the quotation.
Its occurrence at Qumran shows that the covenanters there shared
that assumption. Balaam's oracle (Numbers 24; 4QFlor frg. 5?)
also falls within the category of prophecy, as may the words of

Jacob in Genesis 49 (frg. 4?).

Apart from these two elements of consistency there is
also a consistency of style in two respects. The first, at
least in so far as 4QFlor was written by one scribe, concerns
the divine name. This is written in Aramaic script throughout
1QIsa[a] and other biblical manuscripts at Qumran, but in Palaeo-
Hebrew in the biblical quotations of the non-biblical "sectarian"
manuscripts: 1QpHab, 1QH, 4QpPs[a] and other scrolls contemporary
with or earlier than 4QFlor. According to M. H. Segal this
was done

> so that the sacred name in square script should not
> make the scroll sacred, since the palaeo-Hebrew script
> was at that time considered to be a profane script as
> is said in the Mishna (Yadayin 4:5): "Palaeo-Hebrew
> script does not make the hands levitically impure,"
> i.e. it has no sacredness whatsoever.[220]

4QFlor, however, uses the square Aramaic script for the divine
name in biblical quotations (1:3, 10, 18). This may be an
indication that the particular Ms. discovered is of a later
date than all the other Qumran literature from a time when the
use of palaeo-Hebrew had died out; or it may be that the scribe
is simply breaking a general rule.[221]

The second consistency of style is to be observed in the
introductory formulae to the biblical quotations. F. L. Horton
had described and classified the components of certain introductory formulae as follows:[222] A = אשר אמר, K = כתוב,
c = connective word (conjunction, pronoun or both), s = citation
of source, L = presence of some object to which the quotation
is applied. He proposes that there are two main types of formula,

K and A. Various combinations are found in the Qumran
literature, A formulae being the most extensive.[223] K formulae
are also represented[224] - they are the ones most consistently
found throughout 4QFlor - and, indeed, are to be seen in the
Bible itself.[225]

    This leads Horton to suggest a tradition history for
introductory formulae such that K has developed into KA which
in turn has evolved into A. Yet, comments Horton,[226] 4QFlor
evidences a further and still later development: in 1:16 there
is an example of an abbreviated A formula, as part of a defective
KA formula, where אמר is omitted allowing אשר alone to introduce
the quotation as though an object clause. Thus 4QFlor not only
shows some consistency in its use of introductory formulae, but
also evidences a particular formula that may be further support
for a late date for the manuscript - at least the broad palaeographical date is confirmed.

c. *The liturgical setting of the biblical texts*

    Although D. Goldsmith incorrectly describes 4QFlor 1:1-13
as a pesher, he does provide evidence in his discussion of
Acts 13:33-37 that 2 Samuel 7 and Psalm 2 were known to be
compatible in combination, in that case to show how Jesus is
the Christ, not through random selection of biblical quotations,
but through a carefully conceived linguistic and theological
scheme.[227] The question remains to be asked, however, whether
or not the combination of such biblical texts has a setting,
beyond the literary one, which may have been part of the
covenanters' experience. Such a setting could have provided
the texts already in combination before they were ever commented

upon, and such a combination may partially describe the stimulus
from which 4QFlor derives its final form.[228]

Most scholars now hold that the oracle of Nathan in 2
Samuel 7 has undergone major editing during the process of its
inclusion in the Samuel narrative and during the revision of the
Deuteronomistic period.[229] There is also a large amount of
agreement that Psalm 89 is prior to the inclusion of the oracle
within the Samuel narrative, and is probably even datable to
the tenth century B.C. The underlying oracle of Nathan, whatever
its precise dimensions, comes, therefore, from a period close to
the time described in Samuel. Several settings for the oracle
have been proposed.

H.-J. Kraus has suggested that

in Jerusalem existierte das 'königliche Zionfest' am
15 Tage des 7. Monats, also am ersten Tage des Laub-
hüttenfestes. Jahr für Jahr wurde die Erwählung des
Zion den Wallfahrern Israels zusammen mit der Erwählung
der Davidsdynastie in Jerusalem durch einen kultischen
Akt verkündigt.[230]

He further argues that this "Zionfest" is the festival that
continues the tradition of the ancient amphictyonic covenant
festival. The oracle of Nathan belongs directly to this tradition
as it is a major aspect of the festival in pre-exilic times that
David and his seed should be seen as rulers over Jerusalem and
the kingdom according to the will of God. At no point before
the exile is there an enthronement of Yahweh; however, in a
changed form in post-exilic times the "Zionfest" became assimilated
to the procession cult act of the Jewish New Year feast, but it
still remained primarily a festival of "Offenbarung, Gesetzgebung

und Bundeserneuerung,"[231] even though Yahweh was then spoken
of as the king of his people.

R. A. Carlson has supported but slightly adapted this
theory to show the importance of the oracle in relation to the
Ark narrative and the fact that the Deuteronomic legal tradition
is to be clearly seen in the editing of the oracle within its
own particular covenant tradition as expressed in the Jerusalemite
tabernacles festival during monarchic times.[232]

The major alternative to the above, beyond a purely literary
approach, is that the oracle in 2 Samuel 7 is a historical
transposition of a coronation liturgy. S. Mowinckel concludes
that "from the literary and traditio-historical point of view,
2 Sam vii is a faithful culthistorical reflection of a common
cultic situation,"[233] that is, the installation of a king at
Jerusalem. I. Engnell had earlier stated that 2 Samuel 7 is an
"historicised coronation-liturgy: a dialogue between the god
and the king . . . selection, victory, enthronement . . . followed
by the king's psalm of thanksgiving culminating in a prayer of
fulfillment."[234] However, Mowinckel also mentions in the same
place that Nathan's oracle as a whole "in form and content
corresponds to that which was addressed in the ritual to a new
king at his anointing," and it may be that rather than 2 Samuel 7
containing a historicized coronation liturgy, it is simply only
a part of such a liturgy.

From the enthronements described in 1 Kgs 1:32-48 and
2 Kgs 11:12-20 de Vaux has deduced that the coronation rites
located at the sanctuary consisted of investiture with the
insignia, anointing, acclamation, enthronement and homage, and
he mentions some psalms that may have been used as accompanying

liturgy.[235] Others have hinted at a fuller form of coronation
rite: R. Patai[236] notes that according to Widengren the
ascension of the throne only occurs after an oracle of promise.
Such an oracle is the mark of selection in many places in the
OT,[237] an oracle which is later ritually ratified by the people
either through recognition of the oracle or through acceptance
of its truth as exemplified by some mighty deed performed by
the chosen, in both cases shown by acclamation.

Both of the above theories claim Psalm 2 as part of their
particular rite. For example, Kraus says that "ps 2 ist ein
Gedicht zum königlichen Zionfest, das von der Erwählung und
Einsetzung eines Nachkommens Davids handelt."[238] Engnell, on
the other hand, picks on Psalm 2 as clearly reflecting the
dialogue between the god and the king which is apparent in
2 Sam 7:16-18.[239]

Three comments need to be made at this point. Firstly,
there has been much debate among commentators as to the actual
date of Psalm 2 and few have supported a date for it in its
complete form prior to the reigns of the last few pre-exilic
kings of Judah, and most assign it an exilic or post-exilic
date largely because of its future orientation and messianism.
Secondly, both the above theories of "Zionfest" and coronation
ritual tend to merge in post-exilic times and it becomes
difficult to distinguish them clearly, especially as both are
held to be aspects of the New Year enthronement festivities, or
rather part of the Feast of Tabernacles (celebrated after an
autumnal New Year?).[240] Thirdly, Psalm 1 is identified with
Psalm 2 in rabbinic literature and in the Western text of
Acts 13:33; the similarity of content and the overarching form

of the two psalms has led W. H. Brownlee to suggest that
"Ps 1, though originally only didactic, was aptly joined to
and knitted together with Ps 2 for the coronation of one of
the last kings of Judah, who thereby pledged himself to fulfil
the Deuteronomic Law."[241] Whatever the case may be in pre- or
early post-exilic times, certainly by late post-exilic times
the psalms could have been traditionally used together with
2 Samuel 7 at the Feast of Tabernacles.[242]

To relate this to the Qumran community it is necessary to
see that for the covenanters the most important festival was
that of the renewal of the covenant, when new converts were
admitted to the community, described at the beginning of 1QS.
According to 1QS 2:19, this was to be performed annually. It
is commonly held to have taken place at the Feast of Weeks, an
important festival at Qumran, as is reflected in the popularity
there of the book of Jubilees. If covenant is seen to be the
sole importance of the tradition of 2 Samuel 7 - Psalms 1 and 2,
then these texts may belong to the liturgy of the Qumran Feast
of Weeks.[243]

However, if the basic biblical texts in 4QFlor assert the
kingship of Yahweh and the community as properly reflecting and
allowing that kingship, then it is most likely that some other
festival should be considered. Though a particular enthronement
aspect of the Feast of Tabernacles may have ceased in late post-
exilic times,[244] the Feast of Tabernacles may still have maintained some processional element.[245] In Judaism contemporary
with Qumran, the Feast was probably celebrated from the 15th
to the 22nd Tishri, five days after the Day of Atonement, a
feast which is mentioned several times at Qumran,[246] and to whose

liturgy several of the Qumran texts have been ascribed.[247]

Although the dates of the festivals celebrated at Qumran
and in contemporary Judaism did not coincide,[248] the fragment
of the Book of Priestly Courses shows that the sect observed
the Day of Atonement on the sixth of the course in Joiarib,
and the Feast of Tabernacles from the fourth in Jedaiah, that
is, the 10th and 15th respectively of their seventh month.[249]
This dating of the Feast of Tabernacles should not exclude that
the observance of the festival was carried out with the use of
traditional materials formerly associated with the feast when
celebrated with a different emphasis and possible at a
different time.[250]

Thus, from all these various traditions and comparative
festivals as practised at Qumran, might it not be suggested
that 4QFlor is a midrash on texts that have their setting at
Qumran as part of the liturgy of the Feast of Tabernacles? If
that were the case and that that liturgy maintained some of
the post-exilic traditions, then it accounts for the existence
together of 2 Samuel 7 and Psalms 1 and 2 in both a post-exilic
and a Qumran setting, for the presence of sections of
Deuteronomy 33,[251] for the interest in the midrash in the
community as sanctuary over against the physical temple building
and for the stress on the rule of Yahweh. It also gives
powerful significance to the use of Amos 9:11 as an explanatory
text: "I will raise up the booth (tabernacle) of David that is
fallen." At very least one can conclude that the midrash of
4QFlor is on texts that may have formed part of a testimonia
which was based on the traditional liturgy of the festivals of
post-exilic Judaism.[252]

D. 4QFlor and Qumran Theology

1. *The Latter Days*

Of the theological aspects of 4QFlor, this first to be
considered may well be also first in importance since the phrase
אחרית הימים occurs at 1:2, 12, 15 and 19 (and in Fragment 14?)
in all the major subsections of 4QFlor. To that extent its
discussion will also influence and expand the earlier effort
of this study to describe the intention of 4QFlor. The term
is in fact explained in the second column.

J. Carmignac has observed one point of this explanation:
Par bonheur, le Florilège 1:19-2:1 prend soin de
definir la formule אחרית הימים en ajoutant à titre
d'explication "c'est le temps de la fournaisse à
venir " et nous savons que la "fournaisse" désigne
à Qumran la domination de Bélial et la guerre de
libération (1QM xvi:15, xvii:1, 9) donc que le
"temps de la fournaisse" est l'époque qui précédera
l'installation de la paix inaltérable.[253]

This is also the case for the other occurrences of מצרף in the
Qumran literature.[254] Yet מצרף and אחרית הימים are not always
associated with one another. Indeed, whilst Carmignac argues
persuasively that the primary and usual meaning of אחרית הימים
is "la suite des jours," he acknowledges that at least in CD
4:3-4 and 6:8-11 the phrase refers to the time after the period
of present refining.[255] Such may also be the case in 4QFlor.
In 2:3-4 the time (עת) when the righteous will understand
(Dan 12:10) is described, though that understanding is clearly
inaugurated by the process of refining; similarly in 4QFlor 1:12

the coming of the shoot of David may occur in that time which
sees the restoration of the kingdom after the final victory
when the fallen booth stands again. Yet generally in 4QFlor
the period referred to is the time before the end.

If it is accepted that the primary meaning of אחרית הימים
is not "end of days" but something like "la suite des jours,"
"l'avenir,"[256] then the translation "the latter days" allows
for this sense of futurity whilst embracing something of the
eschatological and historical self-understanding of the
community. This future time, this time before the end,is
already being experienced. The latter days herald and anticipate,
even inaugurate the end but they are not the end except
proleptically in the exceptional texts of CD 4 and 6. So
Carmignac's understanding seems preferable to that of H. Kosmala
who would translate the phrase as "the end of the days" largely
because of his observations that in Daniel קץ and אחרית הימים
tend to coalesce and because the passages in CD mentioned above
can carry this meaning.[257] But against Kosmala's translation
can be cited the use of אחרית הימים elsewhere in the OT; for
example, G. W. Buchanan has argued that "end of days" is an
inappropriate translation for most of the MT occurrences of
the phrase.[258] In addition J. Licht has made two important
observations with regard to Qumran eschatology: firstly "that
the sect distinguished at least four periods, viz. the past
which preceded its own establishment, its historical present,
the coming period of active struggle against the forces of
evil, and the ultimate future of full eschatological peace;"[259]
secondly, that the thought of the Qumran writings is "pre-
occupied by the things to be done in this time . . . not on

the fundamental or abstract apects of the whole question of
the sequence of times."[260]

Although one should not impose a rigid time structure on
the Qumran evidence, one might conclude that the phrase אחרית
הימים is certainly distinct from קץ in Qumran usage though
there may also be some overlap,[261] not resulting from confusion
of terminology but from the different period within the history
of the sect at which the various documents were composed.
Licht's view could perhaps be modified from the perspective
of the scribe: the later he was writing, the more he saw of
the past history of the sect as being in the latter days, and
therefore the more he thought of his own time as being nearer
the end. 4QFlor must be seen, therefore, in a tradition
history the later stages of which are reflected in CD and
4QFlor where אחרית הימים has the two aspects of the time of
trial and the time beyond the trial. Thus in the use of the
phrase in 4QFlor there is further evidence for the late date
of the manuscript, especially as the author's intention throughout the midrash is to stress the referent of the biblical texts
as being in the latter days.

This understanding of אחרית הימים influences the way in
which מקדש אדם is to be understood. This will be considered in
detail in the next section. Suffice it to say that if אחרית
הימים is thought to refer only to the end, then it is easy to
see that scholars can conclude that the references to the
eschatological sanctuary must refer to a building in the future.[262]
On the other hand, if אחרית הימים refers to the time before the
end, the time before the heavenly temple is established on earth,
then it is possible to argue that the primary meaning of מקדש אדם

is "sanctuary *consisting* of men." This human sanctuary is
not conceived apart from the awaited heavenly building; rather
it is that building in anticipation.

2. *Place, Sanctuary, House and Congregation*

The major section of the midrash on 2 Samuel 7 is concerned
with the identification of the house that is punned in the Nathan
oracle. In lines 1-7 the primary identification is made between
the sanctuary and the house (place, in 2 Sam 7:10) through
Exod 15:17b-18 by means of *gĕzērâ šāwâ*.[263] The root used to
link the two quotations, נטע, is commonly applied as a metaphor
for the establishment of the Qumran community as the true Israel.[264]

It is this particular part of Nathan's oracle that is used
for midrash on the house as sanctuary because later the pun in
the oracle reveals that Solomon will build a house.[265] The
intention of 4QFlor, however, is to say that God has established
both houses, the sanctuary and the shoot of David. D. Flusser
has pointed to the belief that was common in Jewish thought at
the time, that God would establish the eschatological sanctuary,
and not man, as being the factor that counted towards the
linking of Exod 15:17-18 with 2 Sam 7:10-11.[266]

But in 4QFlor much more is at play than just a general
contemporary Jewish belief, though that is undoubtedly present
too. In the Exodus quotation another idea is stressed: the
kingship of Yahweh. Interestingly this is also the case in the
text of the oracle of Nathan in 1 Chronicles. For example,
1 Chron 17:14 reads, "I will maintain him in my house and in
my kingdom for ever," over against, "and your house and your
kingdom shall be made sure for ever before you; your throne
shall be established for ever," in 2 Sam 7:16. The sense of the

version in Chronicles is that the king of David's house
occupies his throne as the representative of God, who is the
supreme king. A difficulty remains, however, concerning the
house: is it the royal house or the temple? S. Aalen has
pointed to the difficulty but prefers to emphasize rather that
the kingdom in later texts, including the Targum, was understood
as being a synonym for the people of God.[267] Certainly 4QFlor
supports his contention that at least part of contemporary
Judaism could conceive the house primarily as the proper religious
community and secondarily as the royal line or the temple building.

As soon as the author of 4QFlor has validly established that
the oracle of Nathan is concerned with the sanctuary of the
latter days, he then proceeds to describe that sanctuary in
detail. Firstly, it will be of limited access.[268] The exclusion
of Ammonite and Moabite is based on an ancient Israelite
tradition taken here from the legislation as expressed in
Deut 23:3-4.[269] The bastard is similarly excluded by Deut 23:2;
there is also rabbinic evidence for the idea of the exclusion
of the bastard from the Jerusalem of the latter days.[270]
Although rabbinic tradition has for the most part taken Deut
23:2-4 to refer to marriage restrictions, Philo understood the
exclusions to apply to assemblies: "knowing that in assemblies
there are not a few worthless persons . . . it banishes not only
harlots, but also the children of harlots."[271]

Concerning the בני נכר, J. Baumgarten has demonstrated[272]
the dependence of 4QFlor on the concept expressed in Ezek 44:6-9:
"O house of Israel, let there be an end to all your abominations,
in admitting foreigners (בני נכר), uncircumcised in heart and
flesh, to be in my sanctuary, profaning it . . . No foreigner,

uncircumcised in heart and flesh, of all the foreigners who
are among the people of Israel, shall enter my sanctuary" (RSV).
In his description of the restored temple Ezekiel insists on
the elimination of all foreign temple-servants.

Baumgarten notes the equation of the בני נכר with the
devoted ones, נתינים, of Ezra, Nehemiah and Chronicles, concerning
whose status there is some ambiguity.[273] Isa 56:3-7 assumes a
similar identification and offers encouragement to the בְּנֵי הנכר,
the servants of the Lord. From *m. Qidd.* 4:1, however, Baumgarten
argues that the legal status of the נתינים at the time of Qumran
was equivalent to that of the ממזר. That important text reads:

> Ten classes of definite genealogy came up from Babylon:
> priests, Levites, Israelites, priests of impaired stock,
> proselytes (גירי), freedmen, bastards, netinim, children
> of unknown fatherhood and foundlings. The priestly,
> Levitic and Israelitish stocks may intermarry; the
> Levitic, Israelitish, impaired priestly stocks,
> proselyte and freedmen stocks may intermarry; the
> proselyte, freedman, bastard and Natin stocks, children
> of unknown fatherhood, and foundlings may all intermarry.

Essentially the halakah has put the *nâtîn* in the same category
as the classes excluded in Deuteronomy 23.

M. Qidd. 4:1 also provides evidence concerning the proselyte.
Although he could legitimately intermarry with any Jewish family
(except priests), his position was still inferior to those who
belonged to the community by birth. The proselyte and the בן נכר
were indeed counted as members of the general congregation
governed by the laws of the Torah, both in rabbinic and Qumran
thought.[274] Thus at Qumran CD 11:2 reflects the law that the

בן נכר could not do errands for an Israelite on the Sabbath,
and the proselyte was to be aided by the members of the
community together with the poor and needy (CD 6:21). Yet,
at Qumran, concludes Baumgarten,

> a significant barrier remained; for neither the
> *ger* nor the *ben-nekar* could gain admittance into
> the "congregation of the Lord." The meaning which
> Qumran exegesis attached to the latter phrase in
> the communal law of Deuteronomy 23 was evidently at
> variance with rabbinic interpretation. While the
> rabbis understood to "come into the congregation of
> the Lord" as a restriction on intermarriage, the
> author of *4Q Florilegium* applied it to the exclusion
> of the disqualified classes from the messianic
> sanctuary.[275]

11QT 40:6 describes the third court for the proselyte. If
11Q Temple can be used for providing information about the
sectarians' hopes for the eschatological sanctuary, then 11QT
40:6 may cause us to qualify Baumgarten's statement. In any
case the גר was excluded from the central court of the
worshipping community (קהל).

The reason(s) offered for the exclusion of the five classes
is surrounded by textual difficulties, but given the reading
"His holy ones are there," one must ask who the holy ones are.
Most scholars hold them to be angels and certainly the Qumran
texts, especially 1QM, and possible contemporary external
literature would support this.[276] However, H.-W. Kuhn has
shown that exactly the same arguments can be used to aid those
who prefer to read "His holy ones" as saints. In relation to

1QH 11:1ff. he writes that "von den übrigen Qumrantexten her
keine sichere Interpretation möglich ist - 'die Heiligen'
beziehen sich zweifellos auf Menschen nur noch an folgenden
Stellen in 1QM 3:5, 6:6, 10:10, 16:1; an anderen Stellen der
Texte dagegen sicher auf Engel."[277] Turning to external literature Kuhn sees the holy ones as Israelites in Daniel 7,
Deuteronomy 33, *I Enoch* 65:12, 93:6, *Jub.*2:24 and as particular
pious people in Ps 34:10, 16:3, Tobit 12:15 and 1 Macc 1:46.
He also claims that in late Judaism the expression took on an
eschatological sense designating those who belonged to the
eschatological people of God, and it is this particular meaning
which he wishes to apply at Qumran. He thus concludes that
"auf Grund des ausgebreiteten Stellenmaterials ist es also
durchaus möglich, dass mit 'den Heiligen' . . . Menschen und
nicht Engel gemeint sind."[278]

In relation to the context of 4QFlor, however, three
important passages must be considered: 1QM 7:6, which reads
"And no man shall go down with them on the day of battle who is
impure because of his fount, for the holy angels (מלאכי קדוש)
shall be with their hosts;" 4QD[b] which states that "no fools,
madmen, simpletons and imbeciles, the blind, maimed, lame and
deaf may not enter into the community for the holy angels are
in their midst;"[279] and 1QS 11:7:

> God has given them to His chosen ones
>> as an everlasting possession,
> and has caused them to inherit
>> the lot of the Holy Ones.
> He has joined their assembly
>> to the Sons of Heaven

> to be a Council of the Community,
>
> a foundation of the Building of Holiness,
>
> an eternal Plantation throughout all ages to come.[280]

This last quotation designates the community as the chosen ones
(as in 4QFlor 1:19) in antithetic parallelism to the Holy ones -
the heavenly council. Mention is also made of the building and
of the plantation, both of which are present in 4QFlor 1:1-7.
It can thus be maintained that the criterion for entry into the
community is based on the purity of those already there and that
when purity is being discussed, the Holy Ones refer to the
angels[281] - not as intermediaries, but as those who are already
in the heavenly council. These holy ones are also the guarantee
that all will not be lost to the sons of Belial (4QFlor 1:8),
for in the seventh battle God will intervene with his holy ones
to defeat Belial and his hosts (1QM 18:1-2).[282]

All that is certain concerning the exact meaning of all
three (?) reasons given for the exclusions is that this first
description of the sanctuary is evidence for the general Qumran
concern for purity. Barthélemy, in summarizing the motive for
this concern, points not to a desire for asceticism *per se*, but
rather to the idea, as expressed in 1QSa 2:8-9, that the community
is only "une réalité sainte" because the angels are part of the
congregation and "toute la sainteté humaine n'est que participation de celle des Saints par autonomasse, les anges."[283]

The second description of the sanctuary deals with the fact
that it cannot be desolated. The זרים, foreigners, who live in
other countries, will not desolate the sanctuary like they
desolated the former one.[284] If it is understood that the
former sanctuary was desolated because of Israel's sin, then

this could be a reference, from the perspective of the Qumran
author, to the Solomonic temple which is the concern of part
of the original oracle of Nathan. The desolation, a technical
term applied to that which results from sin or the breaking of
the Law,[285] would in this case be the destruction of the temple
because of Israel's sin in disobeying the Law.

The desolation could also be that which stems from the
זרים and is because of *their* sin. In other words, their presence
is what caused the desolation of the former sanctuary and the
former sanctuary in that case could be the present earthly
temple which was desolated by the admission of זרים. C. Roth
supports this second reading, taking זרים to refer to Gentiles
in general.[286] That may indeed be the case, but "foreigners"
seems a safer translation;[287] certainly this alternative understanding is preferable to any allusion to the temple of Solomon
as it is, above all, the difference between Qumran, as proleptically representing the eschatological sanctuary, and the
existing temple that is the author's concern in describing the
various aspects of the purity of the "sanctuary."[288]

The third point of description concerns the ongoing practice
of that proleptic "sanctuary". God has promised himself that
a מקדש אדם be built. Various translations have been offered
for this phrase. Yadin and D. Flusser translate it as "sanctuary
amongst men" and Flusser comments that the apparent combination
האדם אדוני in 2 Sam 7:19 seems to have enabled the author of the
midrash to call the מקדש אדני of Exodus 15 by the cryptic name
מקדש אדם. This then would refer to the temple to be built for
the coming Messiah.[289] But that is to have missed the point of
the identification in the demonstrative introductory formula

and to insist that מקדש can only be a physical building.

Nor does the phrase mean that the sanctuary will be
"man-made,"[290] for the building is to be done by God himself
according to the Exodus verse under which this description
is still subsumed. Rather it is a simple construct relation
that literally can be taken as a "sanctuary of man"[291] or
collectively as "sanctuary of men."[292] This does not deny that
there will be an eschatological sanctuary but stresses the
position of the Qumran community vis-à-vis the Jerusalem temple.

The purpose of the sanctuary of men is to make smoking
sacrifices, appositionally described as deeds of thanksgiving. It
is interesting that לוא of line 6 is expanded by לפניו in line 7.
The latter expresses both the idea that God observes, that what
is done is seen by him,[293] and also as a technical term shows the
place where the sacrifice was performed; לוא, on the other hand,
shows the direction in which the sacrifice was offered.[294]

In relation to the discussion concerning whether or not
the Qumran sect burnt sacrifices either in Jerusalem or at
Qumran itself, this section of 4QFlor does not deny outright
that no sacrifices are to be performed, for to do that would be
to destroy the cleverly constructed metaphor that has already
convinced some scholars to take מקדש all the time literally as
the temple building! Are the works of thanksgiving simply a
reference to correctly performed sacrifices or to a whole life-
style? It should be remembered that the analogy in 4QFlor is
to מקטירים which are any sort of smoking sacrifice and not
necessarily a bloody animal one.

Those against seeing any actual sacrifice at Qumran use
Philo to support their view. He describes the Essenes as

"especially devout in the service of God, not by offering
sacrifices of animals, but by resolving to sanctify their
minds."[295] O. Betz, for example, does not deny the possible
sacrifices of some of the Essenes but he tries to show how
Philo's observation and the practice at Qumran, deducible from
the Qumran literature, points to his conclusion that at Qumran
"s'est développée non seulement en théorie mais aussi en
pratique, une nouvelle conception du ministère sacerdotal. Le
·culte sacrificiel n'y fut pas supprimé, mais il fut pour une
large part remplacé et spiritualisé."[296]

On the other hand F. M. Cross observes that "Philo's
comment would be appropriate if the Essenes either rejected the
temple cultus on principle or insisted only that God's ethical
and ritual laws be observed as a prerequisite of valid
sacrifices,"[297] and he proceeds to argue that the Qumran texts
show that their authors' objections to the cultus at Jerusalem
fall under the second alternative. Cross stresses the priestly
nature of the Qumran sect, that they expected to perform
legitimate sacrifices in the days of the last war (1QM 2:1-6)
and that it is quite possible, as reported by Josephus (*Ant.*
18:19), that the Essenes at Qumran performed private sacrifices,
for archaeological evidence at Qumran includes the meticulous
burial of animal bones.

Yet Cross omits mention of the relative paucity of bones,[298]
and also he skips over 1QS 9:3-6 where prayer is described as
an acceptable fragrance of sweetness in place of the flesh of
holocausts and the fat of sacrifice.[299] Partly on the basis of
that text G. Klinzing concludes that the Qumran scrolls propose
perfection of life and prayer as equivalents of sacrifice, and

that the perfect life is seen as having an expiatory function.[30C]

It also seems unlikely that מעשי תודה refer explicitly to animal offerings; 1QS 6:18, for example, states how a novice in the community is examined as to his intelligence ומעשיו בתורה, and 1QS 8:1 explicitly describes the council as perfect in all the revealed Law לעשות אמת וצדקה ומשפט such that they can atone for sin. Baumgarten, too, points out that "inasmuch as all of them know the covenant of the law they 'offer a pleasant savor' and 'atone for the earth' (1QS 8:9-10) . . . . The 'oblation of the lips through the (study of) law is like a pleasant savor of righteousness'."[301] Thus the מקטירים in 4QFlor are best understood as a continuation of the metaphoric language of the eschatological sanctuary and, in order that the use of the term remain valid, one must accept that the Qumran sect did not reject sacrifice as such; it may even be the case that they practised it in some way and did not just consider themselves as waiting until the properly ordered cult be restored in Jerusalem.[302]

Thus the threefold description of the sanctuary describes its exclusive nature, the fact that it will not be desolated and that, proleptically, God constitutes it of men whose works of thanksgiving are the smoke-sacrifices of the sanctuary. In light of this two major studies of this section of 4QFlor which antedate the publication of 11Q Temple may be considered; after them more recent studies will be discussed.

B. Gärtner[303] understands that the OT texts quoted in 4QFlor are interpreted as referring to the "house" (i.e. temple) which Yahweh is to establish in the last days; this is none other than the community itself. The community as the "house

of God" bears the seal of eternity; the eternal temple, in
process of realization, practises spiritualized sacrifices that
are lives lived in perfect obedience to the Law. The impotency
of Belial will be a further sign of the realization of the
promises of God in the oracle of Nathan. Also, because the
pesher after 1:14 is concerned with the community, Gärtner
wishes to assume that it is the community that is at the centre
of the interpretation of lines 11-13; by analogy with CD 1:4-11
(and notwithstanding 4QPBless, where the only other occurrence
at Qumran of צמח clearly refers to the Messiah of the house of
David), the shoot of David is a symbol representing the community
which grows up under the leadership of the Interpreter of the
Law who is the teacher of Righteousness. Gärtner finds further
support for this identification in 1:18-19 where he reads משיחו
collectively with Yadin.[304] For the quotation from Amos 9:11
Gärtner compares CD 7:14-21 in which the סוכת is to be identified
with the Law and the king with the community such that the
"tabernacle of the king" is the community and its correct interpretation of the Law; thus the tabernacle of David in 4QFlor is
the community appearing under its teacher in fulfilment of the
promise of a restored "house" of David.

This thesis, seeing the community throughout 4QFlor,
appears to come from an understanding of the exposition which
Gärtner has then read back into the citations of the OT, for
the author of 4QFlor has been most careful to edit the text of
2 Sam 7:11b-14a for his purpose of referring the seed of David
to the future Davidic figure rather than to Solomon. It is
surely difficult to say as Gärtner does that seed, which he sees
as the central relational word between 4QFlor and 4QPBless, is

"an expression, which, according to 4QFlor, refers to the
community."[305] Nowhere else in Qumran literature is זרע to be
taken as the whole community.[306]

Furthermore, Gärtner's use of Qumran texts to support his
interpretation appears arbitrary. He largely ignores the clear
identification of the shoot of David with the Messiah of
Righteousness in 4QPBless preferring to attempt to stress the
"covenant of the kingdom over his people" which is given to
David and his seed, the latter of which he has identified with
the community in 4QFlor. Yet, in relation to the quotation
from Amos 9:11, Gärtner uses every last comparative identification
in CD 7:14-21 in an exposition that leads nowhere. In CD the
king is the community and the tabernacle are the books of the
Law such that the phrase סוכת המלך is the community and its
interpretation of the Law. This cannot be transferred, however,
to 4QFlor, as Gärtner admits, and so is of little use for his
argument beyond that the teacher and the community appear
together, for which he could have cited any number of texts.
It is also unfortunate that Gärtner uses the word "temple" to
translate מקדש, which is more properly rendered as "sanctuary."
Nowhere in Qumran is the community identified as היכל.[307]
Although his overall exposition is faulty, Gärtner provides
a very adequate summary and exposition for 4QFlor 1:1-7.

The second major study of this passage of 4QFlor is that
of G. Klinzing.[308] He begins by questioning the common view
that 4QFlor contains the idea of the community as temple and
asks whether it does not rather contain the notion of the
eschatological sanctuary. That sanctuary is the subject of
Exod 15:17-18 which is followed by comments on how its purity

and holiness are to be preserved by excluding certain groups,
for man with the community of the angels will there partake of
the glory of God. Also, the sanctuary will be built by God, not
by man, and will be built among men for sacrifices to be offered
in it.[309] Late Jewish eschatology supports these ideas of the
eschatological sanctuary,[310] and Klinzing concludes: "So
eindeutig in 4QFl 1 das eschatologische *Heiligtum* gemeint ist."[311]
This idea was used in the other Qumran manuscripts to refer to
the community[312] but in 4QFlor there is no concept of community
and the "house" has solely to do with the future sanctuary.

Several criticisms of Klinzing's view have already been
made implicitly in the discussion of the text so far. His reading
depends on certain highly debatable points; for example, the
understanding of מקדש אדם as "sanctuary amongst men," or his
reading מעשי תודה as actual sacrifices. It also depends upon
establishing a dichotomy between the community as sanctuary and
the eschatological sanctuary, when it is clear, as Klinzing
himself points out, that the two are not mutually exclusive
categories. Furthermore it depends on taking 4QFlor 1:1-7 out
of its (small) context in which it has already been observed
that the exposition of 2 Sam 7:11aᵝ in line 7 depends on the
reader's prior understanding of the sanctuary as community in
the preceding lines. However, Klinzing's overall thesis that
the community as sanctuary is a relatively late development in
Qumran literature supports the date for 4QFlor suggested by the
other analyses above.

The first of three scholars who have considered 4QFlor in
detail since the publication of 11QTemple is the editor of that
scroll himself. Already in a paper given in 1976 and published

two years later[313] Y. Yadin described how the scroll distinguished
between two temples, that built by the Israelites and that
belonging to the end times. He cited 11QT 29:8-10 in support
of his description and in his treatment of those lines in his
edition of 11Q Temple[314] he has argued that they confirm his
interpretation of the sanctuaries referred to in 4QFlor: there
is an earthly temple and there is a heavenly temple built by God
which it is hoped will become a sanctuary amongst men, a
sanctuary like the previous earthly ones except that God will
build it. Thus Yadin has argued against identifying the
community with the sanctuary, even proleptically.

There are two major problems with Yadin's interpretation
of 4QFlor. The first, which has already been discussed,[315]
concerns his translation of מקדש אדם; "sanctuary of men" seems
a more appropriate translation than "sanctuary amongst men."
The second problem concerns the identification of the eschatological temple with a heavenly temple. Even if 4QFlor does not
speak of the community as sanctuary, neither it nor 11QTemple
refers to a heavenly temple. Largely in response to Yadin's
proposals D. R. Schwartz has written an article[316] pointing to
these two problems, though his alternative interpretation is not
without its difficulties. Schwartz argues that there is neither
reference to a heavenly temple nor should מקדש אדם be interpreted as "sanctuary amongst men." Rather the author of 4QFlor
meant his readers to understand that in citing 2 Sam 7:10 he
was discussing the Second Temple, which the sect held to be
desecrated, and the Third Temple to be built by God in the future;
then, even though the phrase מקדש אדם occurs structurally within
the treatment of 2 Sam 7:10, Schwartz proposes that it is a

paraphrase of 2 Sam 7:13a (הוא יבנה בית לשמי) and refers to the "man-made" Solomonic First Temple.

In his turn M. Ben-Yashar[317] has criticized Schwartz's interpretation. Rightly he points out that Schwartz's approach is somewhat too systematic; מקדש ישראל (line 6) refers to both temples that had been violated, the Solomonic Temple and the Second Temple. Yet Ben-Yashar's main argument against Schwartz concerns his interpretation of מקדש אדם. By suggesting that the phrase is dependent on the expression תורת האדם in 2 Sam 7:19 he gives support to Yadin's translation of מקדש אדם as "sanctuary amongst men." But this use of 2 Sam 7:19 depends upon reading תורה in 4QFlor 1:7 (the linkword with 2 Sam 7:19); by following Strugnell's reading of תודה, of which Ben-Yashar seems unaware, we have already rendered this proposal unlikely.

Several other criticisms of Schwartz must be stated here. Firstly he proposes that 2 Sam 7:13a lies behind the phrase לבנות לוא מקדש אדם (which precedes the citation of 2 Sam 7:11aᵝ) yet he also argues that "the order of texts and ideas discussed is governed by that of the biblical text;"[318] this is clearly having it both ways. Secondly he explains that, while 2 Sam 7:13a is used in this indirect way, 2 Sam 7:12aᵅ and 12aᵞ are omitted because they are duplications; this seems somewhat arbitrary given the suggestion under our discussion of line 10 of the text that all three omissions are deliberate editing through the use of homoeoteleuton as an exegetical device.[319] Thirdly Schwartz is far from clear himself what is the referent of each phrase: at one point he says that מקדש אדם refers to the man-made temple of the present,[320] yet the main point of his argument seems to rest in seeing that phrase as referring to the Solomonic Temple.

Fourthly, like many other scholars he has taken אחרית הימים
to mean the end of days; we have already argued against that
above. Lastly he argues that the association of one sanctuary
with another necessarily implies that they are essentially the
same, that is, material; yet no such material identity need be
the case, if one recalls how intricately the author of 4QFlor
is interpreting the pun that is already before him in Nathan's
oracle - not every בית is made of bricks and mortar.

All in all there is nothing in 11QTemple which changes the
way that 4QFlor is to be interpreted except that the "community
as sanctuary" thesis must not be pursued to the exclusion of
any aspiration amongst the sectarians that there would be an
actual temple in the end: 11QTemple is the blue-print for such
a temple because it is primarily the blue-print that should have
been followed for all Israel's temples. In as much as 11QTemple
is a description of what the present temple should have been
like, it gives us insight into why the sectarians were dissatis-
fied with the temple in Jerusalem. In sum, therefore, the
"place" (מקום) of the oracle of Nathan is identified with the
"house" (בית) which in turn is identified with the "sanctuary"
(מקדש). The eschatological sanctuary, part of the manifestation
of the rule of Yahweh,[321] is then described in a threefold way
in sanctuary-language. The whole description is concerned with
identifying the sanctuary proleptically with the Qumran community[322] and its role in the latter days; and the identification
of מקדש with קהל, which is implied in the indirect quotation of
Deut 23:2-4, is clearly the scribe's primary understanding when
he writes his next section on the children of Belial and their
relation to the community members.

3. *The Sons of Belial*

The section of the midrash in which the expression בני
בליעל chiefly occurs is concerned to relate the rest that is
to be given to David, according to Nathan's oracle, to the rest
that will come about when all the plottings of the children of
Belial cease. The rest from the enemies in 2 Samuel 7 is part
of that peace which is the mark of the establishment of מנוחה,
the Deuteronomistic concept that is said to accompany the
proper habitation in the land.[323] Because the enemies in
4QFlor are the sons of Belial, the rest can only come about
with their defeat by Yahweh himself. This is described in 1QM
19 as an aspect of the sovereignty of God, and similarly in
4QFlor, just as Exod 15:17-18 is quoted mentioning the rule of
Yahweh, so in lines 7-9 there is another aspect of that reign:
the rest from enemies promised to the king, David, is to be
realized by Yahweh, "*He* will give them rest."

The phrase בני בליעל occurs only here in the whole of
Qumran literature (and possibly in 4QFlor 2:1-2). It occurs
in the MT several times, however, and appears to denote the
enemy in the holy war.[324] This has led P. von der Osten-Sacken
to suggest that 4QFlor may come closer than any other of the
pesharim to eschatological dualistic thought.[325] He defines
eschatological dualism as being present when Belial is thought
of as the real leader of the forces opposed to God and the
children of Light, and he proposes that that dualism is an
aspect which is clearly visible in 1QM as a feature of Maccabean
times that was dependent on Daniel, on the Yom Yahweh tradition
and the theory of the holy war; it is lacking in 1QS and 1QH
where dualism is ethically oriented and Belial is an abstract

entity - though perhaps no less real.[326]   He understands CD
to be a later document that is in many ways close to the
pesharim, sharing a number of concepts with them alone; the
only eschatological dualism in CD is in the phrases שר האורים
(5:18) and מלאך המשטמה (16:5) which both occur elsewhere in
Qumran literature. The emphasis in CD is rather that Belial
is *the* means whereby the pious in the new covenant are deceived.
However, because he reads 4QFlor solely in terms of rest from
enemies, Osten-Sacken does not draw the conclusions that his
thesis suggests in connection with the understanding of these
lines outlined structurally.

It is clear that lines 7-9 are not only concerned with rest
from enemies but that also they are closely connected with the
preceding discussion of the community as the anticipated
sanctuary. The structure reveals that the important aspect of
the defeat of the children of Belial is the cessation of their
present activity in the community of the children of light.
That activity is also described as having occurred in the past,
"when they came with their plots." The children of Belial are
seen as determined to destroy the community through their sin.

Because of the mention of the past, this section may
actually contain an allusion to an event within the history of
the community which threatened to destroy it. Lines 1-7 have
shown how the sanctuary is to be pure from the outset and to
be maintained as such, yet there is always the possibility until
the latter days cease, because the sanctuary is of men, that it
can be made desolate, impure, from within, through the activity
of Belial. As lines 1-7 are in the language of the eschatological
sanctuary, so 7-9 are in the language of the eschatological

battle, but the referent in both cases is the community. CD
also uses eschatological battle language but its link with
4QFlor is closer than that, for CD 4:12-19, in expounding
Isa 24:17, describes the three nets of Belial.

H. Kosmala has demonstrated how the Qumran concept of the
profanation of the sanctuary, the third net (טמא המקדש), is
derivable from the Torah:

> The defilement of the "sanctuary was in the end the
> defilement or profanation of (the name of) God (Ez
> 43:8; with hll, Lev 20:3) who had his miškan in the
> midst of the people; it was a defilement of the land
> (Lev 20:22-24, 18:24b-28); and it was a defilement
> of oneself and of the whole nation (Lev 18:24a, 29)
> which should be holy (Lev 19:2, 20:6)....The purity
> of the miqdaš was understood as the purity and holiness
> of the people, that is, of every individual member as
> well as of the community of the New Covenant as a whole.[327]

Defilement could be avoided by obeying the Law; this notion in
the thought of the covenanters is shown, for example, in CD 5:
6-7, "also they profane the sanctuary because they do not
distinguish (clean and unclean) according to the Law." This
same concept recurs in 4QFlor: those who are refined or in the
process of being refined will do all the Law (2:2).

Thus the purity of the sanctuary is depicted in eschatological
dualistic language, in terms of the rest that Yahweh will give
the children of Light from the plottings of the children of
Belial; that rest is derived from Nathan's oracle and is an
aspect of the sovereignty of God. The eschatological aspect of
the work of Belial is stressed through such work being a major

characteristic of the latter days as described in 4QFlor 2:1ff.

4. *The Shoot of David and the Interpreter of the Law*

Before discussing these phrases and the section in which they are used, it is necessary to define terms.[328] The frequency of the use of the phrase "the latter days" in 4QFlor, by which is meant both the time of trial leading up to a climax and the period immediately after that climax, as described in terms borrowed from Daniel, indicates an eschatological concern. That eschatology is also founded in history; the Qumran sect believed that their historical experiences were part of the events that constituted the latter days - at least, to be precise, the authors of those manuscripts that contain the phrase אחרית הימים regard their historical position as such. This in turn raises the question as to the development of eschatological expectations and beliefs during the existence of the community; to be able to date all the manuscripts accurately, and to read them without error, would enable a clear line of tradition to be established into which certain other manuscripts could be placed for their clearer understanding.

Alongside eschatology, the other term requiring careful definition is "Messiah." This must be restricted to a specific person or persons who, as anointed, will serve a particular function during the period of the latter days.

In 4QFlor two figures are mentioned: the shoot of David and the Interpreter of the Law, and both these are connected with the latter days (1:12).[329] The only other occurrence of the noun צמח in Qumran literature is in 4QPBless 3.[330] That text expounds Gen 49:10 and clearly talks of the Messiah from the seed of David; the covenant of kingship was given to David

and is being kept, until the coming of the Davidic Messiah,
by the thousands of Israel. At the Messiah's coming he will
resume the responsibility of that covenant. The structure
of 4QFlor 1:10-13 shows that the shoot of David, which is then
identified with the סוכת דויד has the slightly different function
in the future of saving Israel.[331]

The verb ישע is comparatively infrequent in Qumran literature,
though it occurs in diverse manuscripts. In 1QS 6:27, CD 9:9
and 10 it is used idiomatically with יד to denote that one is
the master of his own immediate future; in 1QH 2:23 and 3:6 it
is used of the deliverance of the individual from death; in 1QM
10:4, 8 (both biblical quotations) and CD 5:19 (=6QD 3:2) it is
used in relation to the mighty deliverance of Israel by God; in
1QM 11:3 it is used specifically in relation to the function of
the king, "and also you have delivered us by the hand of our
kings;" and in 4QpHos[b] 2:14 it is said that the nations (גואים)
are unable to save those who break the covenant from their
torments. Thus it could be maintained that there is not a
single use of the verb ישע, apart from 4QFlor, that is specifically
eschatological.[332] And yet, apart from the obvious personal
uses in 1QS, 1QH and CD, it is used in connection with the
activity of God, with that activity as performed by kings and in
relation to the impotence of the nations. Equally, the noun
clearly has eschatological significance.[333] Nowhere does the
community operate "to save Israel," but these other aspects of
salvation can be observed in 4QFlor if צמח is seen to refer to
a particular individual who will have the powers and function
of a king. Thus, once again in 4QFlor, there is an aspect of
the sovereignty of Yahweh, to be carried out through the seed of

David (2 Sam 7:12a), the shoot.

The shoot is described firstly as עומד with the Interpreter
of the Law. J. D. Amussin has taken the verb to mean "to rise
from the dead,"[334] but he cites Dan 12:13, which is far from
explicit, for his support, as well as some epitaphs from Beth
She'arim, which it must be remembered are from the third century
A.D. J. Carmignac, on the other hand, underlines that a correct
understanding of the Interpreter of the Law leads to a correct
understanding of the verb; that title refers to any Essene and
not to the Teacher of Righteousness alone. There is, therefore,
no need to translate the verb as "be resurrected."[335]

G. Klinzing prefers to see the term as used in CD 6:10,
4:4 and 4QFlor 1:11 in association with the latter days, as
meaning "to appear," that is, of historical persons.[236] And
W. Grundmann has argued from NT parallels that at Qumran both
"to stand" and "to fall" belong to the ethical-eschatological
sphere and their significance is "eine Frage menschlicher
Existenz, denn der Mensch kann in seinen Leben Stand haben oder
ohne Stand sein, ein Fallender, ein Getriebener, ein seinen
Standor Wechselnder."[337] Although עמד can have particular
cultic, legal or military connotations, and even though נפל
is frequently used at Qumran to signify stumbling through sin,
because of the occurrence of both עמד and נפל in balance together
in 4QFlor, the clearest meaning comes when they are translated
with their basic meaning and are understood in relation to the
figures with which they are used as signifying their taking
office or having fallen from it.

The Interpreter of the Law features as a specific figure
in CD at 6:7 and 7:18.[338] CD 6:7, in commenting on Num 21:18,

equates the Interpreter of the Law with the stave, but it
also speaks of "staves," which would suggest that there was
a succession of Interpreters, that one founding Interpreter
was particularly important and that the Teacher of Righteousness
of the latter days was an heir of the same function. Little can
be said from this, other than that it would appear as though
the Interpreter of the Law of 4QFlor was to have a similar
function to the Teacher of Righteousness of the latter days, and
could even be the same expected eschatological figure.[339]

The other passage, CD 7:18, reads: "and the star is the
Interpreter of the Law who came (הבא) to Damascus, as it is
written, A star went forth from Jacob and a sceptre shall rise
from Israel (Num 24:17). The sceptre is the Prince of the whole
congregation and when he takes office (בעמדו) he shall smite
all the children of Seth." Although there is much debate concerning whether הבא should be taken as past, present or future,
the quotation of Num 24:17 is clearly divided in the mind of the
writer, one half referring to the Interpreter of the Law and the
other half referring to the Prince of the whole congregation.
If there was a succession of Interpreters with the first and the
last (still to come) being considered the most important, then
any tense is possible for הבא, unless one insists that the
future referrent should be maintained from the original sense
of Num 24:17 such that both the figures referred to are
eschatological.

From both these CD quotations it is thus quite in line with
Qumran thought to consider that there would be an eschatological
figure entitled Interpreter of the Law and that he would not be
alone. As to whether or not these figures are messianic, it is

important to turn to current scholarship which has tried to
establish a line of tradition for Qumran thought on this subject
into which it may be possible to fit 4QFlor.[340]

Until J. Starcky published his article on the four stages
of Qumran messianism,[341] most scholars were concerned to pinpoint
a consistent Qumran messianic doctrine, and although some were
prepared to admit that difference in time of writing may have
caused difference in expression, those differences were divergencies from an orthodox doctrine, and were not understood as a
total shift on the part of the whole community.[342] So, for
example, J. Liver attempted to show that the doctrine of the
two Messiahs, which can be observed in the pseudepigrapha, must
have its historical and social background in the Qumran sect and
the Hasmonean period;[343] although there were various stresses at
different periods in the history of the sect, these are all
accountable and the doctrine of the two Messiahs can be seen
consistently throughout the sect's history.

As more manuscripts were published, the difficulties with
maintaining this consistent approach became obvious. Starcky,
especially, has proposed that the history of the Qumran sect be
seen in two phases, subdivided into four periods.[344] To each
period he assigns certain manuscripts and works out a theory of
the development of Qumran thought concerning messianism as it is
discernible from those manuscripts, which to a great extent
reflect the historical setting in their changing messianic
ideology. Thus he sees an eclipse of messianism in the hellenistic period, a reawakening in Hasmonean times but with the
expectation of both a royal and priestly Messiah, an absorption
of the total messianic office in the one figure of the future

High Priest at the start of the Roman period, and the rebirth of
the traditional concept of the Davidic Messiah at about the same
time as Jesus.

Yet such a scheme also has many difficulties. It depends
largely on the dating of the various scrolls and upon particular
understandings and interpretations of their contents. For
example, Starcky's dating, especially his third period in which
he sees one Messiah and the eschatological prophet, has been
questioned by R. E. Brown who argues in favour of a Hasmonean
date for CD, that it quite possibly contains a two Messiah
expectancy and, therefore, that Starcky's third period is simply
a continuation of the second.[345]

Earlier J. A. Fitzmyer pointed out that a danger in any
treatment of messianism is that the scholar, in relating documents
one to another, may fail to treat distinctly titles which may
represent different trends and beliefs. He also insists that
titles be taken at face value, not watered down: two Messiahs
must be recognized at some points because "the texts do use the
word *māšîāh* as a substantive in the plural and not just as an
adjective, and in an individual, not a collective sense."[346]

Taking Fitzmyer's warning seriously, the structure of the
text and the Qumran understanding of the salvific function of
the צמח allow the conclusion that this eschatological figure of
David's seed is indeed to be understood as the kingly Messiah,
the Messiah of Israel of other Qumran Mss. With this the vast
majority of scholars agree.[347] Yet there is not so much
agreement concerning the Interpreter of the Law.[348] 4QFlor
gives no description of the Interpreter other than that he will
stand with the Davidic shoot in the latter days:[349] he is,

therefore, at least an eschatological figure.

If one examines the manuscripts that are possibly contemporary with 4QFlor, then for the figure of the Interpreter of
the Law, whose title must be taken as the only description of
his function, two options present themselves. Firstly, 4QPBless
stresses the Davidic Messiah alone; 1QM though mentioning the
High Priest, stresses the role of the Prince (נשיא). This might
lead to the conclusion that the Aaronic Messiah was no longer
important, nor perhaps even held to be a Messiah, such that the
eschatological Interpreter of the Law is rather to be aligned
with the eschatological prophet of 1QS 9:11 and 4QTest.

Or, secondly, 4QpIsa^a describes how one priest in particular,
of the priests who will teach the Davidic Messiah how to judge,
"shall go out and garments of . . . shall be in his hands . . . ."
4QpPs^a speaks of a future time of trial for the priest and the
men of his council; if the time of trial is to be identified as
part of the latter days, as 4QFlor 2:1 suggests, then this would
allow that the figure beside David is priestly in the tradition
of Zerubbabel and that therefore one may see the Interpreter as
the Priestly Messiah.

4QFlor has enabled us to conclude that the Qumran covenanters
expected two eschatological figures; one of these was to seek
out, interpret, the Law. The normal usage of the expression in
no way necessitates that the person in the particular office of
"law-seeker," sometimes self-appointed, had to be a priest; in
fact, from Ezra 7:10, Sir 32:15, 1 Macc 14:14 and *Jub.* 1:12 it
might be deduced that the task of seeking the Law is everybody's
though some take it up with special vigour.[350] Alongside 4QFlor
can be placed the priest of 1QM, 4QpIsa^a and 4QpPs^a. Is it

possible to join this priestly eschatological figure with that
of the Interpreter of the Law?

The essential link between the functions of this eschatological figure as Interpreter of the Law and as priest is
provided by the fortunate preservation among the fragments of
4QFlor (6-11) of a section of Deuteronomy 33.[351] It is in
Deut 33:10 that the priestly descendents of Levi are described
as teaching the law. This same passage in Deuteronomy is cited
in 4QTestimonia and there clearly refers to the messianic priest.
If Num 24:15-17 also receives exposition in 4QFlor (Frg. 5) then
there is further support for the messianic function of the
Interpreter of the Law as priest. At Qumran this biblical text
was taken to refer to two eschatological figures (CD 7:18-20;
also 4QTest?) as in *T. Levi* 18:3 and *T. Judah* 24:1-6, in both of
which passages the "star" is specifically designated as the priest.

Just as the king and priest were anointed for office so the
two figures that are expected will be Messiahs in the technical
sense.[352] But also, because of their functioning in the latter
days, they both can be described as Messiahs in the broader sense
as well; they are the eschatological pair who will usher in the
new and just age of God. In 4QFlor 1:10-13 it is the messianic
prince around whom the exposition of the quotation of 2 Samuel 7
is developed. In Fragments 6-8 the messianic priest is probably
the centre of attention. Furthermore the phrase ישראל ואהרון]
in Fragment 4 in all probability either refers to the messianic
priest alone or to both the messianic figures[353] - not to the
kingly messiah by himself.

In sum 4QFlor 1:10-13 describes the royal family aspect of
בית as punned in 2 Samuel 7 and reflects primarily the Qumran

expectation of the Davidic King-Messiah, through whom God's
proper rule will be restored and by whom Israel will be saved.
Alongside the Davidic Messiah is the Interpreter of the Law who,
from other fragments of 4QFlor and from the consistent way in
which certain biblical texts (Deuteronomy 33; Numbers 24)
receive treatment in closely related literature, can be identified
with the Aaronic Priest Messiah. From the perspective of the
author of 4QFlor, both these eschatological figures are still
awaited.

E. Traditio-Historical Study

1. CD 3:12b-8:20

Having investigated 4QFlor from a form-critical point of
view and having discussed certain of its contents in relation
to Qumran theology, we can now attempt to delimit the tradition
in which 4QFlor may belong or the traditions to which it
approximates. First to be considered, of course, is the Qumran
literature itself, but within the Qumran writings there is much
diverse material and just as certain texts have been grouped as
contemporaneous according to content, so it may be possible to
group texts as to their dependence, direct or indirect, on other
Qumran manuscripts.

It has often been remarked that the pesharim are more
closely related to CD than to any other Qumran text. 4QFlor not
only shares this with the other pesharim, but witnesses to it
more than any of them for one particular unit of CD, 3:12b-8:20.
At CD 3:12b there is a clear break in the sense of the document
and the new unit that begins there appears to run until 8:20

where again the sense also breaks; 8:20 is also the point at
which the manuscript traditions for CD diverge - whichever is
followed from that point there are no great parallels between
4QFlor and CD. As to the unit 3:12b-8:20, items 10 and 11 below
might suggest that 4QFlor stands particularly within the
tradition of CD A.

The following list of parallels between 4QFlor and CD
concern overall content, specific phraseology peculiar to these
two passages in Qumran literature, and also the mixed type of
midrash common to both. The parallels are listed in order of
their occurrence in CD

1. CD 4:3 has the only occurrence of the phrase "the sons
of Zadok" in its unqualified form apart from 4QFlor 1:17; 1QS
9:10-11 is widely regarded as a later emendation of that text
from a viewpoint representing a similar tradition to that of CD.

2. CD 4:3-4 contains the identification of the sons of
Zadok with the chosen ones of Israel, as is most likely the case
in 4QFlor 1:17-19.

3. CD 4:4 and 6:11 have the only use of the phrase "the
latter days" in CD and its only use, apart from the title of
1QSa (later ?), in material other than the pesharim; the phrase
is used in each of the major subsections of 4QFlor, at 1:2, 12,
15 and 19.[354]

4. Apart from the quotation of Isa 7:17 at CD 14:1, the
only other clear references to the house of Judah in CD are at
4:11, 7:12 and 13, and that house is thus a specific concern of
this section of CD. To be compared with this is the use of the
quotation of Ezekiel 37 in 4QFlor 1:16-17 where the context is
also concerned with Judah over against the house of Ephraim -

which also is only here in CD apart from the Isaiah quotation
at 14:1. The house of Judah also occurs in 4QFlor Fragment 4
and possibly in 2:1.

5. CD 4:13-18 speaks of the three nets of Belial and
specifically names the desolation of the sanctuary as the third
net. The purity of the sanctuary is also the concern of 5:6-7
and in detail of 6:13-21. This concern is shared by 4QFlor
1:1-6 and Belial is also mentioned in 1:7-9. According to CD,
by doing the Law, the nets of Belial can be avoided; the doing
of the law in 4QFlor 2:2 is mentioned in a similar context.

6. At CD 4:14 occurs the only use of the word פשר in CD,
the statement of identification being the usual formal method
of exposition in CD. In 4QFlor there is both midrash with such
statements and midrash with pesher occurs - perhaps a combination
suggested by this passage in CD.

7. In his article on the use of OT quotations at Qumran,[355]
J. A. Fitzmyer identifies four classes of quotation. In the
classes within which the quotation of 4QFlor fall, those of
"modernized" texts (4QFlor 1:2-3, 14-16, 16-17) and of
"eschatological" texts (4QFlor 1:11-13), are almost all of the
passages in CD 3:12b-8:20 that use explicit OT quotations:
CD 4:12-18, 6:11-14 and 7:15-16 are "modernized" texts; CD 7:
10-12 is "eschatological." CD 7:8-9 is the only explicit OT
quotation that does not share a common categorization with 4QFlor.

8. The only use of the verb ישע in CD occurs at 5:19 in
relation to the saving of Israel. This idea also occurs at
4QFlor 1:13.

9. גר occurs in CD at 6:21 (and 14:4 and 6) and at 4QFlor
1:4. Apart from 11QTemple 40:6 these are its only uses. At

6:21 he is clearly identified as a member of a particular
category of people; גר is also used categorically in 4QFlor.
CD 14:4 and 6 are connected with the position of the גר in the
community and do not necessarily contradict the categorization
of 4QFlor.

10. The Interpreter of the Law appears at CD 6:7 and
7:18 (A only) - the only other places in Qumran literature,
apart from 4QFlor 1:11, that use exactly the same phrase
formally as a title.

11. Amos 9:11 is used in both CD 7:16 (A) and 4QFlor 1:12,
and Isa 8:11 at both CD 8:16 and 4QFlor 1:15. There are also
several quotations of Deuteronomy 32 in this passage of CD with
which one may possibly associate the quotations of Deuteronomy
33 in 4QFlor Fragments 6-11.

These many and detailed parallels between 4QFlor and CD
3:12b-8:20 are sufficient to suggest that one is dependent, to
an extent of literary influence, upon the other. Certain
remarks have already been made from archaeology, palaeography,
style and content concerning the date of 4QFlor. From the early
date normally assigned CD (circa 100 B.C.) and from the several
copies of CD that have come to light, especially in the fourth
cave,[356] we cannot but conclude that the dependence is of
4QFlor upon these five and a half columns of CD. Such dependence
could also reflect that within the Qumran community there were
distinct traditions with their own particular emphases, and
that 4QFlor is the heir of that represented by CD. That,
however, may be an overstatement of the case since so many
different genres of material are present at Qumran.[357] Also
in other literature, for example, in Paul's writings, that is

approximately contemporary with 4QFlor, the same concerns
emerge.

2. Acts 13:33-37; Heb 1:5

2 Samuel 7 and Psalm 2, being messianic texts, are used
frequently throughout the NT,[358] but they are used in combination
in only two places.

Firstly for Acts 13:33-37, D. Goldsmith has drawn attention
to the use of 2 Samuel 7 in both 4QFlor and the Acts passage.[359]
In the latter he sees it as the base text which is used
midrashically to frame other biblical quotations: ἀπαγγελεῖ,
κοιμηθήσῃ, ἀναστήσω, σπέρμα, μοι εἰς υἱόν, ἐλεός μου, and
πιστωθήσεται of 2 Sam 7:11-16 all recur in only a slightly
modified form in Acts 13:33-37. Apart from the fact that 2
Samuel 7 is used in this way, the point of interest in relation
to 4QFlor is that Psalm 2:7 occurs explicitly within this passage's
use of the Nathan oracle.[360] Although the use of other biblical
texts in this portion of Acts can best be described from a
literary standpoint, as certain exegetical principles are
applied,[361] it is possible to suggest that, in light of what
has been said concerning the combination of 2 Samuel 7 and Psalm
2 (1) in 4QFlor, the liturgy was the initial/factor in these
texts' combination for the author of Acts too.

The same can be proposed for Hebrews 1:5. There, there are
side-by-side explicit quotations of Psalm 2 and 2 Sam 7:14a,
used rhetorically in relation to the divine sonship of Christ,
to demonstrate Christ's superiority over the angels. Might not
this combination be based on a similar setting as was suggested
for the 4QFlor texts? Though there may be several literary
layers between the liturgy and the texts we have, we can at best

postulate a combination of biblical texts that is apparent in
a few cases as going back originally to a common source.

3. Acts 15:16

If the combination of certain biblical texts in 4QFlor
and the NT passages mentioned belongs to a common liturgical
tradition, Acts 15:16 suggests that there may have been a common
tradition of the biblical text. No literary dependence is
proposed here; merely that one text tradition is maintained
in two places.

The quotation of Amos 9:11 at Acts 15:16 has textual
differences from both the MT and the LXX, yet it is exactly
the same as that of 4QFlor and CD 7:16. J. de Waard has proposed
a common text tradition for Amos 9:11 as used in 4QFlor and
Acts 15:16 and lists their similarities in detail.[362] These
can best be seen in a presentation of the texts:

MT	ביום ההוא אקים את סכת דויד הנפלת
CD	והקימותי את סוכת דויד הנופלת
4QFlor	והקימותי את סוכת דויד הנופלת
Acts	καὶ ἀνοικοδομήσω τὴν σκηνὴν Δαυὶδ τὴν πεπτωκυῖαν
LXX	ἐν τῇ ἡμέρᾳ ἐκείνῃ ἀναστήσω τὴν σκηνὴν Δαυὶδ τὴν
	πεπτωκυῖαν

The texts of 4QFlor and Acts are identical and those of the
LXX and the MT match. Fitzmyer also points out[363] that the
introductory formula to the quotation is parallel in both 4QFlor
and Acts, כאשר כתוב and   καθὼς γέγραπται, whereas the quotation
in CD is introduced by כאשר אמר   W. H. Brownlee stresses the
similarity of the text tradition[364] by paying particular
attention to the initial *wāw* of 4QFlor and CD and the καὶ of

Acts 15:16. From all this de Waard's postulation seems very
likely though it cannot be said that the author of Acts
borrowed his text of Amos from a Qumran source.

4. 2 Cor 6:14-7:1

There have been four particularly detailed studies of
this paragraph of 2 Corinthians in relation to Qumran literature,
especially 4QFlor: by J. A. Fitzmyer,[365] by J. Gnilka,[366] by
B. Gärtner,[367] and by G. Klinzing.[368] These need to be reconsidered in light of the treatment of 4QFlor in this present
work.[369]

Fitzmyer deals with the whole body of Qumran literature and
having noted the obvious interruption that 2 Cor 6:14-7:1 makes
in the epistle in its present place, he examines the NT text
under five heads: the dualism of uprightness and iniquity,
light and darkness, Christ and Belial; the opposition to idols;
the concept of the temple of God; the separation from impurity;
and the concatenation of OT texts.

Concerning dualism Fitzmyer points to the use of the word
μερίς in 2 Cor 6:15 in close relation to light as parallel to
the Hebrew word used at Qumran for "lot."[370] Noteworthy for
4QFlor is the occurrence of גורל in the first line of Fragment 17.
All the aspects of dualism that Fitzmyer mentions 4QFlor has in
common with the other Qumran documents and 2 Cor 6:14-7:1.

For the opposition to idols Fitzmyer cites 1QS 2:16-17[371]
but the most important passage in this respect is 4QFlor 1:16-17
wherein Ezek 37:23 is cited concerning the revocation of idols.
The Corinthians passage makes use of the nearby text Ezek 37:27
in the same verse as mention is made of the disagreement of the

temple of God and idols. Indeed the same phrase, "I will be
their God, and they shall be my people," occurs in Ezek 37:23
but with the two phrases in reverse order from that of Ezek
37:27 and 2 Cor 6:16.

The third point, the concept of the community as the
temple of God, is not totally foreign to Pauline thought,[372]
but it is definitely not suitable to the context of 2 Corinthians
6. Yet the idea is fairly common at Qumran, where the group,
deprived (in part at least) of the Jerusalem temple, spiritualized its significance for themselves. In this respect the
present study's understanding of 4QFlor 1:4-9, particularly the
phrase מקדש אדם, is highly significant.[373] While not denying
the belief in the existence of an eschatological sanctuary,
4QFlor points to the idea that the Qumran community anticipates
in itself such a building.

As to the interest of separation from all impurity, this
is evident in many places in Qumran literature.[374] Fitzmyer
comments that in light of the Qumran evidence "the counsel in
2 Cor, to 'cleanse ourselves from everything that can taint body
and spirit' in an effort toward perfect holiness, takes on new
meaning. It resembles strongly the general Qumran proscription
of all contact with outsiders."[375] This is exactly the concern
of 4QFlor 1:3-4 in its delimiting who will be allowed into the
eschatological sanctuary and thereby into the Qumran community
itself. Fitzmyer does not mention this passage of 4QFlor.

Lastly Fitzmyer points to the concatenation of OT texts in
2 Cor 6:14-7:1 as resembling in collection those of 4QTest but
he fails to indicate the reason why such collections should be
made or how they were made. Though we would not wish to suggest

a liturgical background for the combination of texts in
2 Cor 6:14-7:1, it is noteworthy that a close Ezekiel passage
and a quotation of 2 Samuel 7:14 are to be found in 4QFlor.

Fitzmyer concludes that so many points of comparison with
Qumran literature implies that "we are faced with a paragraph
in which Qumran ideas and expressions have been reworked in a
Christian cast of thought."[376] For him 2 Cor 6:14-7:1 is a
Christian reworking of an Essene paragraph which has been
introduced into the Pauline letter.

J. Gnilka is his study of the same passage[377] begins by
outlining the thematic connection between the various OT
quotations in the 2 Corinthians passage. He then attempts to
decide the question Fitzmyer leaves open as to the exact source
of the section. Although he notes the large number of NT hapax
legomena in the section, Gnilka particularly stresses the
occurrence of the name βελιάρ as indicative of a certain
dependence upon intertestamental Jewish literature.[378] Yet,
claims Gnilka, in such literature Belial's opponent, when
mentioned, is always God, never the kingly messiah; the dualism
of Christ against Belial is something peculiarly Christian and
suggests that 2 Cor 6:14-7:1 was penned by a Christian author.

Further support for this position is deduced from the
Christian meaning implied clearly in the dichotomy established
between believer and unbeliever. Yet here Gnilka has not taken
account of the concern that the Qumran covenanters show in
respect of the limits of their community (4QFlor 1:2-4). Indeed
Gnilka himself draws a very fine line between language used by
the "Christian" author and theological concepts that he considers
to be Essene in origin, namely, the community as God's temple,

separation from a godless environment and dualism.

The first of these is only found in Essene literature
among material contemporary with the NT; the second is
certainly not Pauline but permeates other literature especially
that of the Essenes; the third certainly indicates Jewish
circles and possibly those of the Essenes. In sum, Gnilka
proposes that although the tradition has been subject to
Christian revision, the basic Essene character of the fragment
is still evident; the editor of 2 Corinthians was responsible
for the passage's interpolation in its present place.

For all Gnilka's contributory suggestions he mentions
4QFlor but twice and only in a secondary fashion, such that
his conclusions are not fully discretionary as to the various
traditions present within Qumran literature itself, and certainly
he does not attempt to limit his options upon slight evidence.
His work points constructively in the right direction. The study
of B. Gärtner, on the other hand, is based on the presupposition
that Paul wrote 2 Cor 6:14-7:1 and so is somewhat restricted
from the start.

As already noted, Gärtner sees 4QFlor as solely concerned
with the community; even the "shoot of David" is understood as
the community. Thus in 2 Cor 6:14-7:1, which Gärtner uses
basically as an example of parallel thought to prove his point
about 4QFlor, he sees a concern similar to that which he observes
in 4QFlor: for the community as temple,[379] for idols; also for
connecting the community as temple with the oracle of Nathan at
2 Sam 7:14 (2 Cor 6:18),[380] for purity and separation, and for
Belial. He works solely upon the basis of literary and conceptual
parallels and is in no way involved with attempting to show the

dependence, interdependence or independence of the traditions
represented by 4QFlor and 2 Cor 6:14-7:1. Perhaps with all
of Gärtner's careful literary analysis, Gnilka could have
proposed a more definite line of tradition for the Corinthians
passage.

G. Klinzing, lastly, is also steeped in his own conclusions
when he approaches the question of the relationship of 4QFlor
and 2 Cor 6:14-7:1. He works from the result of his analysis
of 4QFlor 1:1-7 which he sees, somewhat artificially according
to this study, as solely a literal portrayal of the eschatological
sanctuary. He criticizes Gärtner, therefore, for insisting on
an improbable temple = community identification.[381]

Furthermore, Klinzing notes in detail that "idols" is not
only a conjectural reading in 4QFlor 1:17, but that it also
occurs in a quotation there, whereas in 2 Cor 6:16 it is not in
a quotation. Again in reply to Gärtner in particular, he
observes that to identify the shoot of David with the community,
and thus to see the whole of the Nathan oracle in 4QFlor as
concerning the community, is to misunderstand a clear messianic
term. Moreover, since the sect is not the concern of the midrash
until Psalm 1, according to Klinzing, it is wrong to see a
general concept of purity and separation in relation to 4QFlor
1:1-13 for that depends upon reading those lines as a portrayal
of the sect and not of the temple. All these factors lead
Klinzing to conclude:

> Zusammenfassend ist zu sagen, dass 4QFl 1 bei genauerer
> Untersuchung nicht als der Paralleltext zu 2 Kor 6, 16ff.
> angesehen werden kann, als der er bei Gärtner erscheint:
> als ein Stück mit der Vorstellung von der Gemeinde als

Tempel, das auch in der Einzelzügen weithin mit
2 Kor 6 ubereinstimmt.[382]

Klinzing then continues to say that from a literary
critical point of view 2 Cor 6:14-7:1 can only be seen to have
similarities to 4QFlor if it is understood that in different
ways both might be traced back to Ezek 37:26-28 which speaks
of the eschatological sanctuary; indeed 2 Cor 6:16 even quotes
part of Ezek 37:27. However, from a form-critical perspective,
2 Cor 6:14-7:1 has a clear setting in the baptismal rites of
the early church and that explains the emphasis on purity,
separation, sanctification, admission and the temple.[383]

In sum, Gärtner is certainly correct to have drawn together
so many parallels: 4QFlor is indeed concerned with the community
as is 2 Cor 6:14-7:1 with their common citations of Ezekiel 37
and 2 Samuel 7. On the other hand Klinzing is completely
justified in pointing out Gärtner's inadequate explanation of
the shoot of David. It is somewhat unfortunate that Klinzing
was unable to see the link between the belief in the eschatological
sanctuary and the Qumran selfunderstanding as being that
sanctuary as a community in anticipation, for then his remarks
on the Corinthians passage would have been more than hypothetical:
both 2 Cor 6:14-7:1 and 4QFlor express theological concepts in
connection with entry into the community. Thus 4QFlor may have
in mind the entry ceremony associated with the Feast of Weeks,
2 Corinthians the rite of Christian baptism.

In support of this supposition is the quotation from
Exodus 15 in 4QFlor (and from Isaiah 65) which is traditionally
associated with either Passover or Weeks. And such remarks
imply that any dependence between 4QFlor and 2 Corinthians is

of a literary kind, since it appears that more than one
festival is involved in the selection of the various biblical
texts. At least, and certainly, 4QFlor and 2 Cor 6:14-7:1 are
heirs of a common tradition concerning the eschatological
community. Our suggestion thus bears out some of the proposals
of Fitzmyer and Gnilka, adopts the stance of Gärtner concerning
the content of both passages, except for the overly strong
emphasis on the temple understood solely as the community at
Qumran, and while allowing that Klinzing is correct in part
concerning the eschatological sanctuary, supports his theory
as to the baptismal interest of 2 Cor 6:14-7:1.

F. Conclusion

The Florilegium from the fourth cave at Qumran is a
midrash on festival texts concerning the latter days. The main
texts which are expounded in it are from 2 Samuel 7 and Psalms
1 and 2, "coronation" texts which belonged together in some
traditional liturgical setting with which the author of the
manuscript was familiar, probably the Feast of Tabernacles.

Palaeography, archaeology and style show the date of the
actual manuscript to be somewhere in the first century A.D.;
study of the content enables that date to be fixed with a great
degree of probability in the second or third quarter of the
first century.

While the approach of this study has been to distinguish
carefully between the interpreter's use of exegetical principles
and the hermeneutical result attained, it cannot be denied that
the two are very closely intertwined. The overall eschatological
hermeneutic of the content of many of the scrolls may rest

ultimately on some exegesis by the Teacher of Righteousness,
but in relation to 4QFlor the concern of the author writing
with an eschatological hermeneutical purpose was to describe
the eschatological content of two liturgical texts in terms
of the latter days. In the latter days, a term explained in
detail in column two, the community, described in terms of the
eschatological sanctuary, will have restricted admission, the
resultant purity of which will guarantee that the sanctuary
be not desolated. The ongoing ritual in the sanctuary will be
the performance of deeds of thanksgiving offered to God who,
in turn, will give the members of the community rest from all
the devices of their enemies, particularly those concerned with
profanation of the sanctuary. In that way, one half of the play
on the word "house" in 2 Samuel 7 is expounded. Belief in the
eschatological sanctuary as such is not denied; rather the
community is portrayed as seeing itself to be that sanctuary
in anticipation.

     In 1:10-13 the midrashist uses the other part of the pun
to describe the Messiah of the Davidic "house" who is to come
to save Israel in his divinely delegated role as king. The
eschatological messianic priestly Interpreter of the Law will
accompany him.

     The section of the midrash in the form of pesher shows how
joining the community is the initial step in the reunification
of the houses of Israel and Judah, which Ezekiel 37 describes
as yet another aspect of the reign of David who is prince for
ever. In that reign God will also set his sanctuary in their
midst for evermore that "all the nations will know that I, the
Lord, sanctify Israel" (Ezek 37:28).

From Psalm 2 it is the nations who are identified as
those who will be active against the community in the time
of trial, which is itself a major aspect of the latter days.
Those days are also characterized as the time when the wise
will understand, and the rest given to the community at that
time, along with that understanding, are sure signs of the
sovereignty of God, as is the rule of the Davidic Messiah
in Zion.

Thus, in relation to some larger whole, 4QFlor functions
as a midrash on texts concerned with royalty that in its
exposition of the latter days stresses the kingship of God.
And such stress is achieved through the application according
to generally accepted methods of particular exegetical principles,
recognition of which has often been the first step not only in
understanding the text but also, on occasion, in restoring it.

NOTES

[1]See "Le Travail d'Édition des Fragments Manuscrits de Qumrân," *RB* 63 (1956), 50.

[2]In May 1978 W. H. Brownlee wrote to me from Jerusalem to inform me that both Ms. 286 (Fragments 1, 2 and 3; DJD V, Plate XIX) and Ms. 281 (Fragments 4-26; DJD V, Plate XX) were at the Shrine of the Book for restoration work for their better preservation. In May 1983 I studied Ms. 286 at the Rockefeller Museum; Ms. 281 was then still at the Shrine of the Book.

[3]*The Dead Sea Scrolls,* New York: Viking Press, 1955, 62. Further references to the site of 4Q and to the discovery of its contents may be found in H. Bardtke, *Die Handschriftenfunde am Toten Meer,* Die Sekte von Qumran, Berlin: Evangelische Haupt-Bibelgesellschaft, 1958, 25-29; F. F. Bruce, *Second Thoughts on the Dead Sea Scrolls,* Grand Rapids, Mich.: W. B. Eerdmans, 1956, 30-33; F. M. Cross, *The Ancient Library of Qumran and Modern Biblical Studies,* Garden City, N. Y.: Doubleday and Co., Inc., 1958, 19-22; J. T. Milik, *Ten Years of Discovery in the Wilderness of Judaea,* London: SCM Press, 1959, 16-18; R. de Vaux, *L'Archéologie et les Manuscrits de la Mer Morte,* London: Oxford University Press, 1961, 42-43; G. Vermes, *Les Manuscrits du Désert de Juda,* Paris: Desclée & Co., 1954[2], 22-23. Milik and de Vaux were the first two scholars on the scene after the initial Bedouin excavations.

[4]*The Dead Sea Scrolls,* Harmondsworth: Penguin Books Ltd., 1964[2], 44.

[5]"Fragments of a Qumran Scroll of Eschatological *Midrašim*," *JBL* 77 (1958), 350-51; hereafter cited as "Fragments."

[6]"Further Messianic References in Qumran Literature,"
JBL 75 (1956), 176 (photograph facing page 174). An interesting
photograph (Plate 13a in his book *The Dead Sea Scrolls*) shows
two hands (Allegro's?) holding together what is described in
the caption as "a Fourth Cave document;" it is clearly 4QFlor.

[7]"Spurious Texts from Qumran? I The Question," *PEQ* 90
(1958), 61.

[8]"Spurious Texts from Qumran? II A Reply," *PEQ* 90
(1958), 64.

[9]With a photograph facing page 350.

[10]DJD V; with the collaboration of A. A. Anderson, Oxford:
Clarendon Press, 1968, with Plates (XIX-XX); hereafter cited as
DJD V, ad loc. assumed.

[11]In "Further Messianic References in Qumran Literature,"
JBL 75 (1956), 176. This is apparently capitalized from his
description of the document ("Communication," in "Le Travail
d'Édition des Fragments Manuscrits de Qumrân," *RB* 63 1956, 63),
as "un *florilège* de passages bibliques avec commentaires tirés
de l'Exode, II Samuel, Isaïe, Amos, les Psaumes et Daniel."

[12]*Scrolls from the Judean Desert*, Jerusalem: Machbaroth
Lesifurth Publishing House, 1959, 173; hereafter cited as
Habermann, ad loc. assumed.

[13]*The Dead Sea Scrolls in English*, Harmondsworth: Penguin
Books Ltd., 1968[3], 245; hereafter cited as Vermes, ad loc. assumed.

[14]Which is the title of his article in *IEJ* 9 (1959); Yadin
is supported in this by M. Ben-Yashar ("Noch zum *miqdaš 'ādām*
in 4QFlorilegium," *RQ* 10 1979-81 , 587, n.2).

[15]*The Meaning of the Qumran Scrolls for the Bible,* New York: Oxford University, 1964, 88, n. 52; hereafter abbreviated to *Meaning.*

[16]*The Dead Sea Scriptures in English Translation,* Garden City, N. Y.: Doubleday & Co., Inc., 1956, 337; hereafter cited as Gaster, ad loc. assumed. The title and translation remain the same in the 3rd revised and enlarged edition, 1976, 446-48.

[17]"Fragments," 351.

[18]"An Unpublished Fragment of Essene Halakhah (4Q Ordinances)," *JSS* 6 (1961), 71. Later (*PEQ* 96 1964 , 53), Allegro also likened the script of "The Wiles of the Wicked Woman" to that of 4Q Ordinances.

[19]"Notes en marge du Volume V des 'Discoveries in the Judaean Desert of Jordan'," *RQ* 7 (1967-69), 177; hereafter cited as "Notes."

[20]"The Palaeography of the Dead Sea Scrolls and Related Documents," *Aspects of the Dead Sea Scrolls,* Scripta Hierosoly-mitana IV, Jerusalem: Magnes Press, 1958, 56-87. Avigad acknowledges the work of J. C. Trever ("A Paleographic Study of the Jerusalem Scrolls," *BASOR* 113 1949 , 6-23) who was the first to argue for the age of the scrolls from palaeographic evidence; Trever's later work ("Studies in the Problem of Dating the Dead Sea Scrolls," *PAPS* 97 1953 , 184-93) confirmed his earlier proposals for variously dating the scrolls in the two centuries preceding the fall of the Second Temple.

[21]*The Hebrew Scripts,* Leiden: E. J. Brill, 1971, Part I: the Text, see especially 138-62 on Palestinian square script; Part II: the Plates, see especially Plates 81-89.

[22]"How old are the Cave Manuscripts? A Palaeographical
Discussion," VT 1 (1951), 98-101; also, *The Qumran (Dead Sea)
Scrolls and Palaeography, BASOR* Supplementary Studies 13-14,
Yale: American Schools of Oriental Research, 1952. This latter
was written largely in an attempt to refute certain scholars who
persisted with sceptical attitudes towards the scrolls.

[23]From his table illustrating the development of the final
mem (*The Qumran Scrolls and Palaeography,* 42), it is possible to
affiliate the scribe of 4QFlor with that style which Birnbaum
dates between 37 B.C. and A.D. 70.

[24]*The Ancient Library of Qumran,* 78. Elsewhere Cross
develops his arguments fully ("The Development of the Jewish
Scripts," *The Bible and the Ancient Near East,* ed. G. E. Wright;
Garden City, N. Y.: Doubleday & Co., Inc., 1961, 133-202), though
his conclusions in relation to the Qumran material remain the same.

[25]*L'Archéologie et les Manuscrits de la Mer Morte,* 84.

[26]"A Midrash on 2 Sam. vii and Ps. i-ii (4QFlorilegium)," 98;
hereafter cited as Yadin, ad loc. assumed.

[27]E.g., demonstrable because of the known way in which
scripture was used as shown in Chapter I.

[28]A translation in itself may alter the meaning of the text,
e.g., by excluding puns that occur in the original (see the
discussion on סוכה in 1:12), but it is hoped that no translation
is given here which radically alters the outline structure of
the text.

[29]I owe these readings of the original manuscript and the
earliest photographs to Professor W. H. Brownlee who examined

them in the summer of 1976. Presumably the manuscript and
earliest photographs go some way towards explaining Allegro's
original suggestion in "Fragments" reading אוי[ב; Allegro is
followed closely by Carmignac. Brownlee's conclusions have
been previously supported by Strugnell ("Notes," 220) who
proposes to restore לוא ישיא ע[וד אויב]בו ולוא יוסי[ף]וגי,
mostly from Psalm 89:23.

[30]Yadin preserves עוד from vs 10a and in providing an
object for רגז, intransitive in the *qal*, is forced to suggest
the *hiph*[c]*il*, י[רגיז (?) ע[ו]ד ו[חו ?] , "will move him no more."
From where Yadin obtained his line's initial *yôd* remains a
mystery. Yadin is followed here and for the most part by
E. Slomovic ("Toward an Understanding of the Exegesis in the
Dead Sea Scrolls," *RQ* 7 1969-71 , 7).

[31] ולוא   ע[ו]ד אוי[ב ... .

[32]*Les écrits esséniens découverts près de la mer morte,*
Paris: Payot, 1959, 325: "(. . . dans la ma)in de (ses)
enne(mis)." Hereafter cited as Dupont-Sommer, ad loc. assumed.

[33]*Die Texte aus Qumran,* München: Kösel-Verlag, 1964, 256.
Hereafter cited as Lohse, ad loc. assumed.

[34]The text tradition of all the Samuel quotations in 4QFlor
for the most part is closest to that of the LXX. This is
confirmed also by comparison with 4QSam[a,b,c]. Although none
of the 4QSam texts preserves the section of 2 Samuel 7 quoted
in 4QFlor, it is not insignificant that E. C. Ulrich has argued
convincingly "that the Greek version was originally translated
from a Hebrew text much closer to 4QSam[a] than to M" (*The Qumran
Text of Samuel and Josephus,* HSM 19; Missoula: Scholars Press,

1978, 119; the conclusions of his thesis are stated more fully on pages 257-59).

[35]2 Sam 7:1, 9, 11.

[36]Psalm 89:23 reads: לא ישא אויב בו ובן עולה לא יעננו.
See note 29 for Strugnell's proposed restoration. It is not
necessary to see a quotation from Psalm 89 at this point as
Strugnell suggests. Rather it is possible that 2 Samuel 7 as
reflected in 4QFlor and the text of Ps 89 represent a similar
textual tradition, perhaps with direct liturgical associations.

[37]E. Slomovic ("Toward an Understanding of the Exegesis in
the Dead Sea Scrolls," *RQ* 7 1969-71 , 7) includes the whole
text of 2 Sam 7:10 here because he recognizes the use of the
rule of *gĕzērâ šāwâ* in relation to Exod 15:17-18. D. R. Schwartz
("The Three Temples of 4Q Florilegium," *RQ* 10 1979-81 , 87, n.14)
also argues for the inclusion of the whole of verse 10.

[38]F. M. Tocci (*I Manoscritti del Mar Morto,* Bari: Editori
Laterza, 1967, 319; hereafter cited as Tocci) seems to follow
Vermes. His translation reads "('Ho assegnato un posto ad
Israele, mio popolo, e ve l'ho stabilito perché abiti in casa
sua e non sia) I più (agitato dai suoi) nemi(ci, né seguiti) il
figlio della perversione'."

[39]In DJD V, Allegro restored שפטים, changing an original
plene restoration ("Fragments," 351), perhaps because he thought
there was not really enough room for the plene reading at the
beginning of the line. His earlier reading, however, is to be
preferred.

[40]Dupont-Sommer's restoration of a *niphᶜal*, "sera batie,"
does not recognize the *lāmed* and is not long enough to fill the

lacuna. On the other hand, Gaster restores it as "the House
(which God will cause to be built for his abiding) in the Last
Days." That could offer a variety of *lāmeds* but is altogether
too long - indeed Gaster's translation is of little use to the
text critic although in many places he offers a very clear
understanding.

[41]He is supported in this by J. Maier (*Die Texte vom Toten
Meer*: München-Basel: Ernst Reinhardt, 1960, Bd. I Übersetzung,
185, Bd. II Anmerkungen, 165; hereafter cited as Maier, ad loc.
assumed) and by Slomovic.

[42]In a private communication.

[43]Vermes and Tocci use "build" and "costruira" respectively
in their translations, implying יבנה in support of Habermann.
Moraldi (*I Manoscritti di Qumrān,* Torino: Unione Tipografico-
Editrice Torinese, 1971, 573; hereafter cited as Moraldi, ad loc.
assumed) restores "*sarà edificata.*" 11QT 4:8 implies that בנה
was used of the earthly temple, while 11QT 29:9 suggests that
ברא was used for the future temple.

[44]Cf. 4QPBless Fragment 2:1:2 where בוא = בו.

[45]F. M. Cross ("The Song of the Sea and Canaanite Myth,"
JTC 5 1968 , 16; *Canaanite Myth and Hebrew Epic,* 131, n.70)
notes that אדני of MT is "obviously secondary" and that the
Samaritan text reads יהוה, "a rare instance of its preserving
the older reading." Perhaps Sam. should be followed in the
restoration here, especially because of 4QpaleoExod[m] representing
Exodus in a Samaritan recension. Strugnell suggests that
Fragment 21, יהוה ב is to be placed at this point.

[46]Exod 15:18 may lie behind the לעולם ועד of 11QT 45:14:

אני יהוה שוכן בתוך בני ישראל לעולם ועד

[47]Followed by Moraldi.

[48]Yadin (*The Temple Scroll* Hebrew Edition , Jerusalem:
The Israel Exploration Society, The Institute of Archaeology of
the Hebrew University, The Shrine of the Book, 1977, Vol 2, 136)
mentions the phraseology of Deut 23:3-4 in association with
11QT 45:13 (לוא יבואו לה) which concerns the protection of the
sanctuary (מקדש) from the blind.

[49]Compare the similar stress in rabbinic tradition.
b. *ᶜErub.* 54a reads: "It was taught at the school of R. Eliezer
b. Jacob: wherever (in scripture) the expression . . . waᶜed
occurs, the process to which it refers never ceases 'Waᶜed'.
Since it is written, 'The Lord shall reign for ever and ever'."

[50]"The Exclusion of 'Netinim' and Proselytes in 4QFlorilegium,"
RQ 8/29 (1972), 87-96, especially 92-96; reprinted in *Studies in
Qumran Law,* SJLA 24; Leiden: E. J. Brill, 1977, 75-87, with an
expanded postscript. He is supported in this by G. Blidstein
("4Q Florilegium and Rabbinic Sources on Bastard and Proselyte,"
RQ 8/31 1974 , 431-35). Baumgarten endorses Blidstein's work
in his expanded postscript (*Studies in Qumran Law,* 85).

[51]*Studies in Qumran Law,* 82, n.24.

[52]In a letter to me of July 1978 W. H. Brownlee wrote
concerning the *gimel*: "I had another look at it in Jerusalem
this spring and noticed that the stance of the surviving left
leg is affected by a tiny piece of scotch tape where someone
had tried to raise it into a vertical position but was unable

to do so." This accounts for the stance of the stroke of ink
which is not quite what one would expect for a *gimel*.

[53]The *niph^c^al* variously translated by Allegro, "Fragments"
and DJD V, and Gaster.

[54]The *qal* variously rendered by Dupont-Sommer, Lohse, Maier,
Moraldi, Tocci and Vermes.

[55]The idiomatic understanding of Carmignac, followed by
Strugnell.

[56]In a private communication. In view of the presence of
the *gimel* גלה is the only likely root.

[57]It may be possible to restore a form of מגן in the lacuna.
It is used to symbolize protection and even as a divine epithet
in Pss 18:3, 84:10, 12, 89:19 (a psalm already mentioned in
relation to 4QFlor 1:1). See also 1QH 6:27-28: "For no enemy
(זר) shall ever invade it, since its doors shall be doors of
protection (דלתי מגן) through which no man shall pass." If שם
in 4QFlor 1:4 is the noun "name," it is worth comparing 1QM
3:2-4:16, 6:2-3 and especially 5:1-2 in which the Prince of the
congregation has his name written on his shield. Judges 5:18
(according to the textual restorations of C. F. Burney, *The
Book of Judges,* 1918, reprinted: New York: Ktav, 1970, 117-20)
may be the text upon which the whole phrase depends. Through
binyan 'āb מגן of Psalms 18, 84 and 89 and יראה of Gen 22:14
(according to Yadin) are brought together. A restored text
might read: "Our Shield will reveal himself for ever; continually
he will protect it (the sanctuary)."

[58]Cf. 1QS 8:14, 9:19.

[59]This is also supported by J. D. Amusin ("Iz Kumranskoi
Antologii Eskhatologicheskikh Tekstov," *Kratkie Sodbshcheniya
Instityta Naradov Asii*   Brèves communications de l'Institut
des Peuples d'Asie   86   1965 , 56-66; see the recension of
Z. Kapera *RQ* 6   1967-69 , 146-47) who uses Isa 60:2 as support
for his restoration: הירו עליו תמיד [וכבודו היו]

[60]The appearance of the Lord and talk of the eternal
sanctuary occur together in *Jub.* 1:26-28.

[61]Y. Yadin, *The Temple Scroll,* Vol 1, 143-44; Vol 2, 238;
Vol 3, plates 44 and 14*

[62]"The Three Temples of 4Q Florilegium," 85.

[63]Followed variously by B. Gärtner (*The Temple and the
Community,* London: Cambridge University, 1965, 32) and
G. Klinzing (*Die Umdeutung des Kultus in der Qumrangemeinde
und im Neuen Testament,* Göttingen: Vandenhoeck & Ruprecht,
1971, 80).

[64]Followed by S. Lamberigts, "Le Sens de קדושים dans les
Textes de Qumrân," *ETL* 46 (1970), 27.

[65]In discussing 11QT 29:7-10, which is used above in support
of restoring כבודו, H. Lichtenberger ("Atonement and Sacrifice
in the Qumran Community," *Approaches to Ancient Judaism Volume II,*
ed. W. S. Green, BJS 9; Chico: Scholars Press, 1980, 166-67)
agrees with those scholars who suggest that the Qumran Community
considered itself to be in the service of God with the angels;
that would support understanding קדושו as referring to his holy
(angels).

[66]"His holy name" might appear as שם קדושו as in 1QpHab 2:4.

If there was word inversion it might have been written as

קודשו שמו but not as קדושו שם. 11QT 45:12 (אשר המקדש...

אשכין שמי בה.....) which occurs in a similar context and which
might have been used in support of reading שם as "name" is
qualified by a suffix rather than by any form of קדוש, as is

שם in 11QT 3:4 (ח לשֹום שמי עליו כ]).

[67]K.-G. Kuhn (*Konkordanz zu den Qumrantexten*, Göttingen:
Vandenhoeck & Ruprecht, 1960, 223) lists שם many times, even
with motion implied, especially in 1QM, whereas, apart from
4QFlor 1:3, שמה occurs only once: in 1QH 1:10 (with a possible
second occurrence from a restoration in 1QH 1:2).

[68]Cf. R. E. Clements (*God and Temple*, Oxford: Basil Blackwell,
1965, 104): "Whereas Deuteronomy had spoken of Yahweh's name
as the means of his earthly presence, Ezekiel speaks of his
glory." Cf. also Ps 104:31: "May the glory of the Lord endure
for ever."

[69]Alternatively, this expression could reflect the tradition
of *Sifre Deut* 23:12: "And in the same way you find that Abraham
saw it (the temple) being built, and saw it desolated and saw it
rebuilt (Gen 22:14). 'And Abraham called the name of that place
Yahweh-jireh (Yahweh will see);' behold, there it was desolated.
'Where the Lord will be seen;' behold, there it is rebuilt and
perfect in the future."

[70]In addition to 4QPB, Cf. 1QIsa[a] 3:11, לוא for לו and
37:7, בוא for בו.

[71]See the further discussion below on whether the sanctuary
in 4QFlor is actual and whether the sectarians practised
sacrifices. G. Klinzing (*Das Umdeutung des Kultus,* 83-84) uses

Strugnell's reading at this point for his argument that the whole of 4QFlor reflects the hoped-for practice of the actual eschatological sanctuary. This argues against some of the points made by D. R. Schwartz ("The Three Temples of 4Q Florilegium," 85, especially n.9) and M. Ben-Yashar ("Noch zum *miqdaš 'ādām* in 4Q Florilegium," 588).

[72]Similar phrases are לכול בליעל, 1QH 3:28; בני חשך כחיל
כול המון בליעל, 1QM 15:3; כול חיל בליעל, 1QM 1:1; בליעל, 1QM 18:3.
None of these is identical to the phraseology of 4QFlor at this point.

[73]*The Temple Scroll*, Vol 2, 4. A. Caquot ("Le Rouleau du Temple de Qoumrân," *ETR* 53 1978 , 452) suggests that 11QT 3:3 is reminiscent of Deut 25:19 and 2 Sam 7:1.

[74]In this he is followed by Maier, Vermes and Tocci. Slomovic refers to 1QH 2:16-17 where he reads with restoration
ומזמות בליעל ורשע מחשבותם; he then restores line 8 as לכלותמה
במחשבותמה - but the lacuna is barely long enough to carry this and also the destruction is here conceived as only indirectly caused by the plots, directly, on the other hand, by "their" succumbing sinfully to those plots.

[75]Habermann, Dupont-Sommer, Vermes, Lohse, Tocci and Slomovic all agree with Allegro on this point; Maier alone follows Yadin. Carmignac, in agreeing with Allegro, points to Mt 6:13: καὶ μὴ εἰσενέγκῃς ἡμᾶς εἰς πειρασμόν.

[76]With Maier, Vermes, Slomovic and possibly Strugnell.

[77]"Fragments," 352 n.18.

[78]For a recent discussion of the root שגג see R. Knierim, "*šgg* sich versehen," *THAT* II, 869-72.

[79]If *'āleph* is read, on the other hand, as a *ṣādē*, it is also just possible that the fragment is not put together exactly right (see the באו of line 8), and that very faint traces of the stem of a *lāmed* are visible as second (perhaps third) letter of the final word of line 9. That might then give a reading במשגת צלממה, "by their error of idolatry," as the error seems to concern the sanctuary.

[80]Suggested by W. H. Brownlee: the meaning is not affected.

[81]"Further Messianic References in Qumran Literature," *JBL* 75 (1956), 174-87. Apart from the editions already mentioned, lines 10-13 have also been published in translation by A. S. van der Woude, *Die Messianischen Vorstellungen der Gemeinde von Qumran* (Assen: van Gorcum, 1957), 173, and in Dutch, *Bijbel-commentaren en Bijbelse Verhalen* (Amsterdam: Proost en Brandt N. V., 1958), 85-86; by H. Bardtke, *Die Handschriftenfunde am Toten Meer* (Berlin: Evangelische Haupt-Bibelgesellschaft, 1958, Bd. II), 298-99; by M. Burrows, *More Light on the Dead Sea Scrolls* (New York: Viking Press, 1958), 401; and by W. H. Brownlee, *Meaning,* 88. The transliterated text of Slomovic contains at this point what must be two printing mistakes: כי for כיא, and והכינותי for והכימותי.

[82]Although here again the text quoted follows the type of the LXX, it is interesting to note, in connection with the restoration proposed above in line 2, that whereas MT here uses יעשה, the 4QFlor author uses יבנה. The LXX for 2 Sam 7:11 has καὶ ἀπαγγελεῖ σοι κύριος ὅτι οἶκον οἰκοδομήσεις αὐτῷ, with the variant in L alone of οἰκοδομήσει ἑαυτῷ the third person singular reading of the verb which is in accord with the MT's

use of יבנה, and is corroborated by all Mss. in the LXX of
1 Chr 17:10.

[83]Notwithstanding the much debated lines of 1QH 3.

[84]And confirmed from the original manuscript by W. H. Brownlee.

[85]Attested in 1 Chr 23:25 and 28:7.

[86]L. H. Silberman ("A Note on 4Q Florilegium," *JBL* 78 1959 ,
158-59) reads the final phrase of line 13 as "Afterwards he will
stand up to save Israel." The *ḥēt* is possible, but the earlier
parallel construction makes the *šîn* of אשר preferable.

[87]And which may be left ambiguous according to the restorations of Yadin and Habermann. Slomovic reads the same
restoration in his transliteration, but translates the whole
sentence in an abbreviated form that shows a correct understanding
of the grammar. The ambiguity can, of course, be retained in
an English translation that does not restore the lacuna with a
specifically Davidic action: e.g. that of W. H. Brownlee
(*Meaning*, 88) "who (will reside) in Zi(on . . . "

[88]Pointed out to me by W. H. Brownlee. The association of
מלך with הר ציון in Isa 24:23 and Mic 4:7 might support the use
of מלך at the beginning of the line; yet since there בצי[excludes
the full phrase הר ציון, משל is to be preferred.

[89]*A Comparative Study of the Old Testament Text in the Dead
Sea Scrolls and in the New Testament*, STDJ 4; Leiden: E. J. Brill,
1965, 24-26. De Waard gives a detailed description of how 4QFlor
differs from the LXX, with an answer (26 note 1) to Fitzmyer's
query ("4Q Testimonia and the New Testament," *TS* 18 1957 , 536,
n.74) concerning the minimal importance of the "waw-conversive

perfect in Amos 9:11 for argument about textual tradition."
De Waard supports the *wāw* (ϰαί) in that syntactical function
as part of the quotation in both 4QFlor and Acts 15:16; as does
Brownlee (*Meaning,* 88-89).

[90]*A Comparative Study,* 26, n.2. This will be discussed
further below under Tradition History.

[91]This against Carmignac who denies the possibility of a
lāmed in favour of the rare [פשר הדב]ר המה .

[92]E. Slomovic, on the other hand, shows correctly that in
Qumran and rabbinic sources it is common for the biblical quotation
to be connected with what precedes by a linkword that is not
necessarily even quoted. Thus the העם of Yadin, followed by
Maier, Vermes, Strugnell and Slomovic himself, becomes a less
likely restoration. Although דרך העם occurs elsewhere in Qumran
literature, as Yadin points out (CD 8:16, 19:29, 1QSa 1:2), it
may be that here it is too like the Isaiah citation and too far
from that of Psalm 1. From CD 8:9, 4 and 1QS, where דרך is used
most frequently, all that can be said definitely is that when
used of the incorrect way, דרך is always qualified; when used
of the correct way, it may not be qualified. Thus a qualification
is required here, and preferably one that is close to the Psalm
text.

[93]The restoration of Habermann, Carmignac, Dupont-Sommer,
Tocci, and Moraldi.

[94]This restoration depends form-critically not on the content,
but rather on the intention of the scribe: did he intend a
reference to the whole of Psalms 1 and 2, or just to their first
verses?

[95]Cf. Ps 119:49.

[96]For the article in this common phrase compare its occurrence in lines 2 and 19.

[97]As in the photographs of 1QIsa[a] in *Scrolls from Qumran Cave 1* (from photographs by John C. Trever; Jerusalem: The Albright Institute of Archaeological Research and The Shrine of the Book, 1974), 15. Though many times there is $w\bar{a}w/y\hat{o}d$ confusion in the scrolls, both the $y\hat{o}ds$ in יסירנו are distinctly different in form from the final letter which is, therefore, most probably a $w\bar{a}w$.

[98]"A Suggested Reading for 4Q Florilegium 1:15," *JNWSL* 6 (1978), 25-31.

[99]יהי with $w\bar{a}w$ copulative is also found in 1QH 8:8, 17, 18. Laubscher also remarks that ויהי (imperfect with $w\bar{a}w$ copulative) instead of והיה (perfect with $w\bar{a}w$ consecutive) is supported by 1QIsa[a] 29:15 and 56:12 which have the imperfect with $w\bar{a}w$ copulative as against MT's perfect with $w\bar{a}w$ consecutive.

[100]This then matches 1QSa 1:2-3 which contains much terminology similar to this unit of 4QFlor.

[101]The LXX has ἀπειθοῦσιν which could represent either the text tradition of 1QIsa[a] or that of the MT!

[102]In this he has been variously followed by Dupont-Sommer and Vermes. Moraldi cites both Ezek 44:10 and 37:23.

[103]Agreed upon by all other scholars who have published Hebrew texts, and by most in translation. Furthermore the phrasing of 11QTemple 29:7 resembles Ezek 37:23b; 11QTemple 29:8-10 have already been discussed in association with 4QFlor 1:4-5.

[104]In order to remove at least one letter from line 17, Strugnell proposes a possible emendation to the Ezekiel text, reading בכול at the end of line 16; this nicely accommodates the *bêt*. Certainly no word apart from גלול can account for the double *lāmed*, unless it is שלל, "spoil," in Ezek 39:10: ולא יחטבו מן היערים כי בנשק יבערו אש ושללו את שלליהם. Although the quotation would have to be shortened somehow, נשק would provide a neat link with Psalm 2:12.

[105]J. de Waard (*A Comparative Study*, 81, n.6) says the quotation is from Ezek 20:7 - partly because he wishes to see Ezek 20:34 quoted in 2 Cor 6:14-7:1. However, not only are both de Waard's identifications for the citation highly questionable, but also this clearly denies the author of 4QFlor any precision in his quoting of Ezekiel (at least in relation to MT).

[106]*The Dead Sea Scrolls in English*, 206; in an introductory comment to his translation of 1QSb concerning the blessing of the priests.

[107]F. du T. Laubscher ("A Suggested Reading for 4Q Florilegium 1:15," 27) also argues that Ezek 37:23 fits the context most suitably.

[108]Slomovic describes this exegetical method in relation to 4QFlor in full in his article.

[109]CD 4:3ff., 6:4ff. and 7:12ff. See the remarks below under Tradition History.

[110]Cf. Ps 2:6, "I have set my king on Zion, my holy hill." The general thought of this Ezekiel passage may also be present in Fragment 4, line 7 which speaks of Judah and Israel.

[111]Allegro ("Fragments," 354) saw only one group, "the Sons of Zadok who sought (?) the(ir own) coun(sel) (?), . . . " He has been followed in this by Dupont-Sommer, Habermann, Vermes, Tocci and Gaster. J. Le Moyne (*Les Sadducéens*, Paris: J. Gabalda, 1972, 87) reckons that the text is sufficiently poorly preserved that the בני צדוק in 4QFlor could be a designation for enemies of the community, possibly the Sadducees. His overall conclusion, however, is that the title is used in QL to stress the priestly background of the group and is not a sectarian designation of the kind like Sadducees.

[112]1QpHab 8:1 describes the righteous of Hab 2:4b as those who observe the Law in the house of Judah. Cf. CD 4:11, 7:12 and 13.

[113]בני צדוק occurs only twice in QL, at CD 4:1 in the quotation of Ezek 44:15 and at CD 4:3 in that quotation's explication.

[114]These people are described as those who have turned aside (סרו) from the way of the people 1QSa 1:2-3. Cf. Isa 8:11, 4QFlor 1:15.

[115]As suggested by Vermes' translation, "the Sons of Zadok who (seek their own) counsel and follow (their own inclinations) apart from the Council of the community." Or alternatively וֹעֹ[ו]שִׂי עצ[בי]ם, "and the makers of idols," or, וֹחֹ[ר]שִׂי עצ[י]ם, "and the engravers of wood," or again וֹחֹ[ר]שִׂי עצ[בי]ם, "and the engravers of idols;" any of these could fit the Ms. and be relevant to Ezek 37:23 but are less likely because of their still negative assessment of the second group.

[116]Allegro (DJD V), Yadin, Maier, Lohse, Strugnell and Slomovic.

[117]E.g. Vermes: "and follow (their own inclinations),"
(= Gaster); Strugnell: דק צ[פי רוד]; Dupont-Sommer: "qui
sui(vent les oeuvres de) leurs mains." Moraldi follows Strugnell.

[118]Suggested by W. H. Brownlee in a private communication.

[119]Not אחרית [הימים] as Yadin suggests, for the *hē'* in
אחריהמה is clear and so the only reading could be the suffix.
אחריהמה is read by Allegro (DJD V), Lohse, Strugnell, and Moraldi.

[120]Habermann's line reads: ד[ור] שי עצתמה רו [עיהמה וחב]ריהמה
לעצת היחד. דורשי has already been commented upon; the *ᶜayin* in
רועיהמה is impossible from the photograph and therefore the
parallel הבריהמה is less likely.

[121]Most scholars do not give a restoration for the end of the
line and those that do all admit that they are only attempting
to make some sense by joining the few words that are restorable
by meaningful phrases of the correct length. E.g. Yadin, with
reference to 1QSa 1:1, restores כ[ב] אחרית [הימים בהאספם ל[יחד.
Allegro, Habermann, Dupont-Sommer, Vermes, Tocci, Lohse and
Gaster variously restore לעצת יחד, but לעצת is restored solely
from their respective understandings of the context and not
from Ms. evidence.

[122]Cf. 1QM 10:9, 1QSb 1:2. In fact, based on 1 Sam 26:2,
בחירי ישראל is a military designation. J. Coppens ("L'Élu et
les élus dans les Écritures Saintes et les Écrits de Qumrân,"
ETL 57 1981 , 120-24) argues that the OT term "elect" has passed
from Israel in general to the members of the sect, and in some
passages the title "elect one" is applied to the leader or
founder of the sect.

[123]Followed uncritically by Maier; and in his restoration of
המה at the start of the third lacuna by Lohse.

[124]Followed by Lohse.

[125]For the former cf. Nahum 1:7, Ps 5:12, for the latter
cf. 2 Sam 22:31, Ps 18:31, 31:20, 34:23.

[126]See the proposals of Habermann and Strugnell above.
Dupont-Sommer translates as "L'explication de cette parole (c'est
que les rois des na)tions;" Vermes (followed by Moraldi) has,
"concerns (the kings of the nations) who shall (rage against)
the elect of Israel in the last days . . . " Both suggest a
restoration similar to this second alternative. Gaster supports
this too, as does Tocci: "riguarda i re dei Gent)ili."

[127]For the phrases of dual identification see 1QpHab 1:13,
12:3-4.

[128]In a private communication.

[129]As does 1QM 1.

[130]אשר may possibly be omitted; cf. 4QCatena[a] frgs. 10-11, 9
but the lacuna is sufficiently long that either way is admissable.

[131]Except, of course, for line 4a, which, as an insertion,
does not necessarily fill a whole line; cf. 4QpPs[a] 3:4a.

[132]Cf. 1QpHab 8:1, CD 4:11.

[133]See the discussion of 1:7 for other possibilities.

[134]The participle הנשארים also occurs at CD 19:10, 13. The
noun שאר occurs linked with עם in 1QS 6:8-9 and also at 1QM 2:11,
11:15.

[135]In Daniel 12, עת occurs in vss. 1 (4 times), 4 and 9.

[136]Cf. Psalm 1:6: ‏כי יודע יהוה דרך צדיקים.‎

[137]‏יתלבנו‎ was first proposed by Allegro (DJD V) but with no mention of a possible use of Dan 11:35.

[138]"Notes," 237. The question whether 4QFlor 1:14ff. is the beginning of a commentary on the book of Psalms is discussed.

[139]Or the use of ‏ירא‎ in Ps 2:11, Exod 34:30. It is just possible that this verse is cited in 11QT 7:3 which is in the section describing the fittings of the Holy of Holies; such subject matter fits well with the concern of 4QFlor 1:1-7a.

[140]These possible associations will be mentioned again in the discussion of the possible liturgical setting for 4QFlor. I owe most of the observations in this paragraph to W. H. Brownlee.

[141]DJD V, 67-75. Strugnell ("Notes," 237) may be suggesting this by positioning his discussion of these two fragments under Catena[a].

[142]"Le Document de Qumran sur Melkisédeq," *RQ* 7 (1969-71), 361, n. 33.

[143]"The Use of Explicit Old Testament Quotations in Qumran Literature and in the New Testament," *NTS* 7 (1960), 314.

[144]Cf. Psalm 89:6 - an important secondary text in relation to 2 Samuel 7.

[145]It could be that a passage like Ps 114:2 influenced the interpretation through a syllogism such as 1) Judah = people of God = sanctuary; 2) People = ‏קהל‎ = sanctuary. Many texts could support the significance of ‏קהל‎ as "people."

[146]1QpHab 6:2, 7:3, 9:2, 10:1, 12:6.

[147]A point made strongly by F. M. Cross (*The Ancient Library,* 172, n.74) in attacking Allegro's mathematical equating of eschatological figures; also by Fitzmyer ("The Use of Explicit OT Quotations," 331): "There is no evidence at Qumran for a systematic, uniform exegesis of the Old Testament. The same text was not always given the same interpretation (. . . compare the use of . . . Amos IX:11 in different contexts)." For example, even J. M. Baumgarten ("The Exclusion of 'Netinim'," 95) over-states the case for Amos 9:11 in CD and 4QFlor: "Through the arising of David with the Interpreter of the Law the tabernacle will again be erected, that is the Torah will be restored to its proper understanding."

[148]Cf. 1QpHab 8:9. This goes against the theory of W. Grundmann ("Stehen und Fallen in qumranischen und neutestament-lichen Schrifttum," *Qumran-Probleme,* ed. H. Bardtke; Berlin: Akademie, 1963, 147-66) who insists on purely existential significance for the two verbs. H. Lichtenberger (*Studien zum Menschenbild in Texten der Qumrangemeinde,* SUNT 15; Göttingen: Vandenhoeck und Ruprecht, 1980, 151, n.9) notes the parallelism between נפל and כשל. Cf. ἀναστήσει in Acts 3:22.

[149]"Qumran Pesher: Towards the Redefinition of a Genre," *RQ* 10 (1979-81), 483-503.

[150]I owe these distinctions to the work of R. Wellek and A. Warren (*Theory of Literature,* New York: Harcourt, Brace and World, 1956, 231).

[151]E.g., J. Carmignac, *Les Textes de Qumran,* Vol II, 46; I. Rabinowitz, "Pēsher/Pittārōn. Its Biblical Meaning and its Significance in the Qumran Literature," *RQ* 8 (1972-74), 225-26.

[152]This simple observation speaks tellingly against the
suggestion of D. R. Schwartz ("The Three Temples of 4Q
Florilegium," 86), "Lines 1-13 are more aptly termed a *pesher*
of a single passage, *2 Sam 7,* 10-14."

[153]On the Psalms as prophetic texts see the correct assessment
of W. H. Brownlee, *Meaning,* 69-71. He is now supported by
D. N. Freedman "Pottery, Poetry, and Prophecy: An Essay on
Biblical Poetry," *JBL* 96 (1977), 21-22.

[154]The category of "oracle" recalls the so-called Demotic
Chronicle, a fragmentary papyrus from the early Ptolemaic period
which contains an oracle concerning the re-establishment of the
native monarchy and an interpretation linked to each section of
the oracle by a formula that can be translated as "this is;" see,
M. P. Horgan, *Pesharim: Qumran Interpretations of Biblical Books,*
258-59.

[155]CD 10:6, and 13:2 also record that there is to be study of
the book *Hagi,* and the fundamental elements of the covenant.

[156]*Cont.* 10:75 (translated by F. H. Colson, *Philo,* IX, LCL;
Cambridge: Harvard University, 1954, 159).

[157]*Cont.* 10:78.

[158]"Remarques sur l'Histoire de la Forme (Formgeschichte)
des Textes de Qumran," *Les Manuscrits de la Mer Morte,* Paris:
Presses Universitaires de France, 1957, 43.

[159]*The Ancient Library,* 84. The sources are presumably those
mentioned above.

[160]1QpHab is almost certainly not an autograph.

[161]Cf. Ezra 3:11. The scribe copying Ben Sira 51 considered verse 12 to be an allusion to Psalm 136 such that in the Cairo Hebrew Ms. a psalm is placed at that point beginning with Ps 136:1 but developing differently. The use of incipit verses is widely attested in the Near East, from Ugarit (Text 603) to Nag Hammadi (the first verses of the psalms being written on the entrance to the cave in which the Coptic library was discovered).

[162]The Western text of Acts 13:33 (on Ps 2:7) reads ἐν τῷ πρωτῷ ψαλμῷ γέγραπται as observed by Lövestam (*Son and Saviour*, Lund: C.W.K. Gleerup, 1961, 8,n.3) and as noted in relation to 4QFlor by W. H. Brownlee ("Psalms 1-2 as a Coronation Liturgy," *Bib* 52 1971 , 321-22).

[163]Cf. Isa 63:19; 1 Enoch 90:15, 18, 20, 37 (after God's descent in the pleasant land, Mt. Zion, the messianic king is born).

[164]See above pp. 139-141.

[165]In my article "Qumran Pesher: Towards the Redefinition of a Genre" (*RQ* 10 1979-81 , 497-501) I drew attention to the structural similarity of several texts from among the scrolls whether or not they use a formula including פשר: CD 7:14b-21a, 4QFlor 1:10-13, 1QpHab 6:2-5, 8-12, 12:1-10.

[166]"Midraš ist zunächst *a*, allgemein 'Forschung' u. zwar sowohl in dem Sinne von 'Studium, Theorie,' . . . als auch in der Bedeutung 'Auslegung' . . . *b*, Speziell wird dann M. auf die Beschäftigung mit der heil. Schrift bezogen . . . *c*, . . . Genaueres . . . ist sowohl das Auslegen der Schrift als auch dessen Ergebnis" (*Einleitung in Talmud und Midraš*, Munchen: C. H. Beck, 1976[6], 4). Strack sharpens this definition with further treatment of the form of midrash in

sections delineating the "schriftliche Fixierung des Midraš"
and the "Struktur der Midrašim" (*Einleitung*, 196-98).

[167]Bloch's five part definition of midrash is well known.
Her first point states that "its point of departure is Scripture;
it is a reflection or meditation on the Bible" ("Midrash,"
Supplément au Dictionnaire de la Bible, Vol 5, Paris: Letouzey
et Ané, 1957, 1265-67; as translated, paraphrased and largely
supported by G. Vermes, *Scripture and Tradition in Judaism,*
SPB 4; Leiden: E. J. Brill, 1961, 1973^2, 7).

[168]"The midrashic unit must be so structured that the material
contained therein is placed in the context of a Scripture text,
and is presented for the sake of the biblical text.   Midrash,
then, is a literature about a literature" (*The Literary Genre
Midrash,* New York: Alba House, 1967, 67.)

[169]Bloch's fifth point ("Midrash," 1267); amongst many this
distinction is shared by J. Theodor ("Midrash Haggadah," *The
Jewish Encyclopedia,* Vol 8, New York: Funk and Wagnells, 1904,
550), H. L. Strack (*Einleitung,* 5) and M. D. Herr ("Midrash,"
Encyclopaedia Judaica, Vol 11, Jerusalem: Keter Publishing House,
1971,   07) whose definition is perhaps less clear; for him
midrash consists of "both biblical exegesis and sermons delivered
in public as well as *aggadot* or *halakhot* and forming a running
commentary on specific books of the Bible."

[170]See above p. 242, n.153; also M. P. Horgan, *Pesharim:
Qumran Interpretations of Biblical Books,* 248, n.78.

[171]*"Pesher/Pittaron.*   Its Biblical Meaning and its Significance
in the Qumran Literature," *RQ* 8 (1972-74), 231.

[172]*Pesharim: Qumran Interpretations of Biblical Books,* 230-37.

[173]*Pesharim: Qumran Interpretations of Biblical Books,* 252.

[174]"The Subject Matter of Qumran Exegesis," *VT* 10 (1960), 53.

[175]In *Qohelet Rabbah* 12:1.

[176]"Unriddling the Riddle. A Study in the Structure and Language of the Habakkuk Pesher," *RQ* 3 (1961-62), 328.

[177]"A New Commentary Structure in 4Q Florilegium," *JBL* 78 (1959), 346.

[178]"Unriddling the Riddle," 328, n.10.

[179]*The Midrash Pesher of Habakkuk,* SBLMS 24; Missoula: Scholars Press, 1979, 35-36.

[180]*The Midrash Pesher of Habakkuk,* 31.

[181]The word מדרש occurs in 1QS 6:24, 8:15, 26, CD 20:6, 4QFlor 1:14. Four further unpublished occurrences in Qumran literature are listed by A. G. Wright (*The Literary Genre Midrash,* 39-40). Only in 4QFlor 1:14 does מדרש seem to be a technical term introducing a literary type; in its four other occurrences it seems to mean "interpretation, exposition" and is used in relation to law or legal material, possibly alluding to a tradition of halakah. The presence of מדרש here must in some way have ended the impasse seen by G. Vermes when he asked "is pesher midrash or commentary?" ("A propos des Commentaires bibliques découverts à Qumran," *RHPR* 36 1955 , 102).

[182]"Pēsher/Pittārōn," 225-26.

[183]"The Background of Biblical Interpretation at Qumran," *Qumrân: sa piété, sa théologie et son milieu,* BETL 46, ed.

M. Delcor; Paris: Duculot, 1978, 185, especially n.8.

[184]*The Midrash Pesher of Habakkuk,* 27, 196.

[185]"The Background of Biblical Interpretation at Qumran,"
185; *The Midrash Pesher of Habakkuk,* 27.

[186]"Interpretation" is also the preferred translation of
M. P. Horgan (*Pesharim: Qumran Interpretations of Biblical Books,*
237).

[187]Point 2 in her 5 part definition; see n.169. Both Vermes
(*Scripture and Tradition,* 228-29) and Le Déaut ("Apropos a
Definition of Midrash," *Int* 25 1971 , 272-75) expound on setting
as constitutive of literary categories.

[188]1QpHab 7:4-5. Brownlee's understanding of 1QpHab 2:7-10
(*The Midrash Pesher of Habakkuk,* 57) as referring to the
Righteous Teacher is almost certainly to be preferred to Horgan's
association of the "priest" mentioned there with "selected
interpreters who followed him" (*Pesharim: Qumran Interpretations
of Biblical Books,* 229).

[189]*The Midrash Pesher of Habakkuk,* 31.

[190]Notwithstanding the arguments of F. García Martínez ("El
pesher: interpretación profética de la Escritura," *Salmanticensis*
26 1979 , 125-39) who acknowledges the midrashic methods of the
pesharim but claims that their claim to be revelation distinguishes
them categorically from the midrashim which make no such claim.

[191]Bloch's third and fourth points; see p. 244, n.167.

[192]"Biblical Interpretation among the Sectaries of the Dead
Sea Scrolls," *BA* 14 (1951), 54-76; *The Dead Sea Habakkuk Midrash
and the Targum of Jonathan,* Mimeographed paper issued by the

author, February 1953; *The Meaning of the Qumrân Scrolls for the Bible*, New York: Oxford, 1964; *The Midrash Pesher of Habakkuk*, SBLMS 24; Missoula: Scholars Press, 1979.

[193]"Unriddling the Riddle. A Study in the Structure and Language of the Habbakkuk Pesher," *RQ* 3 (1961-62), 328-29.

[194]"Toward an Understanding of the Exegesis of the Dead Sea Scrolls," *RQ* 7 (1969-71), 3-15.

[195]*Pesharim: Qumran Interpretations of Biblical Books*, 244-47.

[196]E.g., K. Elliger, *Studien zum Habakuk-Kommentar vom Toten Meer*, BHT 15; Tübingen: J.C.B. Mohr, 1953, 156-57; F. F. Bruce, *Biblical Exegesis in the Qumran Texts*, Den Haag: van Keulen, 1959, 59-65; O. Betz, *Offenbarung und Schriftforschung in der Qumransekte*, WUNT 6; Tübingen: J.C.B. Mohr, 1960, 77-78; F. García Martínez, "El pesher: interpretación profetica de la Escritura," *Salmanticensis* 26 (1979), 125-39.

[197]*Pesharim: Qumran Interpretations of Biblical Books* , 249-59. Several scholars extend the association of the pesharim with Daniel to include visions and prophetic material whilst denying any connection with later midrash: e.g., J. Carmignac, "Le genre littéraire du 'Pesher' dans la Pistis-Sophia," *RQ* 4 (1963-64), 497-522; I. Rabinowitz, "Pēsher/Pittārōn," 220-26, 229-31; M. Delcor, "Les Pesharim ou les Commentaires qumrâniens," *Supplément au Dictionnaire de la Bible*, Vol 9, Paris: Letouzey et Ané, 1979, 905.

[198]E.g. R. Le Déaut: "by preserving two essential marks of midrash (scriptural context — adaptation) many of the criteria can be considered . . . The sub-genres of midrash are many when

they are classed *according to content* (aggadic midrash, halakhic midrash, historical, narrative, didactic, 'ethical,' allegorical, mystic, apocalyptic) or *according to form* (pesher, liturgical midrash with homily...). Perhaps one could say that the 'midrashic' context remains as long as the scriptural stimulus continues" ("Apropos a Definition of Midrash," 282, n.85); J. van der Ploeg, *Bijbelverklaring te Qumrân,* Mededelingen der Koninklijke Nederlandse Akademie van Wetenschappen, Letterkunde Nieuwe Reeks Deel 23/8; Amsterdam: Noord-Holland, 1960, 209.

[199]"Unriddling the Riddle," 328-29. A. Finkel ("The Pesher of Dreams and Scriptures," *RQ* 4 1963-64 , 357-70) also finds parallels in both areas. For further bibliography see M. P. Horgan, *Pesharim: Qumran Interpretations of Biblical Books*, 251, n.86.

[200]This enables a distinction to be made between Qumran and both rabbinic literature and 2 Chr 13:22 and 24:27 where the same term occurs.

[201]Thus pesher is not to be set alongside haggadah and halakah as a third kind of midrash as W. H. Brownlee has argued (*The Dead Sea Habakkuk Midrash and the Targum of Jonathan,* 12; *The Midrash Pesher of Habakkuk,* 25); in this he has been supported by K. Stendahl (*The School of St. Matthew,* Lund: C.W.K. Gleerup, 1954, 184), P. Grelot (see Wright, *The Literary Genre Midrash,* 83-84) and Slomovic ("Toward an Understanding of the Exegesis of the Dead Sea Scrolls," 4). For further bibliography on the three positions, that the pesharim are midrash, that they are not, and that they are midrash pesher see A. G. Wright, *The Literary Genre Midrash*, 80; E. Slomovic, "Toward an Understanding

of the Exegesis of the Dead Sea Scrolls," 4-5; M. P. Miller,
"Targum, Midrash and the Use of the Old Testament in the New
Testament," *JSJ* 2 (1971), 50-55; M. P. Horgan, *Pesharim:
Qumran Interpretations of Biblical Books,* 250-52.

[202]11QMelch 25 uses the same Isaiah quotation to refer most
likely to the founders of the sect. R. Bergmeier ("Zum Ausdruck
עצת רשעים in Ps 1, 1 Hi 10, 3, 21, 16 und 22, 18," *ZAW* 79 1967,
229-32) concludes that on the basis of understanding עצה as
fellowship at Qumran one can translate the phrase עצת רשעים as
"fellowship of the wicked" in the original MT context too, and
obtain a clearer meaning. Certainly Ps 1:1 is to be understood
that way in 4QFlor.

[203]Alternatively if some such restoration as proposed in the
textual notes is followed,the pesher may be understood as
referring to apostates of whom there is talk in 1QpHab 2 and
CD 7-8. The two groups of people in Ezekiel are then to be
taken as referring to the trusty members of the community, the
sons of Zadok, and to the idolators, the unfaithful, the apostates.

[204]"The 'Sons of Zadok the Priests' in the Dead Sea Sect,"
RQ 6 (1967-69), 6-7.

[205]"The 'Sons of Zadok the Priests'," 10.

[206]*The Temple and the Community,* 4.

[207]In fact צדוק in 1QS 5:9 is not in the parallel passage
in 4QS[e], which reads צדק; thus the 1QS passage appears as a
later emendation. It is at best ambiguous and may reflect the
starting point of the tradition which identifies the community
as a whole with the Sons of Zadok.

[208]It is just possible that 4QpPs[a] also belongs to this
commentary though probably on a different scroll and certainly
by a different scribe (the *śîn* and *mēm* are distinctly different
in the two scrolls). However, 4QpPs[a] is also arranged slightly
differently with greater distance between the lines and the
columns are, on average, 4 cms. narrower. It is also to be
mentioned that 4QFlor has a pesher on the whole psalm through
mention of the first verse, whereas 4QpPs[a] contains a pesher on
each verse of the Psalm. For a detailed description of 4QpPs[a],
see Allegro, "A Newly Discovered Fragment of a Commentary on
Psalm XXXVII from Qumran," *PEQ* 86 (1954), 69-75.

[209]P. W. Skehan ("A New Translation of Qumran Texts," *CBQ* 25
1963 , 119-23) points to this unity of the scroll: "The section
of 2 Sm represented consists of the promises to David, thought of
as the composer of the Psalter, who arranged it for liturgical
worship whether in an earthly or a spiritual "House" or Temple.
Thus the material from 2 Sm is intended to introduce the running
comments on the Pss."

[210]1QpHab 9:14 is requoted in the pesher at 10:2; 1QpHab 12:1
is requoted in 12:6-7.

[211]The longest pesher in 4QpNah is at 3:3-5; in 4QpPs 37
at 2:17-19.

[212]E.g. at 4QFlor 1:13-14, 17.

[213]This is one argument amongst several against the proposals
of D. R. Schwartz ("The Three Temples of 4QFlorilegium," 86-87).

[214]See below pp. 170-173.

[215]W. H. Brownlee ("Biblical Interpretation," 71) lists the

ancient authorities who devised set rules for midrashic
exegesis. See also Chapter I, pp. 8-17.

[216]This has been examined in detail in relation to 4QFlor
by Slomovic who cites rabbinic texts where the rule is also
used. He is misleading, however, in his treatment of Deut 23:1-4
and Neh 13:1, the latter of which he claims is necessary for the
present understanding of 4QFlor; but קהל is used in both texts,
מקדש in neither so Neh 13:1 is not used for *gĕzērâ šāwâ*.

[217]Brownlee ("Biblical Interpretation," 75) quotes *Sifra* on
Lev 23:40 as an example of this in rabbinic literature.
L. H. Silberman ("A Note on 4Q Florilegium [Esch Midr]," *JBL* 78
 1959 , 158-59) first identified the alternative meaning for
סוכה but he then excluded the original reading from the exposition.
However, the importance of the interpretation is that it is an
alternative which does not deny the original meaning. *B. Šabb*
63a clearly states that a scriptural verse never loses its plain
meaning. In relation to Amos 9:11, from which סוכה comes, it is
noteworthy that the Rabbis were able to derive the Messianic
title בר נפלים from the verse (*B. Sanh.* 97a; cf. Dan 7:13).

[218]There may well be an allusion in the interpretation of
this word with the covenant made between Yahweh and Jacob at
Bethel, "house of God" which is mentioned in 11QT 29:10 and
associated with Tabernacles in *Jub.* 32:16-29.

[219]See W. H. Brownlee (*Meaning,* 69-71) for a full account of
the link between psalmody and prophecy at Qumran; also D. N.
Freedman ("Pottery, Poetry, and Prophecy: An Essay on Biblical
Poetry" *JBL* 96 1977 , 22) summarizes part of his argument thus:
"many of the poets of the Bible were considered to be prophets

or to have prophetic powers, and in some cases at least, the
only tangible evidence for this identification is the poetry
itself. On the other hand, most of the prophets for whom we
have evidence in the form of speeches or oracles, were in fact
poets." Cf. Acts 2:30.

[220]Cited by S. A. Birnbaum, *The Qumran Scrolls and
Palaeography*, 26.

[221]So far a search to locate even a single use of square
script for the divine name in a biblical quotation in any
published Qumran literature has been unsuccessful. Of course
this does not hold, as would be expected for Mss. that contain
biblical text only.

[222]"Formulas of Introduction in the Qumran Literature," *RQ* 7
(1969-71), 505-14. The introductory formulae to explicit
quotations are also listed in relation to other Qumran Mss.
by J. A. Fitzmyer ("The Use of Explicit Old Testament Quotations
in Qumran Literature and in the New Testament," *NTS* 7 1960 ,
299-305). Horton's abbreviations have been provided in the
relevant places in the structural analyses of the first two units
of 4QFlor. Horton's work updates that of M. Burrows ("The
Meaning of אשר אמר in DSH," *VT* 2 1952 , 255-60) but he fails
to take account of the structural significance of the conjunctive
element in his schematisation of introductory formulae.

[223]1QpHab 1:2, 7:3, 9:3, 10:2, 12:6, 4QpIsa[a, b], CD 9:2,
16:6, 11QMelch 1:2, 4QFlor 1:7.

[224]1QS 5:17, 8:14, CD 7:9 - 4QFlor 1:2, 12, 15.

[225]1 Kgs 21:11, Dan 9:13.

226"Formulas of Introduction," 512.

227"Acts 13:33-37: A *Pesher* on II Samuel 7," *JBL* 87 (1968),
321-24.

228To venture here into a discussion of the influence of
liturgy is indeed a hazardous task since so little is known of
the Jewish liturgy at about the time of Jesus. For a brief
summary of present knowledge of synagogue liturgy, see E. Schürer,
The History of the Jewish People in the Age of Jesus Christ,
Vol 2, ed. G. Vermes, F. Millar, M. Black; Edinburgh: T. & T.
Clark, 1979, 447-63.

229The detailed studies of R. A. Carlson (*David, The Chosen
King*, Uppsala: Almquvist and Wiksells Boktryckeri A. B., 1964,
97-128) and of J. Coppens (*Le Messianisme Royal*, LD 54, Paris:
Les Editions du Cerf, 1968, 37-63) outline and criticize the
main views of recent scholarship on this topic.

230*Die Königsherrschaft Gottes im Alten Testament,* Tübingen:
J.C.B. Mohr, 1951, 44.

231*Die Königsherrschaft,* 115. Kraus cites Isa 52:7-10 as
an exemplary passage that indicates the change in the tradition
that the exile brought about.

232*David, The Chosen King,* 121, 125-27. Deuteronomy 17 is
especially important in this tradition.

233*He That Cometh,* Oxford: Basil Blackwell, 1956, 100 note 3.

234*Studies in Divine Kingship in the Ancient Near East,* Oxford:
Basil Blackwell, 1967 (1943 Uppsala edition revised), 175, n.7.

235*Les Institutions de l'Ancien Testament*, Paris: Les
Editions du Cerf, 1958, Vol 1, 158-65. He speaks of Psalm 2

in relation to the enthronement.

[236]"Hebrew Installation Rites," *HUCA* 20 (1947), 145.

[237]For Saul, 1 Sam 9:17ff.; for David, 1 Sam 16:1ff.; for Jeroboam, 1 Kgs 11:29ff.; for Jehu, 1 Kgs 19:16ff. J. de Fraine (*L'Aspect Religieux de la Royauté Israélite*, Rome: Pontificio Instituto Biblico, 1954, 201-2) notes that "l'oracle royal est très souvent suive de l'accession au trône, et de l'investiture au moyen des insignes royaux." However, he would not wish to hold that the oracle was a necessary part of the coronation ritual - rather that it is a common feature which should not lead to "une thèse catégorique" (201, n.6).

[238]*Die Königsherrschaft*, 66 - that largely because of the occurrence of Zion in the psalm.

[239]*Studies in Divine Kingship*, 175 n.7.

[240]For example, Kraus (*Die Königsherrschaft*, 119) concludes that the Zion procession of the New Year Festival in post-exilic times becomes Yahweh's enthronement procession, and, on the other hand, Patai ("Hebrew Installation Rites," 209) emphasizes that the Feast of Tabernacles is a feast of the repetition of the coronation installation ritual.

[241]"Psalms 1-2 as a Coronation Liturgy," *Bib* 52 (1971), 332. Psalm 1 was certainly written by the 3rd C. B.C.; see Hengel, *Judentum und Hellenismus*, 291.

[242]See Zech 14:16 and the tradition represented in Exod 23:16, Num 29:1, 7, 12, and Neh 8:14 for this combination of date and content.

[243]It is just possible that the exposition in 4QFlor reflects

admission rites in its stress on purity and works of thanksgiving
(Cf. 2 Cor 6:14-7:1, discussed on pp. 211-217). However, 4QFlor
talks about more than admission. Of course it remains true that
all festivals and times of worship are times for renewing the
covenant: Cf. 1QS 10. One further possible support for
identifying the liturgical setting of the texts comes from the
Cairo Geniza Ms. G: Exod 15 is therein set for either Passover
or Weeks. See J. Mann, *The Bible as Read and Preached in the
Old Synagogue* (I; Cincinnati: Hebrew Union College, 1940;
reprinted New York: Ktav, 1971), 435, who questions the opening
of the reading and M. Black, *An Aramaic Approach to the Gospels
and Acts* (Oxford: Clarendon, 1967[3]), 306; F. M. Cross ("The
Song of the Sea and Canaanite Myth," *JTC* 5 [1968], 11) also
supports use of Exodus 15 at the spring festival from earliest
times. Yet it is not necessary to insist that the supportive
quotations in 4QFlor come from the same liturgy as the main ones,
since 4QFlor is finally a written construction. On the possible
covenanting ceremony associated with the Feast of Weeks see
W. H. Brownlee, "The Ceremony of Crossing the Jordan in the
Annual Covenanting at Qumran," *Von Kanaan bis Kerala*, AOAT 211,
ed. **W. C.** Delsman et al; Neukirchen-Vluyn: Neukirchener
Verlag/Kevelaer: Butzon & Bercker, 1980, 300-301.

[244]Especially as the Feast of Booths, which may have contained
liturgical traditions reflecting an enthronement, was fixed in
the middle of the first month of the autumnal New Year. A
similar suggestion in favour of the liturgical setting of certain
texts has been made by J. Massingberd Ford who sees, in a general
way, Tabernacles as the source for the biblical themes in the
Shepherd of Hermas ("A Possible Liturgical Background to the

Shepherd of Hermas," *RQ* 6 1967-69 , 531-51).

[245]Perhaps this is the liturgical setting for 1QM.

[246]1QpHab 11:6-8, CD 6:19 and 1QS 3:4 (if taken substantively); also 11QT 25:10-27:10.

[247]M. R. Lehmann ("'Yom Kippur' in Qumran," *RQ* 3 1961-62 , 121) so ascribes the Scroll of Three Tongues of Fire, Priestly Blessings, the Pesher on Jacob's Blessings, Yom Kippur Prayers and The Scroll of the Mysteries. He also sees several parallels between the Qumran and Samaritan rites and notes the frequency with which Deuteronomy 32, part of the Samaritan Yom Kippur liturgy, occurs at Qumran. 4QFlor probably contained midrash on Deuteronomy 33; can that have been part of an alternative blessing for the Feast of Booths?

[248]1QpHab 11:4-8, for example, talks implicitly of a difference in the date of the Day of Atonement.

[249]S. Talmon ("The Calendar Reckoning of the Sect from the Judaean Desert," *Aspects of the Dead Sea Scrolls,* Scripta Hierosolymitana IV, eds. C. Rabin and Y. Yadin; Jerusalem: Magnes Press, 1958, 170-73) works out in detail the priestly courses at Qumran from the texts discovered there and comments on the differences between the solar calendar of Qumran and other late post-exilic writings, and the contemporary lunar one of the Jerusalem temple. These dates are confirmed in 11QT 25:10 and 27:10.

[250]It is unfortunate that 11QT 28 restricts its treatment of the Feast of Tabernacles to description of the animals to be sacrificed. Perhaps the only clue as to the possible content of the liturgy comes from the summary conclusion in column 29 which

follows immediately the discussion of Tabernacles.

11QT 29:10 has already shown to have some remarkable parallels
with 4QFlor.

[251]It is just possible that Fragments 15 and 19 (Isa 65:
22-23) reflect the Synagogue liturgy if considered in combination with the Song of the Sea in Exodus 15; the readings for
the 56th Seder from Exod 14:15ff. have as the haftara Isa 65:
24ff. (Mann, *The Bible as Read*, 430-34). At least according
to the present discussion the 4QFlor Fragments 6-11 (Deut 33)
find their place alongside 2 Samuel 7 and Psalms 1 and 2 in
the festival liturgy; perhaps the combination of supportive
quotations is dependent on a separate liturgical setting.

[252]As suggested by Fitzmyer ("4Q Testimonia and the New
Testament," 531) on first seeing only 4QFlor 1:10-13.

[253]"Notes sur les Pesharim," *RQ* 3 (1961-62), 528.

[254]1QS 1:17, 8:4, 1QH 5:16, CD 20:27, 4QpPs[a] 2:18, Catena
A Fragments 5-6. Notwithstanding the remarks of H. Stegemann
("Der Pešer Psalm 37 aus Höhle 4 von Qumran," *RQ* 4 1963-64 ,
230, n.143): "מצרף ist in den Qumrantexten nicht nur terminus
technicus für die endzeitliche Drangsal sondern häufig einfach
Ausdruck zur Charakterisierung des Leidens der Gläubigen in
der Welt, insofern sie es als läuternde Erprobung der Echtheit
ihres Glaubens durch Gott annehmen." In Qumran the two cannot
be separated: that has been particularly well demonstrated by
J. Daniélou ("Eschatologie Sadocite et Eschatologie Chrétienne,"
Les Manuscrits de la Mer Morte, Paris: Presses Universitaires
de France, 1957, 118-20). He also makes a clear distinction
between the latter days and the end but his presentation on

this point is such that for the covenanters there is no
pre-eschatological time of trial. G. Klinzing (*Das Umdeutung
des Kultus,* 104) understands מצרף as signifying that God
purifies his community through their enforced exile.

[255]"La Notion d'Eschatologie dans la Bible et à Qumrân,"
RQ 7 (1969-71), 25-26. Carmignac has repeated his views on
אחרית הימים more clearly and more forcefully in his article
"La future intervention de Dieu selon la pensée de Qumrân,"
Qumrân: sa piété, sa théologie et son milieu, ed. M. Delcor,
BETL 46; Paris-Gembloux: Editions Duculot, Leuven: University
Press, 219-29.

[256]"La future intervention de Dieu selon la pensée de
Qumrân," 229.

[257]"At the End of the Days," *ASTI* 2 (1963), 27-37. This
translation of the phrase is supported by the earlier arguments
of C. Roth ("The Subject Matter of Qumran Exegesis," 52-53)
who claims that it is the primary characteristic of pesher.

[258]"Eschatology and the End of Days," *JNES* 20 (1961), 188-93.

[259]"Time and Eschatology in Apocalyptic Literature and in
Qumran," *JJS* 16 (1965), 177.

[260]"Time and Eschatology," 182.

[261]K. Schubert (*The Dead Sea Community,* New York: Harper
& Row, 1959, 98-104) expresses the idea that אחרית הימים is
both the latter days and a period beyond that by conceiving of
it as being a phrase that might be rendered in terms of an
"end period." That is, however, perhaps only applicable to
4QFlor and CD and not to the whole body of Qumran literature.

[262]It is this particular understanding of the eschatology
of 4QFlor that leads R. J. McKelvey (*The New Temple: The
Church in the New Testament,* London: Oxford University, 1969,
51) and A. J. McNicol ("The Eschatological Temple in the
Qumran Pesher 4QFlorilegium 1:1-7," *OJRS* 5 1977 , 136) amongst
others to their understanding that מקדש אדם refers to a future
building `amongst men.

[263]A. Gelston ("A Note on II Sam 7:10," *ZAW* 84 1972 , 93)
has pointed out that מקום and מקדש are interchanged in the MT
too; he cites Jer 7:12-14 and especially 1 Chr 16:27 quoting
Ps 96:6, where מקדש has become מקומו.

[264]1QS 8:4-6, 11:8, 1QH 6:15, 8:6-10. CD 1:1 also links
the verb נטע and plantation in relation to the community. The
secondary meaning of נטע, "to pitch a tent," may have some
significance for the present passage when it is recalled that
the tabernacle was originally a tent.

[265]This is expressed most clearly by Y. Congar (*Le Mystère
du Temple,* LD 22, Paris: Editions de Cerf, 1963, 43): "Le
mouvement et l'intention de la prophétie, dans Sam, sont
polarisés par cette idée: Tu veux me bâtir une maison; ce
n'est pas toi qui me bâtiras une maison, c'est moi qui t'en
bâtirai une, à savoir une descendence perpetuelle. C'est bien
ainsi que David comprend Nathan (v. 19)." If 2 Sam 7 is to be
associated with the Feast of Tabernacles then Nathan's pun may
be alluded to in *Jub.* 32:16-29 which describes that feast as
a time of alliance with Jacob at *Bethel*.

[266]"Two Notes on the Midrash on 2 Sam vii," *IEJ* 9 (1959), 103.
He cites Enoch 90:28-29 and Mark 14:58 as evidence for the idea

of the God-made eschatological sanctuary.

[267]"'Reign' and 'House' in the Kingdom of God in the
Gospels," *NTS* 8 (1961-62), 234. He has a detailed discussion
of background texts to the Gospel understanding of the Kingdom
of God, and deals at length with the oracle of Nathan. However,
in relation to Qumran he fails to cite 4QFlor which is clearly
important for his argument that even in Judaism house was no
longer understood in the sense of a royal family but "as the
people of God, the true religious community" (240).

[268]It is somewhat surprising that G. Forkman makes no use
at all of 4QFlor in his work, *The Limits of the Religious
Community* (ConB NTS 5; Lund: C.W.K. Gleerup, 1972).

[269]J. Baumgarten (*Studies in Qumran Law*, SJLA 24, ed.
J. Neusner, Leiden: E. J. Brill, 1977, 85-87) also draws
attention to *Jubilees* 16:25 which describes the exclusion of
aliens from Abraham's celebration of Tabernacles, a remarkable
parallel with 4QFlor if Tabernacles provided the liturgical
setting for the midrash.

[270]G. Blidstein ("4Q Florilegium and Rabbinic Sources on
Bastard and Proselyte," *RQ* 8/31 1974 , 431-35) lists *'Abot
R. Nat.* 12 (3rd C. A.D.), which records that the bastard
travelling to study at Jerusalem must go no further than Ashdod
(applying Zech 9:6), and *t. Qidd.* 5:4, where R. Meir argues
against R. Jose that bastards will not be purified in the
future, as evidence for the exclusion of the bastard from the
sacred geographic boundaries, and hence the temple, of the
future Israel.

271 *Spec* 1:326, translated by F. H. Colson, *Philo*, VII,
LCL; Cambridge, Mass: Harvard University, 1958, 289.

272"The Exclusion of 'Netinim' and Proselytes in 4Q
Florilegium," *RQ* 8/29 (1972), 87-96 = *Studies in Qumran Law*,
75-85.

273Ezra 2:70, 77, Neh 10:29 rank them as the last of the
menial servants and they are clearly servants in Ezra 2:58,
Neh 7:60. However, Ezra 7:24 describes them as having tax
exemption privileges, and Ezra 2:2-65 lists them among the
קהל ; Neh 10:29 includes them among those who pledged that they
would not intermarry with non-Israelites.

274E.g., CD 14:4-6. G. Blidstein ("Rabbinic Sources," 433-
34) points out that no rabbinic teachings prohibit the proselyte
from entering Jerusalem and the temple, but that *m. Bik.* 1:4
says that the proselyte may bring the first fruits to the temple
but may not recite the creed of Deut 26:1ff. as the Patriarchs
were not his fathers. To this could be added *b. Yebam.* 24b
which says that no proselytes will be accepted in the days of
the Messiah because Israel will be prosperous and proselytes
would be attracted for worldly reasons.

275"The Exclusion of 'Netinim' and Proselytes," 93-94. Cf.
1QS 2:4-10. It is surprising that both Baumgarten and Blidstein
have missed *b. 'Abod. Zar.* 3b which links the exclusion of
proselytes in the messianic age with an interpretation of Psalm 2,
both elements of which are present in 4QFlor: "Has it not been
taught that in the days of the Messiah proselytes will not be
received; . . . For when the battle of Gog-Magog will come about
they will be asked, 'For what purpose have you come?' and they

will reply: 'Against God and His Messiah' as it is said,
Why are the nations in an uproar, and why do the peoples
mutter in vain, etc. Then each of the proselytes will throw
aside his religious token and get away, as it is said, Let
us break their bonds asunder, and the Holy One, blessed be
He, will sit and laugh, as it is said, He that sitteth in
heaven laugheth. R. Isaac remaked that there is no laughter
for the Holy One, blessed be He, except on that day." That
גר is translated as proselyte (implying "convert") may be
questioned on the grounds that it only acquires that meaning
in late tannaitic times (so argues S. Zeitlin, "Proselytes and
Proselytism during the Second Commonwealth and the Early
Tannaitic Period," *Wolfson Jubilee Volume* 2, 874) but Philo
uses "proselyte" (LXX rendering of גר) to refer to converts
(H. A. Wolfson *Philo* 2, 364-73); furthermore it can be argued
that the LXX translators understood גר = προσήλυτος as referring
to a convert and גר = γειώρας or πάροικος as not doing so
(P. Churgin "The Targum and the Septuagint," *AJSL* 50 1933-34 ,
47-51). Cf. *Mek. Nez.* 18:32-40.

[276]E.g. *1 Enoch* 12:2, 14:23, 39:5 etc. Elsewhere in *Enoch*
the more specific "holy angels" is used, but always in relation
to the archangels.

[277]*Enderwartung und gegenwärtiges Heil, SUNT* 4, Göttingen:
Vandenhoeck & Ruprecht, 1966, 90. Among the passages where
Kuhn understands angels is 4QFlor 1:4. It may be that sometimes
"holy ones" includes both men and angels; cf. 1QS 11:7.

[278]*Enderwartung,* 93.

[279]Translation of H. Ringgren (*The Faith of Qumran,*

Philadelphia: Fortress Press, 1963, 85). This is a parallel
to 1QSa 2:8-9 cited below. Cf. J. A. Fitzmyer "A feature of
Qumran angelology and the angels of 1 Cor 11:10," *NTS* 4 (1957-
58), 48-58.

[280]Translation of Vermes (*The Dead Sea Scrolls in English,* 93).

[281]This is splendidly put by D. Barthélemy ("Le Sainteté
selon la Communauté de Qumran et selon l'Evangile," *La Secte
de Qumran et les Origines du Christianisme,* RechBib 4, Paris-
Brugge: Desclée de Brouwer, 1959, 205): " . . . l'unique
realité: Dieu et la cour des anges. Car le Très-Haut n'a pas
placé l'homme au sommet de la création, comme celui-ci se plaît
à le croire en des moments d'optimisme béat. Il y a d'abord
les anges...qu'un juif de cette époque n'imaginait pas du tout
comme des êtres féminoides roses ou bleu-pâle, mais comme d'
immenses êtres de feu, d'une pureté et d'une lucidité consumantes,
seuls capables de faire face à Dieu . . . la part de la création
qui seule sait connaître et louer Dieu."

[282]All this makes for a refutation of the pioneering work
of S. Lamberigts ("Le sens de קדושים dans les textes de Qumrân,"
ETL 46 1970 , 24-39). Of the three parallels mentioned above
he considers only 1QS 11:7 in which he acknowledges that the
holy ones are angels. Yet he does not use even that passage
to inform the meaning of קדושו שם in 4QFlor 1:4 nor does he
refer to the wider context of 4QFlor. Rather, taking 4QFlor by
itself, he reckons that the phrase denotes the members of the
sect over against the impure men who are excluded. This also
ignores the structure of the text - those phrases are not
parallel, that containing קדושו שם is a reason for the earlier
statement of exclusion.

[283]"La Sainteté selon la Communauté," 210. If 4QFlor is
an exposition of texts from the covenant service when new
converts were admitted, then the stress on purity can be
understood even more clearly. Barthélemy also summarizes
the Essenes' conception of sanctity "en trois mots: se
convertir, se séparer, s'unir" (204).

[284]בראישונה seems to be borrowed from the quotation of
2 Samuel in line 1, and therefore would most likely carry the
same meaning. Perhaps there is an allusion here to Jer 51:51.

[285]Thus Tamar is desolate because of the sin Ammon committed
against her (2 Sam 13:20), an altar is desolate because of the
idols associated with it (Ezek 6:4), the land is desolated by
the wickedness of men (Jer 12:11), etc. One cannot translate
directly "lay waste" (Vermes, Gaster, Dupont-Sommer) or "destroy"
(Maier and, by implication O. Betz, "The Eschatological Interpretation of the Sinai Tradition in Qumran and in the New
Testament," *RQ* 6 1967-69 , 101; also G. Klinzing *Das Umdeutung
des Kultus,* 82 , who confuses the issue by claiming that "destroy
is the original meaning of the root and that טמא would have
been used for 'desolate'.")

[286]"The Cleansing of the Temple and Zechariah xiv 21," *NovT* 4
(1960), 178-79.

[287]McNicol's translation of זר as "enemy" ("The Eschatological
Temple in the Qumran Pesher 4QFlorilegium 1:1-7," 138) is surely
incorrect as is his identification of them with the priesthood
in Jerusalem.

[288]This is also the understanding of Allegro, Yadin, Flusser
("Two Notes," 102) and Tocci - it certainly better accounts for

the plural suffix of בחטאתמה.

[289]"Two Notes," 102 n.11; followed by Maier. Yet, the simplest way of expressing the translation "among men" would be by the preposition ב which is indeed missing. G. Klinzing (*Das Umdeutung des Kultus,* 83) supports this reading too as it best reflects the thought of the passage wh ch for him is concerned with the eschatological sanctuary, the building, alone.

[290]Allegro and Dupont-Sommer ("un sanctuaire [fait de main] d'homme") read it this way; yet this goes against the contemporary idea (*1 Enoch* 90:28, *Jub.*1:28) that God himself builds the eschatological temple. On Plato, Xerxes, Zeno, Plutarch and Philo all being against the ideal sanctuary as being man-made, see S. G. Sowers, *The Hermeneutics of Philo and Hebrews* (Richmond: J. Knox, 1965), 55. Recently D. R. Schwartz ("The Three Temples of 4QFlorilegium," *RQ* 10 1979-81 , 86) has supported this translation, as also M. Delcor ("Littérature essénienne," *Supplément au Dictionnaire de la Bible,* Vol 9, ed. H. Cazelles et A. Feuillet; Paris: Letouzey et Ané, 1979, col. 912).

[291]So Gärtner (*Temple and Community,* 351; see also n.2).

[292]So Vermes, Tocci. O. Betz ("Sinai Tradition," 101) identifies the sanctuary as the living temple of the eschatological community. This idea that the sanctuary consists of men is also supported by J. Massingberd Ford ("A Possible Liturgical Background to the Shepherd of Hermas," *RQ* 6 1967-69 , 542 and n.43) and by J. Amusin ("Iz Kumranskoi Antologii," *RQ* 6 1967-69 , 147) who says that the expression "a human temple" emphasizes the "spirituality" and "humanity" of this sanctuary.

[293]Cf. Gen 6:13, Isa 65:6, Jer 2:22, etc.

[294]Lev 1:11 makes the distinction reflected in other parts
of the book that the slaughter or sacrificial action is done
before (לפני) the Lord, whereas the sacrifice goes up to or
makes a pleasing smell for (ל) the Lord. 4QFlor uses both
prepositions and so recognizes both aspects of sacrifice -
performance and direction. Cf. also the use of פנים and
sacrifice in Ps 51:9-11.

[295]*Prob.* '75, 75; translation by F. H. Colson, *Philo, IX,* 55.

[296]"Le Ministère Cultuel dans la Secte de Qumran et dans le
Christianisme Primitif," *La Secte de Qumran et les Origines du
Christianisme,* RechBib 4, Paris-Brügge: Desclée de Brouwer,
1959, 202. The same idea is expressed by O. Cullmann ("L'Opposition contre le Temple de Jérusalem, Motif Commun de la
Théologie Johannique et du Monde Ambiant," *NTS* 5 1958-59 , 165).
Perhaps the scholar who has most surely stressed the works of
the Law and Qumran practice in general being legalistically
rather than sacrificially oriented is C. Rabin (*Qumran Studies,*
London: Oxford University, 1957) who wanted to identify the
sectarians with the Pharisees rather than as the priestly-
oriented sons of Zadok.

[297]*The Ancient Library,* 75.

[298]De Vaux (*Archaeology,* 12-14, 86, 120) supports the view
that the animal bones are to be related to some kind of
sacrificial meal and notes that bones were buried throughout
the history of settlement at Qumran, but he makes no comment
on the amount of bones unearthed. Perhaps the bones unearthed
reflect a practice of the burning of the red heifer whose ashes

were needed for purificationary purposes: cf. J. Bowman,
"Did the Qumran Sect Burn the Red Heifer?" *RQ* 1 (1958-59),
73-84; W. H. Brownlee, "John the Baptist in the New Light of
Ancient Scrolls," *The Scrolls and the New Testament,* ed.
K. Stendahl; New York: Harper, 1957, 37-38.

[299]J. Carmignac ("L'Utilité ou l'Inutilité des Sacrifices
Sanglants dans la 'Règle de la Communauté' de Qumrân," *RB* 63
1956 , 524-32) comments in relation to 1QS 9:3-5 and 1QM 2:5-6
that this is just use of language, suitable to their situation,
from a different part of the OT which was held in respect as a
whole at Qumran. However, the sect believed that one day it
would return to Jerusalem to re-establish a true liturgy
conforming to the Law. Yet the very specific term, מקטירים,
may indicate that at the time of 4QFlor actual non-animal
sacrifices were burnt at Qumran. Cf. the discussion by
S. H. Steckoll ("The Qumran Sect in relation to the Temple of
Leontopolis," *RQ* 6 1967-69 , 55-69) who identifies a small
altar at Qumran (p.57) and suggests the area was associated
with a temple.

[300]1QS 3:4-12, 8:2-4, 9:4-5, CD 11:21, 11QPss[a] 18:17 are
mentioned in his treatment. Thus for him the Qumran community
did not offer sacrifices in the literal sense.

[301]"The Exclusion of 'Netinim' and Proselytes," 94.

[302]A. J. McNicol's approach ("The Eschatological Temple in
the Qumran Pesher 4QFlorilegium 1:1-7," 140) seems too straightforward: for him תודה can only refer to the actual sacrifices
performed in the future temple; he does not consider the whole
phrase מעשי תודה.

[303] *The Temple and the Community,* 30-42.

[304] See above, under Textual notes, for discussion of these
lines. We do not take them as having any referent, either
collective or individual, in משיחו of Ps 2:2.

[305] *The Temple and the Community,* 39.

[306] D. R. Schwartz ("The Messianic Departure from Judah
[4Q Patriarchal Blessings]," *TZ* 37 1981 , 258) also rejects
Gärtner's suggestion that the sect saw itself as the sprout
of David.

[307] H. Kosmala ("The Three Nets of Belial," *ASTI* 4 1965 ,
112, n.27) has stressed this in relation to Gärtner's treatment of CD: "Miqdaš itself could be applied to God (Ez 11:16,
cf. Is 8:14) or the land (Ex 15:17); the defilement of the land,
the profanation of the name of God always begins with the self-
defilement of the 'holy nation' (Lev 19f. and often). It was,
therefore, quite natural for the author(s) of the Damascus
Document to apply the word miqdaš (not hekal) also to the new
congregation of Israel."

[308] *Das Umdeutung des Kultus,* 80-87. He tries to determine
to which group of texts 4QFlor belongs: for him 1QS, CD and
1QpHab all contain the concept of the community as temple, 1QH,
1QM and 4QpPs[a] do not. This he attributes to differences of
"Gattung," and of period of writing. J. Murphy-O'Connor (*RB* 79
1972 , 435-40) largely agrees with this and approves Klinzing's
analysis of 4QFlor.

[309] Here Klinzing correctly leans towards the reading of
Strugnell, תודה, "Dankopfer," which is found with קטר in Amos 4:5.

Thus for Klinzing the sacrifices to be offered in the future
will be actual, though he concludes that "in jedem Falle
bleibt die Deutung der Stelle ungewiss " (84).

[310]Klinzing cites *Jub.* 1:17, 27, *Sib. Or.* 5:433, *Midr. Pss* 90:
19 (198a), *1 Enoch* 91:13, *2 Bar.* 32:4, *Sifre* Deut 33:12 (145b).
He also points to a similar concern in intertestamental literature
concerning the eschatological city.

[311]*Das Umdeutung des Kultus*, 84.

[312]At 1QS 5:6, 8:5, 9, 9:6, CD 3:18. Also at 4QD[b], 1QSa
2:3ff. and 1QM 7:6 which are discussed above.

[313]"Le Rouleau du Temple," *Qumrân: sa piété, sa théologie et
son milieu*, ed. M. Delcor; BETL 46; Paris: Duculot, Leuven:
University Press, 1978, 115-119.

[314]*The Temple Scroll, Volume One: Introduction*, Jerusalem:
The Israel Exploration Society, The Institute of Archaeology of
the Hebrew University, The Shrine of the Book, 1977, 140-144.
11QT 8-10 read: "And I will sanctify my sanctuary with my glory
which I will cause to dwell on it, my glory until the day of
blessing when I myself will create my sanctuary to establish it
forever" (my translation).

[315]See pp. 184-185.

[316]"The Three Temples of 4QFlorilegium," *RQ* 10 (1979-81),
83-91.

[317]"Noch zum *miqdaš 'ādām* in 4QFlorilegium," *RQ* 10 (1979-81),
587-88.

[318]"The Three Temples of 4QFlorilegium," 86.

[319]See pp. 111-112.

[320]"The Three Temples of 4QFlorilegium," 86.

[321]Perhaps this interest is a part of the reaction at Qumran to Herod's temple rebuilding.

[322]This identification is supported recently by P. R. Davies, *Qumran,* Guildford: Lutterworth, 1982, 87; and by P. Garnet, *Salvation and Atonement in the Qumran Scrolls,* WUNT 2, Vol 3; Tübingen: J.C.B. Mohr, 1977, 103.

[323]1 Sam 7:1, 12:11, Deut 12:10, 25:29, Jos 23:1, Judg 2:14, 8:34, etc.

[324]Deut 13:14, Judg 19:22, 2 Chr 13:7ff. On "Belial" and its possible meaning in the OT, see D. Winton Thomas, "בליעל in the Old Testament," (*Biblical and Patristic Studies,* eds. J. N. Birdsall and R. W. Thomson; Freiburg: Herder, 1963, 11-19) and the more thorough work of V. Maag, "B^elija^cal im Alten Testament" (*TZ* 21 1965 , 287-99). Cf. W. Foerster " Βελίαρ ," *TDNT* 1, 607.

[325]*Gott und Belial,* SUNT 6; Göttingen: Vandenhoeck and Ruprecht, 1969, 191,n.4.

[326]The difficult passage, 1QS 3:13-4:14, he sees as a direct modification by the editors of 1QS of material drawn from 1QM and influenced by Iranian dualistic thought concerning the world.

[327]"The Three Nets of Belial," 103. He shows how CD speaks of the defilement at 1:20, 3:11, 5:6, 12, 6:11-14, 7:3 and 20:23f.

[328]L. Stefaniak ("Messianische oder eschatologische Erwartungen in der Qumransekte?" *Neutestamentliche Aufsätze,* J. Schmid Festschrift, Regensburg: Verlag F. Pustet, 1963, 294-95) attempts a precise definition but he limits eschatology specifically to

the end, namely the end of history; however, he rightly
describes the Messiah as the figure who will appear and
function at the "Endzeit," that is, "das endzeitlich Gottesreich."

[329]This is not to exclude outright that these figures
possibly stand for collective ideas, such as proposed by
Gärtner for the shoot, and by Brownlee (*Meaning*, 89) for the
booth, which he sees as the renewed and purified temple and cult.

[330]It may possibly be restored in 4QpIsa[a] frgs. 8-10:17
where the interpretation of Isa 11:5 concerns the rule of
the "shoot" in the latter days.

[331]"Israel" is applied variously at Qumran to the whole
people or to the land or to both - but never to the community
alone.

[332]Not the case for the noun; 1QH 5:12, CD 20:20 and the
change in 1QIsa[a] 42:18-19 require a future if not an eschatological understanding. W. H. Brownlee ("Messianic Motifs
of Qumran and the New Testament," *NTS* 3 1956-57, 19) offers a
messianic interpretation of these passages. The possible
restoration of (ועה)שי at 1QH 11:18 is one among a list of the
attributes of God. J. A. Fitzmyer ("The Aramaic 'Elect of God'
Text from Qumran Cave IV," *CBQ* 27 1965, 349-50) cites a
useful bibliography on Qumran Messianism up to 1965.

[333]E.g. in 1QIsa[a] 42 the alteration of the suffixes in Isa
51:4-5 creates an overall sense in which salvation becomes an
alternative designation for the expected ruler (king-messiah);
cf. 1QH 5:11-12. Also compare "salvation" as a messianic title
in Lk 2:30, *T. Naph.* 8:2, *T. Gad* 8:1, *T. Dan* 5:10, *T. Jos.* 19:11,
Jub. 31:19; this last clearly identifies salvation as an aspect

of the work of the kingly messiah rather than of the eschatological high priest. On all this see W. H. Brownlee, "Messianic
Motifs of Qumran and the New Testament," *NTS* 3 (1956-57), 195-98.

[334]"Iz Kumranskoi Antologii," 146. A. S. van der Woude (*Die
Messianischen Vorstellungen der Gemeinde von Qumran,* Assen:
van Gorcum, 1957, 174) speaks out strongly against this idea,
which he sees as alien to Qumran. Yet, since his work scholars
have persisted in pursuing the concept of a resurrected teacher
of righteousness, e.g. A. S. Kapelrud ("Die aktuellen und die
eschatologischen Behörden der Qumrangemeinde," *Qumran-Probleme*,
ed. H. Bardtke, Berlin: Akademie Verlag, 260-61), and in the
same volume, K. Weiss ("Messianismus in Qumran und im Neuen
Testament," 354-55) actually identifies the Interpreter of the
Law of 4QFlor with the resurrected Teacher.

[335]"Le Retour du Docteur de Justice à la fin des Jours?"
RQ 1 (1958-59), 246-48.

[336]*Das Umdeutung des Kultus,* 139.

[337]"Stehen und fallen im Qumranischen und Neutestamentlichen
Schriften," *Qumran-Probleme,* ed. H. Bardtke, Berlin : Akademie
Verlag, 1963, 160.

[338]The general appellative דורש בתורה is used at 1QS 6:6;
1QS 8:12 also speaks of an Interpreter who is not to conceal
anything from the members of the Council of the community. It
is just possible that the title is also used in 4QFlor Fragment
23]דורש [.

[339]P. R. Davies ("The Ideology of the Temple in the Damascus
Document," *JJS* 33 1982 , 301) proposes that the Interpreter of
the Law in CD 6:7-10 is a figure from the past and must be

distinguished from the future Teacher of Righteousness.

[340]The starting point of D. Flusser ("Two Notes," 104) is
questionable. He opens by saying that "our problem is to
explain why the anointed priest of the last days should be
called the 'Interpreter of the Law'." Rather, it is a
question of how the Interpreter of the Law is the anointed
priest.

[341]"Les Quatre Étapes du Messianisme à Qumrân," *RB* 70
(1963), 481-505.

[342]Thus, W. H. Brownlee ("Messianic Motifs," 199); among
others M. Black ("Messianic Doctrine in the Qumran Scrolls,"
Studia Patristica I, Part 1, eds. K. Aland and F. L. Cross,
Berlin: Akademie Verlag, 1957, 441) begins with the caveat
that material from different periods may contain different
beliefs, but then tries to show how Qumran consistently only
expected one Messiah, the Davidic prince.

[343]"The Doctrine of the Two Messiahs in Sectarian Literature
in the Time of the Second Commonwealth," *HTR* 52 (1959), 149-85.
Thus, for him, משיח in CD 12:22, 14:19 and 19:11 "is merely a
scribal error or an emendation of משיחי" (152), and concerning
4QTest and 4QFlor he clearly sees two messianic figures.

[344]Ia Maccabean, from 152 B.C., QS (in earlier 4Q copies), 1QH.
   Ib[1] Hasmonean, from 103 B.C., 1QSa, 1QSb, 4QTest, 4QAhA, 1QS.
   Ib[2] Pompeian, 64-32 B.C. CD, 4QarP, 4QD[b].
   II Herodian, 10 B.C.-A.D. 68, 1QM, 4QFlor, 1QpHab, 4QPB,
          4QpPs[a].

[345]"J. Starcky's Theory of Qumran Messianic Development,"
CBQ 28 (1966), 51-57.

[346]"The Aramaic 'Elect of God' Text," *CBQ* 27 (1965),
355-56.

[347]J. Massingberd Ford's statement ("Can we exclude Samaritan
Influence from Qumran?" *RQ* 6 1967-69 , 120) is incomprehensible:
"the same is true (as in 4QPB) of the Florilegium, where the
prophecy of Nathan to David is applied first to the community
and secondly the branch of David is applied to the Teacher of
Righteousness."

[348]There is no need to rehearse the views of the multitude
of scholars who have written on this subject. Most of the
scholars cited in Fitzmyer's bibliography (*The Dead Sea Scrolls,
Major Publications and Tools for Study,* Sources for Biblical
Study 8; Missoula: Scholars Press, 1975, 114-118) have proposed
that the Interpreter of the Law in 4QFlor is the priestly
messiah of Aaron; most recently A. Caquot has made this association with explicit reference to 4QFlor ("Le messianisme
qumrânien," *Qumrân: sa piété, sa théologie et son milieu,* BETL
46, 1978, 243-44). To Fitzmyer's list might also be added
J. J. Smith ("A Study of the alleged 'Two Messiah' Expectation
of the DSS against the background of Developing Eschatology,"
Dissertation Abstracts International 31A 1970 , 3027) who
suggests that the Interpreter of the Law is the risen Teacher
of Righteousness following, amongst others, Dupont-Sommer (*The
Essene Writings from Qumran,* 313, n.2) and J. Starcky ("Les
Quatre Étapes du Messianisme à Qumrân," 481-505).

[349]D. Flusser ("Two Notes," 108-9) concludes from this that
the Interpreter of the Law would not become the Messiah of
Aaron until the Davidic Messiah came; the Interpreter is thus

a potential Messiah, a Messiah-to-be.

[350]In this regard M. Hengel (*Judentum und Hellenismus,* 404)
argues convincingly that the primary function of the משכילים
of Dan 11:33, 35, 12:10 is to teach the law: cf. 4QFlor 2:4a.

[351]On the importance of the Urim and Tummim in post biblical
Judaism as *high-priestly* symbols of the תורה, see E. L. Ehrlich,
*Die Kultsymbolik im Alten Testament und im nachbiblischen
Judentum* (Stuttgart: A. Hiersemann, 1959), 21-22.

[352]For possible OT sources of the doctrine of two Messiahs
at Qumran see J. R. Villalón, "Sources Vétéro-testamentaires
de la doctrine qumrânienne des deux Messies," *RQ* 8 (1972-75),
53-63. He particularly stresses Malachi.

[353]For the former support can be adduced from such a text
as CD 19:10; for the latter 1QS 9:11. Perhaps the former would
be better because of the other parallels that 4QFlor has with
CD; yet, the word order in 4QFlor Frg. 5 is inverted from the
usual אהרון וישראל and so the talk may be rather of both messiahs.

[354]The eschatology of CD is discussed generally by
H. W. Huppenbauer ("Zur Eschatologie der Damaskusschrift," *RQ* 4
1963-64, 567-73). Interestingly he concludes that CD's
eschatology is primarily ecclesiological rather than messianic -
4QFlor also appears to show that ordering of priorities.

[355]"The Use of Explicit Old Testament Quotations," 305-30.

[356]Fitzmyer says that 8 fragmentary copies of CD have turned
up in Cave 4 ("Qumran and the Interpolated Paragraph in 2 Cor
6:14-7:1," *CBQ* 23 1961 , 276, n.16) apart from those of the
fifth and sixth caves.

³⁵⁷If P. R. Davies is correct in identifying a certain ambiguity in the attitude of CD to the temple, that it is no longer the seat of the law but that it should be used by those who possess the law ("The Ideology of the Temple in the Damascus Document," 300), then CD may support the interpretations of 4QFlor given here: the community, the מקדש אדם, is the seat of the law and its interpreter.

³⁵⁸S. Aalen discusses the 2 Samuel 7 passages in the gospels ("'Reign' and 'House' in the Kingdom of God in the Gospels," *NTS* 8 1961-62, 215-40); cf. esp. Acts 4:25-28.

³⁵⁹"Acts 13 33-37: A *Pesher* on II Samuel 7," *JBL* 87 (1968), 321-24.

³⁶⁰E. Lövestam (*Son and Saviour*, Lund: C.W.K. Gleerup, 1961, 39) saw the allusion to the Nathan oracle in Acts 13:33 but failed to describe the extent of its influence as Goldsmith has now done.

³⁶¹E.g., both Isa 55:3 and Ps 16:10 use the word ὅσιος and these verses are thus analogically combined.

³⁶²*A Comparative Study*, 24-26.

³⁶³"The Use of Explicit Old Testament Quotations," 300.

³⁶⁴*Meaning*, 88-89.

³⁶⁵"Qumran and the Interpolated Paragraph in 2 Cor 6:14-7:1," *CBQ* 23 (1961), 271-80; reprinted in his *Essays on the Semitic Background of the New Testament* (London: G. Chapman, 1971), 205-17.

³⁶⁶"2 Kor. 6, 14-7, 1, in Lichte der Qumranschriften und der Zwölf-Patriarchen-Testamente," *Neutestamentliche Aufsätze* (Festschrift J. Schmid; ed. J. Blinzer et al.; Regensburg:

F. Pustet, 1963), 86-99; ET: "2 Cor 6:14-7:1 in the Light
of the Qumran Texts and the Testaments of the Twelve Patriarchs,"
Paul and Qumran (ed. J. Murphy-O'Connor; Chicago: Priory Press,
1968) 48-68.

[367]*Temple and Community*, 49-56.

[368]*Das Umdeutung des Kultus,* 175-82.

[369]The important article by H. D. Betz, "2 Cor 6:14-7:1:
An Anti-Pauline Fragment?" *JBL* 92 (1973), 88-108, aligns the
theology of this interpolated paragraph with that of the
judaizers of Galatia. Betz does not address the question
whether or not such ideas or people or both might stem from
Qumran or an Essene source, and so his work is not treated here.

The study of M. Thrall, "The Problem of II Cor. vi. 14-vii. 1
in some recent discussion," *NTS* 24 (1977-78), 132-48, is ruefully
inadequate in its argument for the Pauline authorship of this
Corinthians passage.

[370]Cf. 1QS 1:9-11, 1QM 13:9, 5-6, CD: 13:12, also the phrase
גורל אל: 1QS 2:2, 1QM 1:5, 15, 13:5, 15:1, 17:7.

[371]And secondarily 1QS 2:11, 17, 4:5, 1QH 4:19, CD 20:9.

[372]Cf. 1 Cor 3:16-17, Eph 2:21-22.

[373]Fitzmyer also mentions 1QS 5:6, 8:4-6, 8-9, 9:5-7, 11:8.

[374]1QS 4:5, 5:13-14, 9:8-9, CD 6:17. Also see the many
regulations for ritual purity: e.g., 1QS 4:10, CD 7:3, 9:21, etc.

[375]"Qumran and 2 Cor 6:14-7:1," 278.

[376]"Qumran and 2 Cor 6:14-7:1," 279.

[377]Bibliographical information in n.2, above.

[378]Qumran literature, to be sure; but also *T. 12 Patr.*,
Sib. Or. and *Jub.*

[379]*The Temple and the Community*, 50; even though ναός in
the LXX normally translates היכל and not מקדש.

[380]*The Temple and the Community*, 54.

[381]*Das Umdeutung des Kultus*, 175-78.

[382]*Das Umdeutung des Kultus*, 178.

[383]*Das Umdeutung des Kultus*, 179-82.

Chapter III

QUMRAN EXEGETICAL METHOD

The purpose of this chapter is to provide examples of
midrashic techniques at work in the interpretation of scripture
in a wide variety of Qumran literature. All these examples
give support to the proposals presented in the previous chapter
concerning the use of midrashic techniques in 4QFlor. Some
passages from 11QtgJob are considered in order to show that
even in translating or re-presenting the scriptural text the
interpreter is at work; so he is in the amended citation of
2 Sam 7:11b-14a in 4QFlor 1:10-11. Several examples of these
techniques are cited from 1QpHab so that their use can be seen
in a text of similar genre to 4QFlor. 1QM 10:1-8 provides an
explicit example of *gĕzērâ šāwâ*, the most obvious method for
the juxtaposition of scriptural texts in 4QFlor, and the
liturgical midrash in 1QS 2:2-4 demonstrates that the proposals
for a liturgical setting for 4QFlor in no way conflict with the
use of exegetical devices. Three more texts, CD 7:13b-8:1a,
4QTest and 11QMelch, all share a biblical passage in common
with 4QFlor, though those passages are not necessarily treated
in the same way as they are in 4QFlor. These three texts also
show the compatibility of the use of midrashic techniques with

messianic reflection. Furthermore the association of some
of the biblical texts in 11QMelch may well depend on their
common use in a liturgical setting.

A. 11 QTgJob[1]

In Chapter I several examples of the interpreter at work
were cited from the targums. It is appropriate, therefore, to
include a few examples from one of the Qumran targums.[2] To
observe the interpreter at work in the act of translating is
to support the conclusion that the scriptural text may sometimes
be adjusted through the acceptable use of certain exegetical
techniques.

Some work on the hermeneutic of the Job targum has already
been completed by E. W. Tuinistra,[3] but he deals with the
interpretation that 11QtgJob contains and implies, rather than
being concerned with the exegetical method whereby those interpretations were reached.

Since it is difficult to determine in what text-type the
Qumran community possessed the book of Job in Hebrew,[4] remarks
at this time will be limited to a few places where it clearly
appears that the targumist depended on a consonantal Hebrew
text the same as that represented by MT.

1. אוּר or אוֹר

The first example concerns the targum's reading of the
Hebrew אוּר. Three times it is translated by נורא, "fire," in
the targum (11QtgJob 8:3 [Job 24:13a], 29:2 [Job 37:11] and
36:4 [Job 41:10a]) and F. J. Morrow proposes[5] a possible fourth
reading at 9:6 (Job 25:3) where the change from a masculine verb

(MT: יקום) to a feminine (11QtgJob: תקום) would suggest that
once again אור is rendered by נורא, thus making the verb
feminine: unfortunately the subject of the verb is lacking.
The LXX rendering diverges considerably from the MT at Job 24:13a,
but at Job 37:11 it translates אור by φῶς and at 41:10a by
φέγγος.[6] When it is considered that at 11QtgJob 23:7 (Job 33:28)
and 29:6 (Job 37:15)אור is rendered as נהור (LXX φῶς both times),
then it seems likely too that at 11QtgJob 10:1 (Job 26:10) נהור
should be restored just before the initial word of the line[7] and
that the end of 28:7 (Job 36:30) is correctly read as נה]ורה.
All this points to the possibility that the targumist, or the
tradition that he represents (on occasion possibly similar to
that of the LXX), deliberately chose to read אור either as אגר
or as אוֹר, over against the consistent understanding of אוֹר of
the MT text-type. These choices not always to read (*'al tiqrē'*)
אור as "light" are the result of the application of the
targumist's exegetical concern to make the text of Job as
understandable as possible for his audience.[8]

2. 11QtgJob 37:8

At 11QtgJob 37:8 (Job 42:6) the targumist has not taken
נחמתי of his Hebrew text as a *niphᶜal* from the root נחם as MT
("I will repent in dust and ashes") but rather as a *niphᶜal* from
the root חמם, "to be heated,"[9] with the result that he had to
supply a verb for "dust and ashes" at the end of line 8. Thus
11QtgJob reads for the whole verse, "Therefore, I am poured out
and boiled up, and I will become dust and ash."[10] This is a
further example of *'al tiqrē'*.

3. 11QtgJob 21:4-5

A. D. York discusses the targumist's treatment of ירפנו
(Job 32:13) at 21:4-5.[11] Although the meaning of the Hebrew
is very uncertain, York reckons that the context of the targum's
interpretation requires that God is no longer considered as the
verb's subject (which, if that is the case, then has a 1st or
3rd pers. suffix) as has been the traditional understanding of
the MT (e.g., Vulgate), but rather it is the friends of Job who
"condemn" God by their silence. That silence acknowledges Job
as righteous in *their* eyes (Job 32:1): the LXX (ἐναντίον αὐτῶν),
the Peshitta (בעיניהון), Symmachus (ἐπ'αὐτῶν) and at least one
Hebrew manuscript (Kennicott 248) all support this reading of
Job 32:1, unfortunately not preserved in 11QtgJob, and the LXX
also presupposes two plural verbs for Job 32:13: εὕρομεν
σοφίαν προσθέμενοι κυρίῳ.[12] Thus the targumist represents a
tradition in which the Hebrew verb is understood as a 1st person
plural perfect; he did not read *('al tiqrē')* a 3rd person
singular verb with a suffix which would have been presented to
him as an option if the Hebrew *Vorlage* was pronounced as MT is
currently pointed.[13]

4. 11QtgJob 29:1

W. H. Brownlee has proposed that the plural pronominal
suffixes at Job 37:11ff. were understood by the targumist as
referring to "personal agents who listen to God's voice and go
forth to their assigned tasks."[14] These are not the clouds and
water of Job 37:10-11 but angels, the targumist taking אל of
MT Job 37:10a in this sense. Unfortunately the first half of
verse 10 is not preserved in the targum, but although the
targumist consistently translates אל by אלהא everywhere in his

targum, it could be that at this one place, possibly influenced
by his understanding of בני אלהים at Job 38:7 as the מלאכי אלהא
and by the general use of אל for angel(s) at Qumran,[15] the
targumist interpreted the whole passage deliberately to reflect,
"the cosmic role of angels."

B. 1QpHab

Much scholarly work has been done to illuminate the
biblical exegesis that is present in 1QpHab. W. H. Brownlee's
initial work on the commentary's exegesis[16] has been supplemented,
adjusted and criticized by various scholars,[17] not least by
Brownlee himself.[18] Doubtless there is still much work to be
done.[19]

It is necessary, firstly, to distinguish clearly between
hermeneutical principles or presuppositions and exegetical
techniques. Brownlee initially confused the two by defining
his first hermeneutical principle as "Everything the ancient
prophet wrote has a *veiled eschatological meaning;*"[20] the rest
of the principles he outlines more or less closely approximate
exegetical techniques that the commentator may have used. He
has, however, provided enough material to show that his first
principle never really describes more than the content or, at
most, the underlying assumption of the interpretation and cannot
explain how that particular content was attained.[21] For example,
the Kittim are not seen to be the subject of Hab 1:8-9 (1QpHab
3:7-13) through the understanding that there is a "veiled
eschatological meaning," as Brownlee proposes; rather "veiled"
and "eschatological" describe the content of the prophecy in
relation to an already and otherwise obtained interpretation -

obtained most probably through the application of Num 24:24,
Dan 11:30 and Isa 23:12b-13 in traditional exegesis.[22]

Of Brownlee's twelve remaining principles nearly all fit
into the standard pattern of rabbinic exegesis, more or less
contemporary, in approximately the following way. Principle
number two, that the meaning is to be "ascertained through a
forced, or abnormal construction of the biblical text,"[23] is
really an overarching category under which can be grouped several
of the other principles; it is unfortunate that the words "forced"
and "abnormal" were used, for the exegesis was surely an attempt
through normative and accepted techniques to understand the
meaning of the text and many of the basic teachings of Habakkuk
come through in the Qumran pesher.[24] That exegesis may appear
"difficult" to obtain, in fact it was only done by experts, but
it should not be considered "forced." All the examples Brownlee
gives of the use of this second principle can in fact be
described otherwise.[25]

The principles, numbers three, the use of "*textual or
orthographic peculiarities*" in the study of a text, four, the
use of "*a textual variant*," and ten, the use of "*the substitution
of similar letters* for one or more of the letters in the word
of the Biblical text" which is being interpreted are all
variations of the rabbinic technique of *'al tiqrē'*.[26]

Of the two examples which Brownlee gives for his fifth
principle, interpretation through the application of "*analogous
circumstance*," the first, the identification of the כשדים
(Hab 1:6, 1QpHab 2:11-15), more properly is an interpretation
derived from the eschatological use of Num 24:24 and Dan 11:30
in relation to an understanding of Isa 23:12b-13 which could be

read so as to imply the identification of כתיים and כשדים.[27]
The second example, in the interpretation of Hab 2:5-6 (1QpHab
8:3-13), is better explained through the application of the
technique of 'asmaktâ as tentatively but precisely laid out
by E. Slomovic.[28] Thus the fifth principle, like the second,
is more a description of the final interpretation than it is
of the method of exegesis whereby that interpretation was reached.

Similar remarks can be made about the sixth principle, that
of "*allegorical propriety*." The two examples classified under
this principle require further explanation to elucidate how the
"allegorical" interpretation was obtained. Firstly Brownlee
notes how the understanding of מגמת פניהם (Hab 1:9; 1QpHab 3:6-14:
"The mutterings of their face are . . .") as "the heat of his
nostril" and "the snorting of his nostrils" in the interpretation
is most likely dependent upon taking מגמת as from the Aramaic
root גמם, and that the association of heat with anger and of
the wind with speech both depend upon common themes in the OT.[29]
The identification of מגמת פנו with קדים is already made in the
text of Habakkuk through the reading of Hab 1:9 in the form of
מגמת פנו הם קדים over against MT's מגמת פניהם קדים;[30] this was
either traditional or a deliberate use of *nôṭārîqôn*, division
of words, by the author of 1QpHab.

Secondly, in relation to Hab 1:16 (1QpHab 6:2-5) Brownlee
understands the equation of חרם, "net," and אותות, "standard,"
as depending solely upon allegorical propriety, whereas for the
equation of מכמרתו, "his seine," and the phrase "weapons of war
are the object of their religious reverence" he gives an elaborate
clarification of the application of certain interpretative
techniques. A. Finkel has however pointed to the means of

equation in the first pair: חרם is to be considered in both
its meanings of "banned, sacred object" and "net."[31] It may
also be possible to understand Finkel's identification of the
paronomasia in greater detail by allowing that any word with the
root letters חרם could provide the basis for the identification
of חרם and אוח: at Josh 2:10 occurs the phrase החרמתם אותם
normally and properly understood as, "you utterly destroyed
them," but perhaps the commentator took אותם as "their standard"
and conceived the destruction otherwise.[32] Thus in both cases
the "*allegorical propriety*" is most likely to be dependent on
the use of some exegetical technique.

Principles seven and eight, the attachment of "*more than
one meaning*" to a word in the prophet's vision and the use of
"*synonyms*" are to be derived from the employment of the technique
of paronomasia.[33] For examples Brownlee shows that אף means
both "anger" and "face, nostrils" in the exposition of Hab 1:9
(1QpHab 3:6-14), that משל in Hab 2:6 "proverb" is taken as משל,
"to rule" (1QpHab 8:9)[34] and that בלע is used to interpret
Hab 2:15 in both its senses of "to swallow" and therefrom "to
destroy" (1QpHab 11:2-8).[35]

Brownlee's principle number nine, "*rearrangement of the
letters in a word,*" is the rabbinic exegetical technique of
ḥillûf:[36] its clearest use is in the interpretation of היכל
(Hab 2:20) by means of יכלה (1QpHab 12:15;13:4). Because the
interpretation of destruction can be seen as parallel to that
of the Targum of Jonathan which takes חם as signifying just that,
Brownlee has since denied the use of this anagram technique at
this point.[37] However, the particular choice of words that the
commentator makes in 1QpHab would still seem to depend on a

deliberate anagram, whether or not that entails the destruction
of the temple as part of the thought of the commentary.[38]

Principles eleven and twelve, interpretation through " *the
division of one word into two or more parts*" and "*interpretation
of words, or parts of words, as abbreviations,*"[39] are two forms
of *nôṭārîqôn*, used actually within the text of Habakkuk itself
(Hab 1:9: פניהם—פנו הם)[40] by the commentator (1QpHab 3:8-14)
and in the interpretation too. Among examples Brownlee cites the
interpretation of כולו (Hab 1:9; 1QpHab 3:7-13) as "to devour
all the peoples as a vulture, *but* without being satisfied;"[41]
the exegesis of עבטט (Hab 2:6; 1QpHab 8:3-13) so that it is
divided in the sense of "thickness of mud" and so understood as
"the guilt of transgression" and as "all impurity of defilement;"[42]
the understanding of עור לת (1QpHab 11:13) as two words, the
second being an abbreviation for לב תועבה (Cf. 1QpHab 8:13);[43]
and the interpretation of בהיכל (Hab 2:20; 1QpHab 13:2-4) as an
abbreviation of the phrase ביום המשפט יכלה.[44]

The thirteenth and final principle, that "*other passages of
scripture* may illumine the meaning of the prophet," applies to
almost all the other techniques and descriptions mentioned.
Brownlee himself admits of the elusive nature of the principle
though he is correct in ascertaining that other scriptural
passages do indeed form the basis for certain interpretations.[45]

In sum, Brownlee presents 13 principles from which can be
distilled certain techniques of exegesis that are clearly
midrashic; given their rabbinic names, Brownlee gives examples
from 1QpHab of the use of *'al tiqrē'*, *ḥillûf*, *nôṭārîqôn*, paronomasia and there is possibly an implied use of *gĕzērâ šāwâ* where
there may be two or more biblical texts, linked by a common word

or phrase, behind an exegetical tradition that is represented
in the commentary. Even allowing for adjustments by other
scholars and by Brownlee himself, the use of all these techniques
would still seem to be evident in 1QpHab.

Further evidence for the use of the technique *'al tiqrē'*
in 1QpHab has been gathered by A. Finkel.[46] He cites seven
examples in which he considers that there is more to a proper
understanding of the text than the recognition of the existence
of a textual variant.

1) 1QpHab 3:1: במישור יכלו לכות, "in the plain they
came to smite," suggests the dual reading of Hab 1:6, למרחבי,
"in the plain," and להחריב, "to smite, to destroy."[47]

2) 1QpHab 4:9 reads וישם, "he will make waste," instead
of the MT's ואשם (Hab 1:11) but the interpretation understands
both: בית אשמ[ה], "house of guilt," and לשחית, "to lay waste"
(1QpHab 4:11, 13).[48]

3) 1QpHab 6:8 reads חרבו instead of the MT's חרמו and
thereby the dual meaning of חרם introduced in 1QpHab 6:2-5 is
reinforced.

4) 1QpHab 7:14 reads עופלה, "is puffed up," as in the MT
(Hab 2:4), yet the interpretation contains יכפלו, "they will
double" (1QpHab 7:15) - an auditory pun.[49]

5) 1QpHab 9:14 reads קצוות, "the ends of" (or, better,
"confines"), but the judgment of 1QpHab 10:2-5 suggests rather
an understanding or play on the verb קצה, "to cut off, finish."[50]

6) 1QpHab 11:3 reads מועדיהם over against the MT's מעוריהם,
yet, claims Finkel, the interpreter betrays an understanding of
the MT in his phrase "his house of exile" (1QpHab 11:6).[51]

7) 1QpHab 11:9 reads הרעל, "stagger," instead of the MT's

הערל, "be uncircumcised" (Hab 2:15), but the interpreter takes
account of both since alongside the staggering there is mention
of the uncircumcised heart of the (wicked) priest.[52]

Another technique the use of which has been pointed out
by E. Slomovic[53] is that of *'asmaktâ*, the support of an interpretation through the use of other biblical texts in which occur
either the words of the text interpreted or those of the interpretation or both. Slomovic gives as his example the interpretation of Hab 2:5a-b (1Q̣Hab 8:3-13). The biblical text reads:
ואף כיא הון יבגוד גבר יהיר ולוא ינוה אשר הרחיב כשאול נפשו והוא
כמות לוא ישבע "Moreover the arrogant man siezes wealth without
halting. He widens his gullet like Hell and like Death he has
never enough."[54] The pesher for this section of Habakkuk reads:
פשרו על הכוהן הרשע אשר נקרא על שם האמת בתחילת עומדו וכאשר משל
בישראל רם לבו ויעזוב את אל ויבגוד בחוקים בעבור הון "Interpreted,
this concerns the Wicked Priest who was called by the name of
truth when he first arose. But when he ruled over Israel his
heart became proud, and he forsook God and betrayed the precepts
for the sake of riches."[55]

Slomovic comments: "The general idea of the *pesher* is
apparent. The Wicked Priest, after a period of enjoying a
reputation for truth, grew arrogant and betrayed God and his
precepts for the sake of wealth. The commentator derives this
from the introductory phrase כי היין utilizing the *al tikrei*
rule to change the masoretic היין to הון."[56] Slomovic then
continues by outlining how each phrase of the biblical quotation
finds its parallel in the history and activities of the Wicked
Priest. In this way כי הון is interpreted by הכוהן הרשע: through
ḥillûf, anagram, כי הון is adapted to כוה(י)ן. יבגיד of Hab 2:5

becomes in interpretation אשר נקרא על שם האמת בתחילת עומדו
through the support of Isa 48:8: כי ידעתי בגיד תבגוד ופשע
מבטן קרא לך "For I knew that you would *deal very treacherously,*
and that from birth *you were called* a rebel" *(RSV)*.

Furthermore Slomovic proposes that the use of גבר in
Hab 2:5, as interpreted to signify that the Wicked Priest ruled
in Israel, כאשר משל בישראל, is supported by 1 Chr 5:2:[57] כי
יהודה גבר באחיו ולנגיד ממנו , "though Judah became strong among
his brothers and a prince was from him" *(RSV)*. Then, after
יהיר has been paraphrased by רם לבו , the phrase ולו ינוה is
interpreted by ויעזב את אל which Slomovic sees as supported by
Exod 15:2:[58] זה אלי ואנוהו , "This is my God and I will praise
him" *(RSV)*. Next, אשר הרחיב כשאול נפשו interpreted as ויבגד
בחוקים is supported by Isa 5:14: לכן הרחיבה שאול נפשה ופערה
פיה לבלי חק , "Therefore Sheol has enlarged its appetite and
opened its mouth beyond measure" *(RSV)*. Lastly the exegesis
of והוא כמות ולא ישבע as בעבור הון is supported by Prov 30:15-16:
שלוש הנה לא תשבענה ארבע לא אמרו הון שאול , "Three things are never
satisfied, four never say, 'Enough': Sheol . . ." *(RSV)*.

Slomovic concludes his study with a note of caution that
since "the Exegete of the Scrolls does not specify the method he
employs, any discussion of that method must of necessity contain
an element of speculation."[59] Yet the overall presentation of
material by Slomovic would seem to provide sufficient evidence
in support of an understanding of 1QpHab 8:3-13 such as he outlines.

The value of Slomovic's caveat cannot be overestimated in
a study such as this for without indication of the method that
he uses the interpreter links commentary in many and various ways.
Most of what has been said thus far would imply that the use of

certain exegetical techniques has been discerned in 1QpHab
with a corresponding increase in likelihood as to the precise
meaning of the interpretation. Yet, in actuality, that there
is a particular technique of exegesis being used in any one
place is almost the only thing that is reasonably certain.

The uncertainty of the complete content of the interpretation
can be seen well from the following example. Much of the text
of Hab 2:2 is missing in the lacuna of 1QpHab 6:15-17 but it
is partly requoted in the interpretation in column seven, thus:[60]

וידבר אל *אל* חבקוק לכתוב את הבאות על על הדור האחרון ואת גמר
הקץ לוא הודיעו ואשר אמר למען *ירוץ* הקורא בו פשרו על מורה הצדק
אשר הודיעו אל את כול רזי דברי עבדיו הנבאים   "Then God told
Habakkuk to write the things that are coming upon upon (*sic*)
the last generation; but the fulness of that time He did not
make known to him. And as for that which He said, 'for the sake
of him who reads it' (or, 'that he who reads it may run [may
divulge]'), its interpretation concerns the Righteous Teacher
to whom God has made known all the mysteries of the words of
His servants the prophets."[61]

In his extensive commentary Elliger made no attempt to
correlate the biblical text and the interpretation, but since
then several connections have been identified between the two.
L. H. Silberman[62] asks if there is any possibility that ירוץ
be understood in such a fashion as to point to the ability of
the Teacher of Righteousness to discern the meaning of the text.
He offers three suggestions: firstly, *b. Sanh.* 34a on Jer 23:29
reads, "'And like a hammer that breaketh (פצץ) the rock in
pieces,' id est, just as the rock is split into many splinters,
so also may one Biblical verse convey many teachings." Just as

in this passage פצץ is taken to mean "interpret a text," so
ירוץ, if taken from the root רצץ, "crush," could mean "interpret."
Secondly, there may be a play on the Aramaic root תרץ, "make
level," used in *b. Yebam.* 11b-12a of interpretation: "Did you
not, however, have recourse (ולתרוצי) to an interpretation
(מתרצת)? You might as well interpret (תריץ) . . ." Lastly,
Silberman notes the medieval Hebrew תרוץ, "an answer to a
difficult question."

Brownlee adds to these suggestions of his own:[63] he
compares the root רצח, which in the *hiph°il* may mean "to arrange
subjects for debate, to discourse:" to make ירוץ an understandable pun on רצח the commentator would have had to have read יָרִיץ,
possible through the ambiguity of *wāw* and *yôd* in the scroll. To
that reading might have been added a pun on יליץ, "he may
interpret."[64] Furthermore a verbal play on the letters רץ might
also yield the suggestion for רז, for the Teacher's interpretations divulge the mysteries (רזי) unknown to Habakkuk.[65] Which
one or more of all these possibilities approximates something
that was in the mind of the interpreter at Qumran? The answer
is most likely beyond our present understanding of the text, but
surely there was some association of commentary with lemma akin
to the proposals outlined above.

C. 1QM 10:1-8

J. Carmignac was the first to describe the allusions to and
citations of scripture in 1QM.[66] He noted that there were five
explicit quotations of the Bible; three of these occur close
together in column 10 of the scroll and are worthy of study in
relation to one another. All three quotations occur within the

discourse of the High Priest to be used before the
eschatological battle.

    1) 1QM 10:1-2 (Deut 7:21): "And as (Moses) declared to
us that 'You are in our midst (בקרבנו) a great and terrible
God, causing all our enemies (אויבינו) to flee before us'."

    Only the first part of the quotation is represented in MT's
Deut 7:21: כי יהוה אלהיך בקרבך אל גדול ונורא with the persons
variously changed.[67] The latter half of the quotation has been
otherwise described as an adaptation of Deut 7:22 (ונשל),[68]
Deut 23:15 (לחת איביך לפנר),[69] or Deut 6:19 (להדף את כל איביך)
(מפניר).[70] The quotation could be an indirect summary of these
several passages.[71]

    2) 1QM 10:2-5 (Deut 20:2-5): "And he taught our generations
from of old saying, 'When you draw near to battle (בקרבכם למלחמה),
the priest shall stand and speak to the people saying, "Hear,
O Israel, you are drawing near to battle today (קרבים היום
למלחמה) against your enemies (אויביכמה). Do not fear, do not let
your heart waver, do not be terrified and do not be horror-struck
before them, for your God walks with you to fight (להלחם) for you
against your enemies (אויביכם) to save you." And our officers
shall speak to all those prepared for the battle'."[72]

    The citation of Deut 20:2-5 in 1QM 10:2-5 is very close to
the text of the MT; there are a few minor differences of word
order and vocabulary. In relation to Deut 7:21 it can be seen
that קרב occurs in both: בקרבנו in Deut 7:21 (1QM 10:1), בקרבכם
and קרבים in Deut 20:2, 3 (1QM 10:2, 3). Furthermore, the use
of אויב in Deut 20:3, 4 (1QM 10:3, 4) may provide a link with
the phrase in which that word occurs in 1QM 10:1 and which is
attached to Deut 7:21 in the form of being part of the quotation.

3) 1QM 10:6-8 (Num 10:9): "And that which you spoke
through Moses, 'When war (מלחמה) comes[73] in your land against
the oppressor who oppresses you, you shall blow on the trumpets
and you shall be remembered before your God and saved from your
enemies (מאויבכם)'."

This quotation, different only in orthography from the MT,
provides the interpretation of Deut 20:5 by describing what the
captains of the eschatological army are to say. But the link
between the two quotations is more than one of general content
alone; rather, it is through the occurrence of the word מלחמה
in Num 10:9 that this quotation is most suitably attached to
that of Deut 20:2-5. The analogy of vocabulary enables the use
of the particular text of Numbers.

From this it can be seen that the phrases בקרבכם למלחמה
(Deut 20:2; 1QM 10:2) and קרבים היום למלחמה (Deut 20:3; 1QM 10:3)
are the means whereby the citation of Deut 20:2-5 is attached to
and used as an interpretation of Deut 7:21: the priest exhorts
the army not to fear because of the presence of God with them.
Also those phrases enable the development and interpretation of
Deut 20:5 by means of Num 10:9, relating what the captains say.

The dependence on one another of the three biblical
quotations of 1QM 10:1-8 and the method through which they are
linked by their analogous terminology is an example of the use
of the exegetical technique of *gĕzērâ šāwâ*.[74] Thus both Deut
20:2-5 and Num 10:9 are interdependent interpretations of the
first text, Deut 7:21, since, although Num 10:9 is closely
linked to Deut 20:2-5 in the scroll, it can be connected with
Deut 7:21 (in its version quoted in 1QM 10:1) by their common
terminology, אויבינו (1QM 10:1) and מאויבכם (1QM 10:8). With

this understanding Deut 20:2-5 interprets Deut 7:21 concerning
the lack of fear that the presence of God brings with it,[75]
while Num 10:9 develops the second half of the quotation in
1QM 10:1-2 through the declaration that at the trumpet blow
God will save the covenanters from their *enemies*.[76]

D. 1QS 2.2-4 [77]

The expanded Aaronic benediction of Num 6:24-26 in 1QS
has received considerable treatment from scholars, largely
because of its position within the Manual of Discipline where
it functions in a traditional manner as part of an overall
section concerned with the community's covenant ceremony,[78] be
it either the annual renewal of the covenant or the ceremony at
which new members were initiated into the covenant or both.[79]
With all the scholarly discussion of the passage, however,
there has been no ascertainable elucidation of the use of the
Bible as the means whereby the benediction receives its expansion.[80]

To answer how the text of Numbers was enlarged requires a
detailed analysis of the three lines under consideration.
They read:

יברככה בכול טוב וישמורכה מכול רע

ויאר לבכה בשכל חיים ויחונכה בדעת עולמים

וישא פני חסדיו לכה לשלום עולמים

"May He bless you with all good and keep you from all evil.
May He enlighten your heart with life-giving wisdom and grant
you eternal knowledge. May He raise his merciful face towards
you for everlasting peace."[81]

Far from being simply an *ad hoc* treatment of the biblical
benediction, each phrase has received interpretative additions

in the following way.

1) To יברכך of Num 6:24 is added the phrase בכול טוב.
Surprisingly, כל טוב and its corollaries is very infrequent
in the Hebrew Bible,[82] and only once does it occur with the
preposition ב, at Deut 26:11: בכל הטוב. Although the article
on טוב is not represented in 1QS 2:2, neither is it represented
in the use of the aprepositional phrase in Ps 34:11 and could,
therefore, be a minor textual variant in the book of Deuteronomy
present at Qumran.[83] It seems highly probable that the person
who expanded this whole phrase was citing Deut 26:11 in the
version he knew. O. Betz prefers to see an allusion to Deut 30:15
at this point, and throughout 1QS 2:2-3, because of the occurrence
of החיים, הטוב and הרע in that verse and in 1QS; yet the more
direct citation of Deut 26:11 and the accountability of the
other expansions through other biblical texts would seem to
lessen the suitability of Deut 30:15 at this point.[84]

2) Many scholars have pointed out that the second phrase
of the expanded benediction is comparable to Ps 121:7.[85] In
fact, with the expected orthographic variants it is a direct
citation of that psalm as represented in the MT tradition.[86]
Together with יאר of the following stich there is a play on
words: while the Lord keeps (שמר) and enlightens (אור) the
covenanter, he attends to (שמר) the destruction of and curses
(ארר) those who follow Belial (1QS 2:6-7).[87]

3) Num 6:25a reads, יאר יהוה פניו אליך; the phrase לבכה
בשכל חיים has therefore been added and substituted in 1QS 2:3,
at least for the text tradition of MT and LXX. The only passage
in the Hebrew Bible where שכל and חיים occur together is Prov
16:22a[88] which phrase reads in MT: מקור חיים שכל בעליו.

Literally translated this becomes, "The good sense of those
who possess it is a fountain of life."[89] Yet the phrase in the
LXX, πηγὴ ζωῆς ἔννοια τοῖς κεκτημένοις, may suppose a Hebrew
Vorlage of מקור חיים שכל לבעליו.[90] Herein lies the key to
the expansion of Num 6:25a in 1QS 2:3, for, taken together with
Prov 16:21 and 23 in both of which verses לב occurs, it seems
probable that the author of the expanded benediction understood
Prov 16:21 through the deliberate division of לבעליו, a use of
nôṭārîqôn, into לב and עליו. He therefore read the verse either
as "prudence of mind is a fountain of life upon him (i.e. the
man of discernment of Prov 16:21)," or by seeing מקור as מְקיר -
possible since *wāw* and *yôd* are very alike in contemporary script -
the phrase could be understood as "prudence of mind causes life
to gush upon it (i.e. the mind)," or, "upon him (i.e. the man
of 16:21 again)." With the suffix of the preposition אל translated to לב in 1QS 2:3, all three words of the expansion, לבכה
בשכל חיים are derivable from Prov 16:22.[91]

4) To ויחנך of Num 6:25b is added בדעת עולמים.[92] This
phrase does not occur in the Hebrew Bible but the aura of wisdom
that the phrase has and which makes it a "complementary cor-
relative"[93] to the use of Prov 16:22 in expanding Num 6:25a is
the result of a combination of words and ideas that may ultimately
derive from Jer 31:31-34.[94] In Jer 31:33 the law is to be written
on the heart (לבם) and "no longer shall each man teach his
neighbour and each his brother, saying, 'Know (דעו) the Lord,'
for they shall all know (ידעו) me, from the least of them to the
greatest, says the Lord" *(RSV)*. The correlation of Jer 31:31-34
with Prov 16:22 at this point comes through the occurrence of
לב in both passages; the use of Jer 31:31-34 here to link the

phrases of the expanded benediction almost amounts to practice
of *gĕzērâ šāwâ*. The eternal aspect of the knowledge[95] is
implied from the context of Jeremiah and may also have been
introduced because of the use of עולמים in the expansion of
Num 6:26 that follows in 1QS 2:4.

5) Num 6:26 is altered considerably: with the excision
of וישם the two clauses of the MT are reduced to one; the subject,
יהוה, is also not mentioned specifically.[96] To what is left are
added חסדיו, the preposition ל, and עולמים: put together in the
order in which they are used in 1QS 2:4, it is clear that the
refrain כי חסדו לעולם has been put in the plural in both its
parts and split up. This refrain belongs most overtly to Psalms
105, 106, 118 and 136, but it is also echoed extensively
elsewhere.[97] It is, therefore, not surprising that the expansion
maintains the unity of this allusion in reducing the number of
clauses of Num 6:26 from two to one.[98]

These five alterations of the text produce a benediction
that contains three lines with five clauses over against the
three sets of parallel clauses in the MT.[99] Although the
deliberate omissions and additions are suggestive of an adjustment
of the text so that there would be 18 words in the blessing,[100]
O. Lehmann forces the text of 1QS when he claims that the
expanded benediction has six stanzas of three stresses each,
for it cannot be avoided, unless one exclude a word, that the
middle pair of clauses is either 3:2 or 4:3, not 3:3.[101]

Rather than being an adaptation to certain number symbolism,
the use of these five biblical texts as expansions of the
benediction of Num 6:24-26 is a clear example of the exegetical
technique of '*asmaktâ*, the use of biblical citations and allusions

to support a biblical quotation. But why should the Aaronic
blessing require support at this point? A complete understanding
of the use of 'asmaktâ can only come from some further remarks
on the context of 1QS in which the expanded blessing occurs.

Although scholars soon noticed the liturgical correspondence
of 1QS 1:16-2:25a to a covenant ceremony,[102] it was several
years before the section received detailed treatment, and the
benediction within that section. O. Betz brought to light the
way in which the expansions to the blessing emphasized the
nature of the blessing over against the curses that are for
Belial and his own which follow; Betz also noted the way in which
the additions pointed to the eschatological life in which the
members of the Qumran community believed themselves to be, in
part at least, already participating.[103] But although he observed
"die midraschartige Veränderung der einzelnen Aussagen,"[104] Betz
failed to describe the change exactly.

M. Weise[105] has similarly shown the setting of the blessing
to be antithetical to the curse that follows. For Num 6:24 he
notes the dualistic stress of the expansion as characteristic of
Qumran,[106] and he clearly expounds with quotations from Qumran
literature the use of יאר in 1QS 2:3, whereby it is no longer
God who lightens his own face but rather He enlightens the heart
(mind) of the blessed.[107] Furthermore Weise expounds שכל חיים
without mention of Prov 16:22; he prefers to understand the
phrase solely on the comparative basis of the Qumran texts from
which he derives the notion that שכל חיים is the gift of God and
his Torah,[108] as is דעת, and דעת is not only an expression of a
wisdom theme but also forms part of the dualistic vocabulary of
Qumran.[109] Weise's most important contribution, however, to the

understanding of the Aaronic benediction in its expanded form
is his observation that not only is Torah a frequent illuminating
agent in Jewish liturgical texts, but that those texts are
themselves frequently expansions or adaptations of the Aaronic
blessing.[110] Weise thus establishes that at least during
tannaitic times there was a *liturgical* tradition of the adaptation
of Num 6:24-26, and 1QS 2:2-4 most probably belonged in the
mainstream of that tradition; such liturgical formulation he
considers traceable to texts like Ps 67:2 and Ps 119:29.[111]

K. Baltzer has also outlined the covenant liturgy as it is
represented in prose form in 1QS 1:18-2:18[112] and he sees it as
the only testimony there is for the actual liturgical order of
a covenant ceremony that might have taken place in post-exilic
times - not that there was a regular covenant ceremony in
normative post-exilic judaism attached to the celebration of a
particular festival (either Weeks or Booths)[113] but that such
a covenant ceremony was celebrated whenever the need for it was
felt. At Qumran the covenant liturgy was to be used every year
(1QS 3:19) while the dominion of Belial lasted.

From these remarks and from the identification of the
expanding phrases in Num 6:24-26 proposed above the most probable
conclusion is that 1QS 2:2-4 is no *ad hoc* interpretative passage,
but that the additions themselves are dependent upon the covenant
liturgy that may or may not be associated with a major feast day
at Qumran. Thus Deut 26:11 is from the "creed" associated with
the offering of first fruits[114] (Feast of Weeks); it is then
followed in Deuteronomy 27 by the command of Moses to those who
have "become the people of the Lord your God" that they keep all
God's commandments and statutes (Deut 27:9-10). This in turn is

followed by the set of twelve curses (Deut 27:15-26; cf.
1QS 2:5-9) to which all the people say, "Amen" (Deut 27:26;
cf. 1QS 2:10).

Similarly Ps 121:7 is a quotation from one of the "songs
of ascent,"[115] and the Psalm is so classified at 11QPss[a] 3:1.
These songs were most likely used by those on their way to
Jerusalem for one of the major feast days,[116] or, as Mowinckel
understands it, the psalm was part of the great festal procession
of the early harvest festival.[117] The use of Prov 16:22, too,
not only shows up the antithesis between the foolish and the
wise (the cursed and the blessed) but also, as Weise has shown,
it reflects the liturgical application of the theological
understanding of the Torah with which wisdom through various
particular words was associated. Jer 31:31-34 shares such
wisdom traits in its use of "knowledge" but it is primarily
connected to the ceremony of covenant renewal through its talk
of the "new covenant." And lastly the basis of the adaptation
of כי חסדו לעולם is most likely to be found in either Psalm 105
or 106. Both these Psalms have been variously connected with the
covenant ceremony.[118]

In conclusion, therefore, 1QS 2:2-4 is not simply the
elucidation of Num 6:24-26 through cross-references. Rather it
shows the midrashic validation of the use of the Aaronic blessing
at the covenant ceremony through the support (*'asmaktâ*) given it
by its expansion with texts or allusions to biblical texts that
could certainly be reminiscent of the covenant ceremony of old
if not in actual fact themselves texts used in the liturgy of
that ceremony.

E. CD 7.13b-8.1a

It has already been noticed that Amos 9:11 is quoted at
both 4QFlor 1:12 and CD 7:16. Its quotation in CD occurs in
the so-called "Amos-Numbers Midrash" which is present only in
Text A (CD 7:13b-8:1a).[119] Much has been written on the
literary construction of CD, especially columns 6-8,[120] but
the most plausible theory yet proposed in relation to the
literary history surrounding the Amos-Numbers Midrash is that
of J. Murphy-O'Connor.[121] His overall suggestions will be
considered summarily before a detailed investigation of the
Amos-Numbers Midrash itself.

In analyzing CD 6:2-8:3 Murphy-O'Connor concluded that it
contained two distinct literary units, 6:2-11a (the Well Midrash)
and 6:11b-8:3a.[122] The second of these he suggested contained
a list of precepts (6:11b-7:4a) and a hortatory epilogue (7:4b-
8:3) which is designed to motivate obedience to the precepts and
itself has two parts: a promise (7:4-6) and a warning (7:9-8:3).[123]
Having extracted 7:6b-8 and 7:13b-8:1a, Murphy-O'Connor demonstrates that 6:11b-8:3a forms a complete literary unit. His
decision to describe 7:13b-8:1a (the Amos-Numbers Midrash) as an
interpolation rests primarily upon his comparative analysis of
Texts A and B at this point.

In a separate article[124] Murphy-O'Connor compared Text A
(7:9-8:3) with Text B (19:5-14) and, far from ending up in the
same state of bewilderment as Carmignac,[125] he proposes to
reconstruct an original text consisting of 7:9-13b followed by
19:7b-14 from which both A and B diverge in explicable ways.[126]
Prior to the identification of such an original text, however,
is Murphy-O'Connor's conclusion that 7:13b-8:1a is an interpolation

inserted into an already divergent A text. The interpolation
is pointed to by the repetition of the phrase הנסוגים הוסגרו
לחרב in 7:13 and 8:1,[127] neatly bracketing the Amos-Numbers
Midrash. Furthermore, the concluding phrase of the interpolation
is a redactional summary statement whereby the sense of the
passage is brought back in line with what is to follow in 8:1b-3
and later.[128]

Having exercised the Amos-Numbers Midrash in the way
described, Murphy-O'Connor outlines his original text of 7:9-13b
+ 19:7b-14. The Zechariah quotation and its complete explanation
(19:7-13a) is lacking in A through haplography, the occurrence
of the phrase הוסגרו לחרב at 7:13b and 19:13a resulting in an
accidental omission. The Amos-Numbers Midrash was inserted after
the Zechariah material had dropped out to provide for the theme
of salvation needed to counterbalance 7:13b.[129] As for the text
of B, that it does not contain the Amos-Numbers Midrash is no
longer a problem; the absence of the Isaiah quotation preceding
that from Zechariah is to be accounted for through the similarity
of their respective introductory formulae.[130]

All this appears as the best proposal to date for explaining
the different texts of A and B at this point. Yet one wonders
whether or not such a large number of scribal accidents is so
very accidental. When it is considered that the very same phrase
is both the redactional sign for an interpolation and also the
cause of the omission of the Zechariah quotation from Text A,
the coincidence seems too great. Furthermore, the reason that
Murphy-O'Connor gives for the inclusion of the interpolated Amos-
Numbers Midrash is somewhat weak: maintenance of "the theme of
salvation."[131]

In the quotation of 2 Sam 7:11-14 in 4QFlor we have
observed that what appears to be a scribal error is in fact the
deliberate use of homoeoteleuton to edit a text; in like manner
the original text of CD that Murphy-O'Connor sets up appears to
have been deliberately adjusted. At the same time as the
Zechariah material was omitted by the original scribe of Text A,
the Amos-Numbers Midrash was included.

Moreover, the content provides the reason for the deliberate
switch of material. In CD 19:10-11 what we may suppose was the
original text talked of the "Messiah of Aaron and Israel."[132]
The later A text, on the other hand, was written by somebody
with different messianic expectations. The analysis of the Amos-
Numbers Midrash that follows below shows that two eschatological
figures were expected and that it is very likely that these two
were considered equally as Messiahs.

With the various redactional material isolated and with
recognition that even in the redaction itself there has been
the deliberate use of an exegetical principle, an analysis of
the Amos-Numbers Midrash can be offered from which some further
comments will be made. The redactional material is excluded
from the unit that is here analyzed.

Qumran Midrash of Amos 5:27 with insertion   CD 7:14b-21a
of 5:26a$^{\alpha 2-\beta}$

I. Quotation of Amos 5:27 with insertion   14b-15a

II. Interpretation
    A. Concerning סוכת מלככם   15b-21a
        1. Statement of identification
                סוכת המלך ⟵ ספרי התורה

2. 2 appositional statements of explanation

   a. Comparison

      1) Introductory formula

      2) Quotation (Amos 9:11a$^{\beta}$)

   b. Identification המלך ←—— הקהל

B. Concerning כיון צלמיכם

   1. Statement of identification

      כיון הצלמים ←—— ספרי הנביאים

   2. Statement of explanation (relative clause)

C. Concerning הכוכב

   1. Statement of identification

      הכוכב ←—— דורש התורה

   2. Statement of explanation (relative clause expanded)

      a. Relative clause proper

      b. Expansion

         1) Introductory formula

         2) Quotation with explanation

            a) Quotation (Num 24:17b$^{\alpha}$)

            b) Explanation

               (1) Statement of identification

                  השבט ←—— נשיא כל העדה

               (2) Further description

                  (a) Protasis: temporal clause

                  (b) Apodosis: quotation (Num 24:17b$^{\gamma}$)

Exegetical principles can be observed at work at the very beginning of the unit in the quotation from Amos 5. The first word is from Amos 5:27; we can therefore suppose that it is that verse which is cited. Through *nôtārîqôn* אתכם is taken as an

inclusive abbreviation of phrases from the previous verse:
two are included at this point, את סכות מלככם and את כיון צלמיכם.
The phrase concerning the star is not included in the citation
since it cannot fully subscribe to the exegetical device and, in
any case, is appositional to the second phrase;[133] the interpreter
wishes to understand it apart from the other two subjects, as
the three-part interpretation makes clear.[134]

Also, the MT's מהלאה ל is altered to מאהלי, a possible use
of the technique of *'al tiqrē'* to produce an understanding such
as that proposed by C. Rabin: "from My tent to Damascus."[135]
For P. R. Davies this alteration was made to show that the tent
of God, that is, the Sanctuary, is the Temple from which the law
has been exiled.[136] In any case these various explanations of
the Amos text as cited in CD seem far preferable to some such
comment as R. H. Charles' to the effect that CD's differences
from the MT were due to the accidents of copyists.[137]

The three parts of the interpretation also give ample
testimony to the use of exegetical principles. In the first
subsection, concerning סכות מלככם, there is initially a statement
in which the books of the Law are identified with the Tabernacle
of the king; that is, the Tabernacle represents the books of the
Law, since the king is later identified with the congregation.
The exact basis for this first identification is not known, but
because it is solely the סוכת which is interpreted as the תורה,
one might suggest that it was the final letter of סוכת that is
the clue to the equation.[138] Support for such a proposal comes
from כיון, if it should prove to be a similar pointer towards
the books of the prophets (נביאים).

The first of the two appositional statements of explanation

is a citation of Amos 9:11.[139] It is linked with the main
quotation of Amos 5:27 through *gĕzērâ šāwâ*, סכות being taken
as סוכת. The identification of the king with the assembly (קהל)
is difficult to trace to a biblical source;[140] it may simply
have been a traditional exegesis derived from the Aramaic (also
Akkadian) use of the root מלך to signify "taking council." The
קהל (council? 1QSa) is the source of counsel in its correct
interpretation of the Law. Rabin has suggested that here we
have a midrash that has been abbreviated from "the king is the
prince of all the congregation."[141] Davies has made the
attractive proposal that the קהל is best considered as the
worshipping congregation: the Law has been exiled to the
community's place of worship from the previous place of worship,
the Temple.[142]

In the second part of the three-part identification כיון
צלמיכם is identified with the books of the prophets. Mention
has already been made of a possible abbreviation at this point.
The midrash may be based, however, on an anagram, צלמים being
read as מליצים, "interpreters" or "intermediaries."[143] This is
attractive from the point of view of the explanation that follows,
since ליץ normally means "to scorn" or "to despise." The
explanation of the books of the prophets is that Israel despised
(בזה) their words.[144] Or again, Dupont-Sommer suggests that as
סכות was read as סוכת, so כיון can be read as כִּיּוּן, "fidélité;"
the books of the prophets are faithful images of the Law.[145]

The third part of the interpretation is based on the
identification of the star. Just as the pesher on Psalms 1 and 2
in 4QFlor presupposes more than the text of the psalms that is
quoted, so here the interpretation can be concerned with elements

close to the quoted scriptural section that are not themselves
actually cited. In support of the midrash cited here Num 24:17bᵅ
is quoted through *gĕzêrâ šāwâ* (כוכב) and from the explanation
that follows it is clear that the Numbers passage is understood
as referring to two figures.[146]

From an understanding of the redactional use of certain
principles of exegesis and from the analysis of the Amos-Numbers
Midrash above it is possible to suggest that the messianic
expectations of the community changed in the course of time,[147]
and that such change can be observed in the literary development
of a single document. Thus the Amos-Numbers Midrash (two Messiahs)
is substituted in a later version (Text A) of the original text
of CD for the Zechariah material (one Messiah) that is preserved
in another version (Text B). If משיחו in the phrases ביד משיחו
רוח קדשו (CD 2:12) and וגם במשיחו הקודש (CD 6:1) is taken to
refer to the prophets, as is quite possible[148] and as Rabin[149]
and others suggest,[150] then the expectation of the editor of
Text A[1] may be considered as of two Messiahs, while the copyist
of Text B expected only one.[151]

Although the messianic expectation of CD will never be known
exactly, partly because the precise significance of the term
משיח for the covenanters cannot be known, there may be a road
toward the understanding of CD's messianism that lies between
the insistence on the one hand that CD talks of only one Messiah[152]
and on the other that there is nothing against taking all the
references in CD as referring to two Messiahs.[153] Furthermore,
in a more restricted way, the recognition of the use of certain
exegetical principles has pointed to a clearer understanding of
the method of the composition of the Amos-Numbers Midrash. The

understanding of early Jewish exegesis that has been brought
to this text, as to 4QFlor, helps with both redactional and
interpretative problems, helps to give reasons why
various materials were included and others excluded.

F. 4QTest

4QFlor Fragments 6-11 contain several verses from
Deuteronomy 33, some of which appear to be accompanied by
interpretation. Fragments 6 and 7 include Deut 33:8-11; these
verses occur again in 4QTest 14-20. Apart from various textual
problems[154] which are unfortunately increased by the damage to
the right hand bottom corner of the text, study of 4QTest has
been concerned with its literary genre, its messianism and its
possible historical allusions.

Those concerned with the genre of the piece have been eager
to discuss it as an exemplar of a pre-Christian testimonial
document from which support can be given to earlier theories
represented, above all, in the work of Rendel Harris.[155] The
most comprehensive analysis of the several positions with which
4QTest must now be reckoned is still that of J. A. Fitzmyer.[156]
Other scholars have added little to his work except in as much
as they use 4QTest as exemplary for collections of texts in
other documents.[157]

Scholars interested in the messianism represented in the
collection of texts in 4QTest fall into two groups. On the one
hand there are those who follow Allegro's original proposal
that Exod 20:21 (Sam),[158] Num 24:15-17 and Deut 33:8-11 refer
to the prophetic, kingly and priestly functions of the Messiah(s).[159]
On the other hand the three texts are often taken separately as

referring to three eschatological figures: the prophet, the
Messiah of Israel and the Messiah of Aaron. This is the view
of Dupont-Sommer,[160] van der Woude,[161] Vermes,[162] and others.[163]
Fitzmyer notes and accedes to this latter majority opinion but
he warns that care should be taken in relation to Num 24:15-17,
since in CD 7:18-20 it is applied to two figures and not solely
to the Messiah of Israel.[164]

In relation to the historical allusions that may exist in
4QTest, scholarly attention has been focused mainly on the last
part of the document which contains a citation from Josh 6:26
and commentary. The whole section (4QTest 21-30) is represented
in the Psalms of Joshua whose partially preserved text (4QPssJosh)
enables several restorations to be made in corresponding places
in 4QTest. Yet at one important point in line 25 the text
remains fragmentary. The phrase in question reads: [24]ועמד
[25]חמס כלי שניהמה יות [לה ....] מ [.... Nearly all scholars
restore some such phrase as Milik's: "And he stood forth / and
(made his sons) rulers and both of them became vessels of
violence."[165] Vermes prefers to understand שניהמה as referring
to a total of two people and so proposes reading, "And (his
brother) arose (and ruled), both being instruments of violence."[166]
It would appear, however, that the majority opinion is more likely
to be correct since the quotation of Josh 6:26 mentions three
people: the accursed, the first-born and the youngest son.

According to Allegro's original publication the three people
are to be identified as Alexander Jannaeus (ruled 103-76 B.C.)
and his two sons, Hyrcanus II (76-40 B.C.) and Aristobulus II
(67-63 B.C.).[167] Milik attempts to show that the reference is
to Mattathias, father of Simon and Jonathan.[168] Cross argues

strongly for equating the accursed man with Simon (ruled
143-135 B.C.) and the vessels of violence would then be Judas
and Mattathias, two of Simon's sons who died with him at Doq
near Jericho in 135 B.C.[169] Although Cross' theory accounts
for many historical details, still a fourth and possible
proposal has been made by O. Betz.[170] He is in favour of
identifying the Wicked Priest, the man accursed, with John
Hyrcanus I (135-105 B.C.), the other members of the trio being
his two sons Aristobulus I (104 B.C.) and Alexander Jannaeus.[171]
To this Brownlee adds that since the Joshua material almost
certainly refers to actual historical figures, so also the
prophet described in Deut 18:18 may be the Righteous Teacher.[172]

Whatever the answers may be to all these questions, this
present study intends rather to look at the composition of
4QTest; from such an investigation others may draw support for
their various conclusions. The significant aspect of 4QTest
from the compositional point of view is that it appears as an
independent document of one column; as a unit we can clearly see
its beginning and its end, even though there is some damage to
the bottom right hand corner of the text. The following structural
outline is offered for the unit.

*4QTestimonia The cast of the eschatological struggle
and reckoning*

I. Those favoured by God   4QTest 1-20
   A. Exod 20:21 (Sam)   1-8
      1. Introductory formula
      2. Yahweh speech proper
         a. Concerning Yahweh's attitude to the
            people (MT: Deut 5:28b-29)

1) Concerning the correctness (הטיב)

   of their words

2) Wish for their continual well-being (הטיב)

b. Concerning future action with the prophet

   (MT: Deut 18:18-19)

   1) Raise him up

   2) Put words in his mouth

   3) Require account of those who do not

      heed him

B. Num 24:15-17   9-13

   1. Introductory formula

   2. Oracle

      a. Announcement

      b. Oracle proper

         1) Concerning הגבר

         2) Concerning כוכב and שבט

C. Deut 33:8-11   14-20

   1. Introductory formula

   2. Content of blessing

      a. Command

      b. Statement of future work of priesthood

         1) To cause precepts to shine to Jacob,

            Law to Israel

         2) To offer incense and burnt offerings

      c. Blessing proper

         1) Blessing

         2) Request for smiting of haters

II. Those cursed by God   21-30

    A. Introduction

B. Quotation and Commentary (4QPssJosh)

    1. Josh 6:26b (less את יריחו = LXX)

    2. Commentary

        a. Concerning the accursed man

            1) Announcement of existence of man
               of Belial

            2) Description of purpose of existence

               a) To be a fowler's net to his people

               b) To be a cause of destruction of
                  his neighbours

b. Concerning two sons	(or) b. Concerning one
1) Identification as	brother
vessels of	a. + b. Actions of the
violence	two as vessels
2) Their actions	of violence

The text as a whole lists, and to an extent implies description of, those involved in the affairs of the latter days, the cast of the eschatological struggle. The document has two parts: in the first those favoured by God are mentioned, in the second are those cursed by him. Since the second part is shorter, we may more easily discuss its structure, especially as that may have bearing upon the first part which is composed solely of three biblical citations.

After an introduction part two is developed according to the Psalms of Joshua in commentary upon Josh 6:26b. Firstly there is a clear description of the existence and purposes of the accursed man, the "one of Belial." The second half of the commentary is fragmentary and depending upon the way in which restoration is made in line 25, alternative structures can be

given. If the text is understood of two sons, then the second
half is simply notice of their existence as vessels of violence
followed by description of their violent actions. If the text
is seen to refer to one figure, then after mentioning him, the
rest of the column deals with the joint actions of the accursed
man and the second figure (represented as a. + b.). Because
the Joshua quotation speaks of three people and because the
reading of three figures makes better sense syntactically, the
first alternative and simpler structure is to be preferred.

This most likely reference to three figures and the people
with which they are involved should be kept in mind when treating
the content of the first major part of 4QTest. It contains three
scriptural quotations: Exod 20:21 according to the Samaritan
version,[173] Num 24:15-17 and Deut 33:8-11. There is no commentary
between these citations and so the questions of most importance
concern why these three quotations in particular were chosen and
why they are in the order that they are.

In relation to the section on those cursed by God it is
noteworthy that the three quotations in the first section have
in common a note of doom for those who do not listen to the words
of the prophet, those who are the "temples of Moab" or the
"children of Sheth," or who are the enemies of the blessed
priest(hood). Yet, if this destruction is the major concern of
the collection of texts, then since all three quotations mention
it, one cannot but ask why it is that only one text was not
quoted, and perhaps one that would have been more suited to the
purpose of describing destruction than any of those mentioned.

Rather, the inclusion of three citations suggests that each
serves a specific purpose. Unless it is that the three are

ordered according to their appearance in the Pentateuch, a
possibility that it is difficult to deny outright, then it is
the order of the quotations that points towards their various
functions. Over against those cursed by God the author would
have included in his first section on those favoured by God
mention of the agent through whom the destruction of the cursed
would be achieved, which destruction is indeed an element of
commonality between the three biblical texts. Such antithesis
would not necessarily reflect person-to-person combat, but could
be merely one of the supporters of Yahweh against those of Belial.

The general Jewish expectation, certainly shared by the
Qumran covenanters, was that such an eschatological struggle
would be lead by a princely Messiah, an anointed individual who
would save Israel; neither prophet nor priest would have a direct
part to play in the battle. One could suggest, therefore, that
the quotation of Num 24:15-17 was sufficient in itself, as
portraying the messianic prince, to balance the second section
concerning the accursed of God and their followers.

That Num 24:15-17 should be preceded and followed by
quotations implies that in some way it required elucidation or
clarification. Comparative study shows that it is very likely
that in two places the Numbers quotation would require further
comment, achieved here through the citation of additional biblical
material. The first of these is the term גבר. G. Vermes has
pointed most clearly to the ambiguity of this term as encountered
in the MT text-type by the versions.[174] For 1QH 3:7-10 and
1QS 4:20-22, in both of which passages גבר occurs, Vermes
analyzes the other possible messianic terms used and concludes
that the various usages point to "two different figures: 1) a

King Messiah (*Geber* and its synonyms) and 2) a messianic
Teacher (crucible and its parallels)."[175] And yet Vermes also
stresses that in Palestinian exegesis there is a noticeable
inclination to attach a teaching mission to the גבר.[176]

Such ambiguity in the term גבר within Qumran literature
itself is highlighted by the oscillating opinion of W. H. Brownlee.
In 1954[177] he hinted at the messianic significance of גבר in
1QS 4:20 in relation to his reading at that time of 1QH 3:7-10.
In 1964,[178] having considered many alternative possibilities, he
proposed that in 1QS 4:20 גבר refers to the Teacher of Righteousness and in 1QH 3:5-10 to the personified sectarian society; he
concludes that there is a "thematic agreement between the
emergence of the *gever* as a corporate figure and also as the
eschatological prophet"[179] since both must pass through the
refining furnace of affliction. More recently, in 1966,[180]
Brownlee adjusted his opinion in light of the description of
David in 11QPs[a] 27:2-4 as a sage, full of insight, and so concludes
that the גבר in 1QS 4:20-22 and 1QH 3:7-10 is to be understood
from the aspect of his wisdom role as the individual Messiah of
Israel. Lastly in 1972 Brownlee noted that at least for 4QTest
גבר refers to the future prophet since in the text of Numbers
24 גבר is applied by Balaam to himself.[181]

In light of this one can only propose that it may be pre-
mature for any scholar to suppose that there is a uniform use of
the term גבר in Qumran literature. It could be used either of
the King or of the eschatological prophet in early Jewish
literature and the Qumran scrolls seem to reflect such ambiguity.
As it stands, גבר in Num 24:15-16 refers to the prophet Balaam,
and the author of 4QTest, while not denying the ambiguity, wanted

to ensure that the term be understood as referring to the eschatological prophet.[182]

To ensure that the prophet was included in his role as teacher the author placed Sam. Exod 20:21[183] in front of the Numbers quotation. He put it there either because of the order of the Pentateuch itself or because the prophet was temporarily to precede the Messiah of Israel or because of the analogous concern of the two passages that the word of God should be heard.[184] Likewise the terms analogous to one another in Num 24:15-17 and Deut 33:8-11, and in Deut 33:8-11 and the PssJosh material can be used to support the literary construction of the order of those texts.

The second ambiguous passage of Num 24:15-17 occurs in the second part of the oracle where the talk is of the star and the sceptre. Normally taken as referring to one figure,[185] the author of 4QTest was almost certainly aware of the tradition witnessed by CD A 7:18-20, that the star was the eschatological Interpreter of the Law (whose high priestly status now seems secure), while the sceptre and the activity of the destruction of the children of Seth were understood in relation to the kingly Messiah of David. In order to make certain that the priestly Messiah was not overlooked, the author included the section from Deuteronomy 33 in which, along with mention of the symbols of the priest's office, there is a statement of the future work of the priesthood. One of the tasks of the priest will be to make the precepts shine (the work of a star?)[186] for Jacob and the Law for Israel; this function of the messianic priest is also described specifically in 4QpIsa[a] frgs. 8-10:24.[187]

The final part of the quotation from Deuteronomy 33 concludes

with the request of Yahweh that those who hate the priest be
smitten (מחץ). Together with mention of Jacob and Israel it is
the smiting which can be seen as a link-word between Num 24:15-17
and Deut 33:8-11 for it also occurs in Num 24:17. Also, whether
one restores "brother" or "sons" in line 25, such terms could be
the catchword links between Deut 33:8-11 and the 4QPssJosh
material;[188] both "brother" and "sons" occur in Deut 33:9. It
is also interesting to note that just as in 1QS 2:3, part of a
blessing, there is the verb יאר followed in 1QS 2:5 by ארור, so
in 4QTest 17 יאירו occurs before ארור of lines 22 and 23.[189]
That may represent yet another reason for the present order of
the texts in 4QTest.

    Overall it can be said that the structure of the first part
of 4QTest concerning those favoured by God shows that the three
texts quoted therein are interdependent in as much as they
represent a particular understanding of the participants in the
eschatological struggle.[190] Such interdependence rests on the
collector's desire to clarify the messianic text of Numbers 24.
Taking the first three citations alone, it seems as if it is not
necessary to suppose the existence of a testimonial document from
which they are copied. If the fourth quotation of Joshua material
is included, it is possible to understand the whole document in
a testimonial role, for then reasons can be given for the
exclusion of certain messianic texts (e.g., Genesis 49).

    In sum, the two major parts of 4QTest form a unit of texts
that lists the cast of the eschatological struggle. Those
favoured by God are the people who listen to his prophet, the
prophet himself, the kingly Messiah and the priest; those to be
destroyed are the people who follow or are ensnared by the

accursed man of Belial and his sons or brother and these
figures (antichrists) themselves. If three figures are cursed,
then there is an attractive balance with the three eschatological
figures of the first three quotations. If nothing else, the
structural approach has shown that, while far from removing all
ambiguity from Num 24:15-17, there appears to be a set of precise
reasons for the present order of the texts. This is apparent
from the analogous words and phrases that occur between the
particular quotations as now ordered (*gĕzērâ šāwâ*) and in the
way in which the content of each scriptural text relates
peculiarly to that of its neighbours.

G. 11QMelch

11Q Melchizedek has been chosen as the concluding illustration
because it contains in line 25[192] an indirect quotation of
Isa 8:11. This verse is quoted with an introductory formula
in 4QFlor 1:15-16;[193] it is there connected to the main text of
the unit, Psalm 1, through *gĕzērâ šāwâ*, the analogous term being
דרך. Isa 8:11 is also quoted indirectly at 1QSa 1:2-3 and CD
8:16 = 19:29; it was, therefore, an important text in the self-
understanding of the Qumran covenanters and is worth closer study.

When the citation of Isa 8:11 in Qumran literature is
indirect, it always occurs in the context of the covenant:
" . . . the establisher(s of) the covenant are those who turn
away from walking (in the p)ath of the people" (11QMelch);[194]
". . . the men of their Covenant who have turned aside (from
the) way of the people" (1QSa);[195] " . . . thus shall it be with
the converts of Israel who depart from the way of the people.
Because God loved the first who testified in his favour, so will

He love those who come after them, for the Covenant of the
fathers is theirs" (CD).[196]

Such a contextual repetition would suggest that wherever
the covenant was mentioned it could be deemed suitable to allude
to Isa 8:11. It mattered not whether it was the title of a
tract (1QSa) or in the text of an interpretation of a biblical
passage (11QMelch: on Isa 52:7; CD: on Deut 9:5 and 7:8).
Indeed it is probably some such text as Deut 7:8 that is to be
understood as the parent of the association, for its immediate
context is a discussion of the Israelistes as the people (עם)
holy to God, the faithful God who keeps covenant (ברית).[197]

In 4QFlor 1:15-16 there is no mention of covenant and
Isa 8:11 is quoted explicitly to stress the distinction between
the righteous and the wicked of Psalm 1. The difference in the
use of the Isaiah quotation is apparent also in the length in
which it occurs in 4QFlor on the one hand and in the remaining
Qumran locations on the other. This is stressed by the fact that
whereas 4QFlor 1:16 includes the demonstrative adjective after
העם, 1QSa, CD and 11QMelch omit it. Thus there appears to be
two close but distinct uses of Isa 8:11 in Qumran literature.
Such a feature re-emphasizes the fact that there should be no
attempt to understand the use or interpretation of a biblical
passage as necessarily consistent throughout Qumran writings.
This in turn supports the distinction that has already been made
between the use of Amos 9:11 in CD 7:16 and in 4QFlor 1:12.

As in 4QFlor, 1QM 10:1-8, CD 7:13b-8:1a and 4QTest it seems
as if the scriptural texts cited in 11QMelch are associated with
one another through *gĕzērâ šāwâ*. From a literary point of view
de Jonge and van der Woude have noted[198] that Lev 25:13 (line 2)

can be connected with Deut 15:2 (lines 3-4) through an analogous
word-use represented only in the LXX text type: ἐν τῷ ἔτει τῆς
ἀφέσεως σημασίᾳ (Lev 25:13), ἄφεσις (Deut 15:2). Also they
observed that "11QMelch connects Isa. lxi. 1 and lii. 7 probably
because of the words לבשר and מבשר occurring there."[199] Again,
they see a connection between Isa 52:7 and Lev 25:8-17 as
reflected in an apparently similar combination in *Pss. Sol.* 11:1,
though they give no reason for the association.[200]

In a closer analysis of 11QMelch itself J. A. Fitzmyer has
proposed that "the thread which runs through the whole text and
ties together its various elements is Lev 25."[201] He also sees
the jubilee year as involving atonement for iniquity, and the
Day of Atonement as playing a special part in it (11QMelch 7).
On the other hand, M. P. Miller has noted[202] that the interpretative comments upon the biblical citations in 11QMelch (Lev
25:13, Deut 15:2, Isa 52:7, Pss 7:8-9, 82:1-2) can all be related
to Isa 61:1-2 which "passage stands behind our document and
appears in the form of Stichwörter at crucial points."[203]

J. A. Sanders has accepted Miller's identification of the
use of Isa 61:1-2 in 11QMelch and has added some further phrases
which most likely are taken from Isaiah 61,[204] at least one of
which (Isa 61:2 in line 20) he had already included in an earlier
description of the use of "The Old Testament in 11Q Melchizedek,"
entitled just that.[205] In that study Sanders set out firstly the
text of 11QMelch according to van der Woude with all the biblical
citations and allusions italicized; secondly he did the same for
the text as proposed by J. T. Milik,[206] thus highlighting
several further possible references.[207] Sanders' work is
descriptive of 11QMelch in its literary construction and although

he has provided good explanations for the present composition,
describing the use of various exegetical principles,[208] the
scriptural combination and the midrashic intention of the author
remains detached from any setting other than Qumran, even though
Isa 61:1-2 is expounded by Jesus in the synagogue at Nazareth
(Lk 4:16-30).[209]

The study of C. Perrot, "Luc 4, 16-30 et la lecture biblique
de l'ancienne Synagogue,"[210] provides the most complete proposal
for the setting of the combination of Leviticus 25 and Isaiah 61[211]
each of which, as we have seen, has been proposed as the key text
behind 11QMelch's composition. That Isaiah was handed to Jesus
in the synagogue service suggests that at that time there was
"un cadre général déjà fixé"[212] within which Jesus focused on
the two verses Luke quotes or has Jesus read. Having given the
standard warnings about reconstructing first century lectionaries,
Perrot argues convincingly, on the basis of the work of J. Mann,[213]
that the seder which accompanied Isa 61:1ff. was that of Gen 35:
9ff. *Tg. Neof.* Gen 35:9 mentions the death of Deborah with that
of Rachel; according to *Jub.* 32:30 Deborah died on the 23rd of
Tishri. The targum of Gen 35:9ff. also speaks of the circumcision
of Abraham which Perrot states happened according to Jewish
tradition on the 10th of Tishri, the Day of Atonement. Perrot
concludes, therefore, that the lection of Gen 35:9ff. and
Isa 61:1ff. took place sometime in Tishri, close to the feast of
Tabernacles or the Day of Atonement.

The association of Isa 61:1-3 with the Day of Atonement
appears old from another aspect. The readings for that day
included Isa 57:15-58:14 but, since the day also marked the
beginning of the jubilee year, the passages from Leviticus 25

and Isaiah 61 were alike appropriate.[213] Perrot points out
that among other things Isa 58:5 and 61:2 (LXX) are connected
through their use of δεκτὸν. In the later triennial cycle the
seder Lev 25:14ff. is followed by the haphtara Isa 52:3ff. Such
liturgical association of these texts may already be reflected
in 1QH 8:14 and Acts 10:35-38. 11QMelch acts as the confirmation
of Perrot's theory. One may at least suppose some fluidity of
the choice of the Isaianic text that accompanied the Leviticus
seder, yet any such haphtara was consistently read with Isa 61:
1-3 in mind.

Apart from the quotation of Leviticus 25 and possibly also
of Deuteronomy 15, the only biblical verses to receive introductory formulae in 11QMelch are Pss 82:1, 2 and 7:8-9,[215] Isa
52:7 and Dan 9:25. Such an observation leads to the proposal
that, apart from Dan 9:25 which may have been introduced later
for midrashic purposes,[216] the most prominent texts in 11QMelch
are based on a liturgical combination of readings. These were
put together with the use of certain exegetical principles and
these can still be seen at work in the particular homily on the
texts that may lie behind the midrashic composition of 11QMelch.

The significance of Isa 61:1-3 then rests in its being
associated with the Day of Atonement readings, directly in terms
of Isa 57:15-58:14 and indirectly as it performed the function
of haphtara to the seder Gen 35:9ff. which almost certainly was
read at a time in Tishri close to the Day of Atonement, if not
on that day itself. Thus, as for the combination of 2 Samuel 7
and Psalms 1 and 2 in 4QFlor, so also for the group of texts in
11QMelch we may understand them to have had their setting within
early Jewish liturgy.

NOTES

[1]The principal text used is that of J.P.M. van der Ploeg
and A. S. van der Woude, *Le Targum de Job de la grotte XI de
Qumrân*, Leiden: E. J. Brill, 1971.

[2]This is not necessarily to suggest Essene authorship for
11QtgJob which J. A. Fitzmyer (*A Wandering Aramean: Collected
Aramaic Essays,* SBLMS 25; Missoula: Scholars Press, 1979, 9
and n.47) argues strongly against.

[3]*Hermeneutische Aspecten van de Targum van Job uit Grot XI
van Qumrân,* Groningen: Dissertation, 1971. Tuinistra attempts
to show that 11QtgJob models its figure of Job after the
Righteous Teacher and that the interpretation of 11QtgJob is
overtly Essene. I owe these observations to J. A. Fitzmyer
("Some Observations on the Targum of Job from Qumran Cave 11,"
CBQ 36 1974 , 507-8) and to M. Sokoloff *(The Targum to Job from
Qumran Cave XI,* Ramat-Gan: Bar-Ilan University, 1974, 237-39).

[4]*2Q 15* is a small fragment of Job 33:28-30 that M. Baillet
describes as "un texte du type massorétique" (M. Baillet,
J. T. Milik, R. de Vaux, *Les 'petites grottes' de Qumrân:
Exploration de la falaise. Les grottes 2Q, 3Q, 5Q, 6Q, 7Q à 10Q,
Le rouleau de cuivre* [DJD 3; Oxford: Clarendon, 1962], 71). See
Fitzmyer, "Targum of Job from Qumran Cave 11," 524, for inform-
ation on the responsibilities of F. M. Cross for publishing
4QJob[a], [b] and of P. W. Skehan for publishing 4QpaleoJob[c].

[5]"11 Q Targum Job and the Massoretic Text," *RQ* 8 (1972-74),
254. φέγγος is ambiguous being used of both "light" and thereby
of the light from flame, especially of "torch" (LSJ, 1920).

[6]At Job 25:3 LXX reads ἔνεδρα παρ᾽αὐτοῦ: a Hebrew *Vorlage*
of ארבו? (MT: אורהו).

[7]As does Sokoloff (*The Targum of Job*, 117). For the
textual difficulty at 11QtgJob 31:2 where there is a gap
corresponding to MT אור and for which the context requires
רוח (as BH[3] and LXX: πάχνη) Sokoloff inserts "wind" in
brackets (*The Targum of Job*, 89).

[8]In fact, for 11QtgJob 29:2 the reading of אור as אור
must lead the targumist to understand ענן, construct in the
MT, as an absolute (Sokoloff, *The Targum of Job*, 143). This
desire for clarity has also been observed by B. Jongeling,
"Détermination et indétermination dans 11QtgJob," *Qumrân: Sa
piété, sa théologie et son milieu*, BETL 46, 131-36.

[9]The *niph^cal* pt. of חמם occurs at Isa 57:5.

[10]Trans. Sokoloff, *The Targum of Job*, 101, 167.

[11]"11QtgJob XXI, 4-5 (Job 32, 13)," *RQ* 9/33 (1977), 127-29.
MT reads פן-תאמרו מָצָאנוּ חכמה אל יהפנוּ לא-איש; 11QtgJob reads:
להן אלהא חיבנא which Sokoloff (*The Targum of Job*, 69) translates
"but God has declared us guilty."

[12]York notes that when this is rendered into Ethiopic two
first plural semitic verbs are used ("11QtgJob XXI, 4-5 [Job 32,
13]," 129, n.6).

[13]Of course, the unpointed text remains ambiguous, as does
the Aramaic of the Targum (cf. Sokoloff's trans. in n.4, pp. 78-
79).

[14]"The Cosmic Role of Angels in the 11Q Targum of Job,"
JSJ 8 (1977), 84.

[15]"The Cosmic Role of Angels," 84, n.2. Brownlee also notes
the function of angels in *1 Enoch*.

[16]"Biblical Interpretation among the Sectaries of the
Dead Sea Scrolls," *BA* 14 (1951), 54-76. Ever since this
article Brownlee has insisted that 1QpHab deserves the title
midrash.

[17]E.g., for criticism, K. Elliger, *Studien zum Habakuk-
Kommentar,* 157-64; for supplementation, K. Stendahl, *The School
of St. Matthew,* Lund: C.W.K. Gleerup, 1954, 190-94.

[18]*The Dead Sea Habakkuk Midrash and the Targum of Jonathan,*
mimeographed paper, 1953, 10-11; *The Text of Habakkuk in the
Ancient Commentary from Qumran,* JBLMS 11, Philadelphia: Society
of Biblical Literature and Exegesis, 1959, esp. 118-23 ("The
Presence of Dual Readings"); *The Midrash Pesher of Habakkuk,*
SBLMS 24; Missoula: Scholars Press, 1979.

[19]M. P. Horgan (*Pesharim: Qumran Interpretations of Biblical
Books,* CBQMS 8, Washington: The Catholic Biblical Association
of America, 1979, 10-55) appeared before Brownlee's *The Midrash
Pesher of Habakkuk;* she is concerned with establishing the best
text and translation for 1QpHab but with little reference to
exegetical techniques. The few examples she gives of "modes of
interpretation" are listed in her book, pp. 244-247, where she
discusses the exegetical method in 1QpHab 1:16-2:10 and in
1QpHab 11:2-8 in detail.

[20]"Biblical Interpretation," 60.

[21]J. V. Chamberlain (*An Ancient Sectarian Interpretation,* 96)
describes this fault in Brownlee's principles by noting that
"the validity of Brownlee's first 'hermeneutical principle' is
dependent on the other eleven" - eleven, because Brownlee
retracted the need for his 12th principle, "interpretation of

words, or parts of words, as abbreviations," in relation to
1QpHab (*The Dead Sea Habakkuk Midrash and the Targum of
Jonathan,* 10). Brownlee has now expounded the eschatological
hermeneutic of Qumran in detail (*Midrash Pesher,* 28-35).

[22]1QpHab 2:11-12 identifies the כשדים as the Kittim; also
the evidence of Peshitta, Vulgate and Targums points to a
traditional identification of the two (cf. Num 24:24, BH[3])
with the Romans; this is supported above all through the work
of A. Dupont-Sommer (*Les écrits esséniens,* 351-61).
Cf. H. H. Rowley ("The Kittim and the Dead Sea Scrolls," *PEQ*
88 1956 , 92-109) who was one of the stronger advocates for
the identification of the Kittim as the Seleucids.

[23]"Biblical Interpretation," 60.

[24]See Brownlee, *Meaning,* 66-69.

[25]I.e., the division of Hab 1:8 and 9 a word later than
usual (1QpHab 3:7-12) is paralleled in the technique used by
R. Gamaliel (*b. Sanh.* 90b) in his punctuation of Deut 31:16,
arguing for resurrection. Elliger mentions this verse division
(*Studien,* 160-61) but ignores it in his notes to the text (174-76).
Secondly, the reading of וצור of Hab 1:12 as יצור is an example
of *'al tiqrē'*; or, as Brownlee now remarks (*Midrash Pesher,* 88-89),
this may be an interpretation much older than Qumran since the
LXX reads a verb here too (καὶ ἔπλασέν με): the Qumran commentator may thus never have understood צור as "rock" (against
Elliger, who reads only "Rock" here [*Studien,* 181]). Thirdly,
'al tiqrē' is also the basis for the understanding of מרחו of
Hab 1:16 "as the construct of *mr'* rather than that of *mrh*"
(1QpHab 6:2-5), if one accepts there is exegesis of למכמרתו by

nôtārîqôn; Brownlee has now dropped this proposal *(Midrash Pesher,* 101). Brownlee has also dropped his earlier under-standing of משקה as having רעיהו as its object (Hab 2:15; 1QpHab 11:2-8; *Midrash Pesher,* 180). Lastly the interpretation of תסוב in its rare meaning synonymous with בלע (Hab 2:16; 1QpHab 11:8-14) is an example of the use of paronomasia; on בלע in 1QpHab see Brownlee, *Midrash Pesher,* 181.

[26]Brownlee in fact cites the same Rabbinic examples for principles 3 and 4: *Gen. Rab.* 20:12, 40:5 ("Biblical Inter-pretation," 73). He gives the use of Ps 45:5 in *b. Šabb.* 63a as an example of principle 10.

[27]"Arise, pass over to Kit im; even there you will have no rest. Behold the land of the Chaldeans (כשדים), this is the people; it was not Assyria. She (i.e., ארץ כשדים) builds up ships (צייו, cf. ציים, Dan 11:30; צים, Num 24:24)." Isa 23:12b-13 is notoriously obscure; W. H. Brownlee suggests that the Massoretic accentuation may show that לא הזה was a scribal comment incorporated into the text. Whatever the actual history of the text, it may have been the basis at Qumran for under-standing that כשדים refers to כתיים: the latter as referring to the present oppressor would be left to the audience familiar with Dan 11:30. 1QIsa[a] 23:12b-13 contains nothing to contradict this understanding. Surprisingly, exactly how the Chaldeans are exegetically related to the Kittim has not been a scholarly concern: e.g., Elliger (*Studien,* 172-73) only mentions their traditional identification with the Cypriots and thence allegorically with the sea-faring Romans.

[28]"Exegesis in the Dead Sea Scrolls," 14-15. The resulting

exegesis may be that of "analogous circumstance" but that
is not the technique whereby the relationship of interpretation
to biblical text can be legitimately explained.

[29]"Biblical Interpretation," 63-63. In *Midrash Pesher*, 71,
Brownlee translates the interpretation, "With the hot breath
of his nose and the fierce storm of their face."

[30]L. H. Silberman ("Unriddling the Riddle," 339) reached
the understanding of קדים as "East wind" and מגמת as being
what it carries without accepting the division of פניהם; that
would, therefore, vindicate Brownlee's more complete understanding
of 1QpHab at this point (for which, see *Midrash Pesher*, 69-70).

[31]"The Pesher of Dreams and Scriptures," 363.

[32]Cf. Deut 3:6: נחרם אותם; 7:2: החרם תחרים אתם, "You
destroy the net, their sign?" The Targum renders חרם as זיניה,
"implement of war." The theory of N. Wieder ("The Habakkuk
Scroll and the Targum," *JJS* 4 1953 , 14-18) that the equation
of אותות and חרם depends upon an understanding similar to that
of the Targum to Hab 1:17 where חרמו is rendered משירייתיה, "his
troops," a secondary meaning of *signum,* does not explain why
the targumist translated חרם in that way, and seems a more
roundabout road to the exegesis of 1QpHab than the ideas suggested
above. Cf. also Exod 22:19.

[33]A. Finkel ("The Pesher of Dreams and Scriptures," 369)
points to several other examples of this, e.g., 1QpHab 4:4-6:
שחק has the dual meaning of "laugh" and "mock;" 1QpHab 10:2-5:
חוטי (Hab 2:11) is taken in its two senses of "condemn" (רשע)
and purify, i.e., "sentence to fire and brimstone" - this example
is questionable: Silberman ("Unriddling the Riddle," 352-53)

supports this identification of the part of the interpretation
that goes with חוטי, but he does not see any need of a double
reading here; 1QpHab 2:11-14: המר והנמהר (Hab 1:6) can be
rendered, "the courageous and the swift" (2:12) or "to be sharp
as a razor and to carry headlong" (2:13). To this Silberman
("Unriddling the Riddle," 336-37) prefers to see המר as related
to מר, identified by Jastrow as from מרא II, "to be fat, strong,"
hence directly rendered in the interpretation by גבורים. These
understandings are complementary and both need to be taken into
account. For a complete list of the understandings of the phrase
and its restored pesher, see Brownlee, *Midrash Pesher*, 60-61;
Brownlee himself translates, "the Kittim, w(ho ar)e swift and
mighty / in war to destroy the s(of)t (and dainty)" (וענונים).
Cf. Isa 47:1.

[34]On משל in its various meanings, see Brownlee, *Midrash
Pesher*, excursus, 143-44. This pun is also noticed by Horgan
(*Pesharim: Qumran Interpretations of Biblical Books*, 245, n.67).

[35]Silberman ("Unriddling the Riddle," 356) proposes linking
this interpretation to מספח in the biblical citation through
'al tiqrē'; reading מספג, "to smite," for מספח, the commentator
was able to play on the double sense of בלע. For further
elucidation of the use of בלע in 1QpHab, see Brownlee, *Midrash
Pesher*, 181-82: he still supports the wordplay here.

[36]See above, p. 70, n.141.

[37]*The Dead Sea Habakkuk Midrash and the Targum of Jonathan*, 10.

[38]As J. V. Chamberlain, *An Ancient Sectarian Interpretation*,
115-16.

[39]"Biblical Interpretation," 62.

[40]Both I. Rabinowitz ("The Second and Third Columns of
the Habakkuk Interpretation Scroll," *JBL* 69 1950 , 48) and
A. Finkel ("The Pesher of Dreams and Scriptures," 370) read
it as two words; Rabinowitz translates (36), "my wrath are they."

[41]Supported by Silberman ("Unriddling the Riddle," 338) and
maintained by Brownlee (*Midrash Pesher,* 69).

[42]Or, better, "cloud of mud," as Elliger ("Wolke von Kot;"
Studien, 146), Finkel ("The Pesher of Dreams and Scriptures,"
370), and now Brownlee (*Midrash Pesher,* 134) who suggests that
עבטו could be construed as either "pledges" or "cloud of mud."

[43]Maintained hesitatingly by Brownlee (*Midrash Pesher,* 192).

[44]This was dropped by Brownlee in his mimeographed paper,
The Dead Sea Habakkuk Midrash (10-11), to which he keeps
(*Midrash Pesher,* 216); but the actual choice of words may still
depend upon some such *nôtārîqôn.*

[45]"DSH makes no direct appeals to other passages of Scripture,
but their influence upon interpretation is nevertheless to be
detected" ("Biblical Interpretation," 75); i.e., no quotation
with an introductory formula, but Isa 13:18 (in reading of 1QIsa[a])
may be cited at 1QpHab 6:11-12.

[46]"The Pesher of Dreams and Scriptures," 367-68. In
Midrash Pesher, Brownlee takes little account of this work,
but see his *Text of Habakkuk,* 118-23 on dual readings.

[47]This second part of the wordplay may derive rather
from the interpreter's reading לרשׁ of Hab 1:6 as from the root
רשׁשׁ, "to beat down, shatter" (Jer 5:17) (Silberman, "Unriddling
the Riddle," 337). There is no attestation for חרב meaning

"smite", so there may be just a midrashic pun here rather than
a dual reading (so Brownlee, *Midrash Pesher*, 65).

[48]Reading וישם as from שמם (as Brownlee, "Biblical
Interpretation," 64); Elliger ("gemacht zu seinem Gott,"
Studien, 178-79) understands, on the other hand, the root שים.
Brownlee (*Midrash Pesher*, 81) allows that וישם is understood
as ואשם, וישם (root: שמם) and וישם (root: שים), and he shows
that the interpretation requires this multiple understanding of
Hab 1:11.

[49]Proposed already by Silberman ("Unriddling the Riddle," 347).

[50]Actually, MT can be read in this way too; there would then
be no double meaning here. Alternatively, the suggestion of
R. Weis to see here the Arabic *qdy*, "to judge," in connection
with Silberman's note of the use of קצין in Dan 11:18 to denote
a judge or commander ("Unriddling the Riddle," 352), may allow
a wordplay whereby קצוות is interpreted by the use of שפט in
the commentary.

[51]I.e., "the house of his uncovering," using the root גלה,
as Brownlee (*Midrash Pesher*, 183). Horgan (*Pesharim: Qumran
Interpretations of Biblical Books*, 247) sees a play on words
between מעד, "to stumble," and לכשילם, "to make them stumble."

[52]Silberman ("Unriddling the Riddle," 361) maintains that
the commentator deliberately metathesized the biblical text for
interpretative purposes, and that this is not a witness to a
textual variant as Elliger (*Studien*, 219) claims.

[53]"Toward an Understanding of the Exegesis in the Dead Sea
Scrolls," *RQ* 7 (1969-71), 3-15, here 14-15. Surprisingly,
Brownlee does not mention this part of Slomovic's work in his

recent exhaustive study of 1QpHab, *The Midrash Pesher of Habakkuk,*

[54]Tr. Vermes, *The Dead Sea Scrolls in English,* 239-40.

[55]Tr. Vermes, *The Dead Sea Scrolls in English,* 240.

[56]"Exegesis in the Dead Sea Scrolls," 15. There may indeed be a use of *'al tiqrē'* here, but it could also be a simple textual variant belonging to the interpreter's text.

[57]In order to maintain correspondence with exact word usage it would be better to see either 2 Sam 23:1-3 or Prov 29:2-5 as referred to here. Or, if one allows the use of paranomasia, then it is likely that Hab 2:5-6 (or possibly Mic 2:2-4) is the support for the interpretation here: e.g., Brownlee, "Biblical Interpretation," 67.

[58]Perhaps Isa 65:10-11 is a better support.

[59]"Exegesis in the Dead Sea Scrolls," 15.

[60]Words between * * are supralinear in the Ms.

[61]Tr. Brownlee, *Midrash Pesher,* 107.

[62]"Unriddling the Riddle," 344-45.

[63]*Midrash Pesher,* 111.

[64]Brownlee notes that in 4QpPss[a] 1:27 the Teacher is called מליץ דעת.

[65]Suggested also by Horgan, *Pesharim: Qumran Interpretations of Biblical Books,* 245, n.67.

[66]"Les citations de l'Ancien Testament dans 'La Guerre des Fils de Lumière contre les Fils de Ténèbres'," *RB* 63 (1956), 234-60, 375-90.

[67]Jer 14:9 reads ואתה בקרבנו יהוה, a similar adaptation
of the phrase. J. van der Ploeg (*Le Rouleau de la Guerre,*
STDJ 2; Leiden: E. J. Brill, 1959, 135) also notes similar
phrases at Exod 17:7, 34:9, 1 Sam 4:3, Mic 3:11.

[68]Implied by J. A. Fitzmyer ("The Use of Explicit Old
Testament Quotations in Qumran Literature and in the New
Testament," *NTS* 7 1960-61 , 327) and favoured by van der Ploeg
(*Le Rouleau de la Guerre,* 135) and Carmignac (*Les Textes de
Qumran*; Paris: Letouzey et Ané, 1961, 107).

[69]Favoured by Y. Yadin, *The Scroll of the War of the Sons
of Light against the Sons of Darkness* (London: Oxford University,
1962), 303, and by A. Dupont-Sommer, *Les écrits esséniens,*
199, n.2.

[70]Mentioned by J. Carmignac, "Les citations de l'Ancien
Testament."

[71]Cf. 1Q22 wherein have been created summary speeches of
Moses (DJD 1, 91-97).

[72]The text here has paraphrastic allusions to Deut 20:5-8 (MT).

[73]1QM agrees with LXX, Peshitta; MT reads תבואו.

[74]The use of *gĕzērâ šāwâ* in 4QFlor has been outlined by
E. Slomovic ("Exegesis in the Dead Sea Scrolls," 7-10).

[75]Thus these verses are exhortations that "doivent rendre
les Fils de lumière plus courageux qu'ils ne le sont déjà"
(J. van der Ploeg, *Le Rouleau de la Guerre,* 136).

[76]This understanding of the use of Num 10:9 in 1QM is clearly
preferable to the proposal of G. Morawe ("Vergleich des Aufbaus
der Danklieder und hymnischer Bekenntnislieder (1QH) von Qumran

mit dem Aufbau der Psalmen im Alten Testament und im Spätjudentum,"
RQ 4 1963-64 , 333-37) that Num 10:9 introduces a hymn that
goes as far as 1QM 10:18 and is parallel in structure to material
in 1QH. Rather the whole set of biblical interpretations should
be seen as part of one of the battle prayers of 1QM, in this
case 1QM 10:1-12:17.

[77]For a detailed analysis of how 1QS 2:2-4 is related to its
context, see E. F. Roop, *A Form-Critical Study of the Society
Rule (1QS) at Qumran*, Dissertation: Claremont Graduate School,
1972, 47-118.

[78]E.g., as outlined by J. Gnilka, "Die Essenische Tauchbäder
und die Johannestaufe," *RQ* 3 (1961-62), 189-90.

[79]F. J. Helfmeyer ("'Gott Nachfolgen' in der Qumrantexten,"
RQ 7 1969-71 , 101, n.123) outlines summarily how the various
parts of the ceremony could be formulated into a service for
those entering the community and as a festival of renewal of the
covenant - not just covenant renewal alone.

[80]Similar results could be obtained from a detailed analysis
of the expansion of the Aaronic blessing in *Jub.* 12:29.
M. Gertner ("Midrashim in the New Testament," *JSS* 7 1962 ,
273-82) has carefully worked out how Lk 1:67-75 is a midrash on
the Aaronic Blessing.

[81]It is noticeable that whereas MT uses יהוה, 1QS 2:2-4 omits
any designation of God. H. Stegemann ("Religionsgeschichtliche
Erwägungen zu den Gottesbezeichnungen in den Qumrantexten,"
Qumrân: Sa piété, sa théologie et son milieu, BETL 46, 203)
suggests this is deliberate: the supposed antiquity of the new
prayer is put over by avoiding the use of אדוני, while writing

יהוה is avoided for obvious reasons.

[82]Ps 34:11: כל טוב; Exod 18:9, 1 Kgs 8:66, Jer 33:9 (bis):
על כל הטובה; 1 Sam 15:9: על כל הטוב; Judg 10:15, 1 Sam 11:10:
ככל הטוב; Jer 32:42: את כל הטובה; Deut 26:11: בכל הטוב. Cf.
T. Jos. 18:1, "He will bless you with good things for ever and
ever" (*APOT* 2, 352).

[83]LXX (and the Peshitta) support a *Vorlage* of בכל הטובים
(ἐν πᾶσιν τοῖς ἀγαθοῖς).

[84]Against O. Betz, *Offenbarung*, 167, n.1.

[85]E.g., P. Wernberg-Møller, *The Manual of Discipline* (STDJ 1;
Leiden: E. J. Brill, 1957), 52; he also cites *Jub.* 12:29, 31:24;
O. Betz, *Offenbarung*, 167; W. H. Brownlee, *Meaning*, 82.

[86]11QPss 3:5 reads, [   ]יש [   ]ישומרכה מכו, best explained
as metathesis.

[87]For this and other wordplays and for the use of certain
Stichworten, see A. Finkel, "The Pesher of Dreams and Scriptures,"
369-70.

[88]As observed by Wernberg-Møller, *The Manual of Discipline*, 52.

[89]Tr. W. McKane, *Proverbs* (OTL; Philadelphia: Westminster,
1970), 490.

[90]As proposed in BH[3].

[91]On enlightenment at Qumran cf. 1QH 3:3, 4:5, 27, 1QSb 4:27.
Compare also 2 Cor 4:6 " . . . *light* of the *knowledge* of the
glory of God in the *face* of Christ" (RSV).

[92]W. D. Davies ("Knowledge in the Dead Sea Scrolls and
Matthew 11:25-30," *HTR* 46 1953 , 125) classifies דעת in 1QS 2:3

as knowledge "of a personal or intimate kind." J. Worrell
(*Concepts of Wisdom in the Dead Sea Scrolls,* Dissertation:
Claremont Graduate School, 1968, 203) correctly assesses the
general view of scholarship when he states that "da'at in the
scrolls is more akin to its connotations in the wisdom literature
than to the esoteric *gnosis* of developed Gnosticism."

[93]The phrase is that of Worrell, *Concepts of Wisdom,* 240.

[94]Cf. 1QS 10:12, 1QM 17:8: בדעת כולם; מקור דעת at 1QS 8:9
is often emended to בדעת עולם: e.g., Brownlee, *The Dead Sea
Manual of Discipline,* (*BASOR* Supstud 10-12; New Haven: American
Schools of Oriental Research, 1951), 33, Lohse, *Die Texte aus
Qumran* (München: Kösel, 1971[2]) 30 n.b., Wernberg-Møller, *The
Manual of Discipline,* 127, n.26.

[95]Whether the phrase be understood as "knowledge of things
eternal" (T. H. Gaster, *The Dead Sea Scriptures in English
Translation,* Garden City: Doubleday, 1964[2], 47) or as "eternal
knowledge" (Brownlee, *The Dead Sea Manual of Discipline,* 10;
G. Vermes, *The Dead Sea Scrolls in English,* Harmondsworth:
Penguin, 1968[3], 73).

[96]See above, n.81.

[97]E.g., Jer 33:11, Pss 89:2, 29, 138:8, Ezra 3:11, 1 Chr 16:34,
41, 2 Chr 5:13, 7:3, 6, 20:21.

[98]On this clause cf. 1QSb 3:5: לם יחד לכה[ו]ע ם[שלו; 1QSb
3:20: יסד שלומכה לעולמי עד. Brownlee (*The Dead Sea Manual of
Discipline,* 11) also points to T. *Dan* 5:11: "eternal peace."

[99]As pointed out by Betz, *Offenbarung,* 166. M. Weise
(*Kultzeiten und kultischer Bundesschluss in der 'Ordensregel'
vom Toten Meer,* SPB 3; Leiden: E. J. Brill, 1961, 84) notes

that *Num. Rab.* 11 (43d) retains the tradition that blessings
are said in groups of three: both Num 6:24-26 and 1QS 2:2-4
can fit this pattern.

[100]18 is the number of blessings in the *camidah* because of
the 18 times God is mentioned in Psalm 29 (*b. Ber.* 28b).   The
tetragrammaton occurs 18 times in the song of Miriam.   For
other uses of 18 in rabbinic tradition, see O. H. Lehmann,
"Number-symbolism as a Vehicle of Religious Experience in the
Gospels, Contemporary Rabbinic Literature and the Dead Sea Scrolls"
(*Studia Patristica* IV:2, ed. F. L. Cross; Berlin: Akademie, 1961),
129, n.2.

[101]Nor is it possible to claim, as Lehmann does ("Number-
symbolism," 129, n.4) that the Hebrew original of the blessing
of Terah at *Jub.* 12:29 had 18 stresses.

[102]E.g., Brownlee, *The Dead Sea Manual of Discipline,* 53, 56;
D. F. Baumgärtel, "Zur Liturgie in der 'Sektenrolle' vom Toten
Meer," *ZAW* 65 (1953), 263-65.   Most recently, see W. H. Brownlee,
"The Ceremony of Crossing the Jordan in the Annual Covenanting
at Qumran," *Von Kanaan bis Kerala,* edd. W. C. Delsman et al.,
AOAT 211; Neukirchen-Vluyn: Neukirchener, Kevelaer: Butzon &
Bercker, 1982, 295-302, esp. 297-98.

[103]*Offenbarung,* 166-69.

[104]*Offenbarung,* 169.

[105]*Kultzeiten,* 82-93.

[106]*Kultzeiten,* 85.   Weise also cites Deut 30:15 and Amos 5:14
as well as some later rabbinic literature in which a similar
expansion of the Aaronic blessing may be apparent.

[107]*Kultzeiten,* 87. He compares this interpretation with 1QS 4:2, 11:15 and 1QH 4:5, 27. On the possibility that this refers to inspiration, see Betz, *Offenbarung,* 113.

[108]*Kultzeiten,* 88. He cites 1QS 4:3, 18, 5:21, 6:18.

[109]*Kultzeiten,* 89. He compares 1QS 3:15, 4:4, 10:12, 11:11.

[110]Weise notes that both *Sifre* Num 6:25 and *Num. Rab.* 11:6 mention the Torah as the illuminating agent, and that Torah is part of the application of Num 6:25 in the 19th benediction of the Babylonian recension of the *Tefilla;* חיים also occurs in the 19th benediction.

[111]*Kultzeiten,* 92.

[112]*The Covenant Formulary,* Philadelphia: Fortress, 1971, 168-69, 189-91.

[113]G. von Rad ("The Form-critical Problem of the Hexateuch," *The Problem of the Hexateuch and Other Essays,* New York: McGraw-Hill, London: Oliver and Boyd, 1966, 35) is the most notable supporter of the Feast of Booths as that at which the covenant was renewed. Most other scholars support the Feast of Weeks because of the stress in *Jubilees* (esp 6:17) on the renewal of the covenant at Weeks: e.g. W. H. Brownlee, *The Dead Sea Manual of Discipline.* Appendix G, 53; "Light on the Manual of Discipline (DSD) from the Book of Jubilees," *BASOR* 123 (1951), 31-32; E. Roop, *A Form-Critical Study of the Society Rule,* 101.

[114]E. Kutsch ("Feste und Feiern," "II In Israel," *RGG*[3] 2:912) supports the association of the Qumran covenant ceremony with the Feast of Weeks, as does A.R.C. Leaney (*The Rule of Qumran and its Meaning,* Philadelphia: Westminster, London: A. & C.

Black, 1966, 95-107) who relies for the most part on evidence
from *Jubilees* which was much used at Qumran. Traditionally
(*m. Pesah* 10:4) Deut 26:3ff. belongs to the Passover Haggadah.

[115]Called "A Pilgrim Song" by A. Weiser, *The Psalms*
(Philadelphia: Westminster, London: SCM, 1962), 744.

[116]Weiser, *The Psalms*, 744.

[117]*Psalmenstudien*, V, (Kristiania: Jacob Dybwad, 1925), 48.
Mowinckel classifies Ps 121 as a *Segenpsalmen*, another pointer
to the suitability of its use for expanding Num 6:24-26, since
the psalm itself may have been used as a blessing.

[118]D.F. Baumgärtel, "Zur Liturgie," 263: A. Weiser, *The Psalms*,
673, 679; K. Baltzer, *The Covenant Formulary*, 133, 189, 190.
Weiser states definitely that this Qumran ceremony was part of
the autumnal festival with its tradition of *Heilsgeschichte* (cf.
von Rad [see above, p. 339, n.113]). If the phrase is borrowed
from Ps 118:1 then a connection with Booths is also supported by
Mowinckel (*Psalmenstudien*, V, 34) for that psalm, especially through
its link with a possible enthronement festival (*Psalmenstudien*,
II, 4, 89).

[119]Hebrew text with translations: S. Schechter, *Documents of
Jewish Sectaries, Volume 1, Fragments of a Zadokite Work*, Cambridge:
Cambridge University, 1910; reissued with a prolegomenon by
J. A. Fitzmyer, New York: Ktav, 1970; C. Rabin, *The Zadokite
Documents*, Oxford: Clarendon, 1954; E. Lohse, *Texte*, 63-107.

[120]E.g., I. Rabinowitz, "A Reconsideration of 'Damascus' and
'390 Years' in the 'Damascus' ('Zadokite') Fragments," *JBL* 73
(1954), 13, 25; J. Carmignac, "Comparison entre les manuscrits
'A' et 'B' du Document de Damas," *RQ* 2 (1959-60), 53-67;

A. M. Denis, *Les thèmes de connaissance dans le Document de
Damas* (Studia hellenistica 15; Louvain: Publications univers-
itaires, 1967), esp. pp. 124, 139, 144-46, 200. For a structural
outline of the whole of CD see J. A. Fitzmyer, *The Dead Sea
Scrolls, Major Publications and Tools for Study* (SBLSBS 8;
Missoula: SBL and Scholars Press, 1975), 90-91.

[121]I have supported Murphy-O'Connor in my article which draws
out the implications of his understanding in relation to Qumran
messianic expectation ("The Amos-Numbers Midrash [CD 7,13b-8,1a]
and Messianic Expectation," *ZAW* 92 1980 , 397-404); P. R. Davies
offers similar support ("The Ideology of the Temple in the
Damascus Document," *JJS* 33 1982 , 299, n.29).

[122]"A Literary Analysis of Damascus Document VI, 2-VIII, 3,"
RB 78 (1971), 210-32.

[123]Murphy-O'Connor points ("A Literary Analysis," 220) to the
structural parallel to the blessings and maledictions that end
the Holiness Code (Lev 26:3-46).

[124]"The Original Text of CD 7:9-8:2=19:5-14," *HTR* 64 (1971),
379-86.

[125]"Comparison entre les manuscrits 'A' et 'B'," 65-66; he
categorizes the divergencies between CD 7:10-21 and 19:7-9 as
a "cas inexpliqué."

[126]The resulting text is laid out clearly in "The Original
Text of CD," 384.

[127]8:1 actually reads הנסוגים הסגירו לחרב, the second word
being a scribal error of a later scribe: Lohse, *Texte*, 80.

[128]המחזיקים thus refers to (7:21b) אלה מלטו בקץ הפקודה הראשון

(7:13b; Dan 11:32) "those who held fast," and not to the sons
of Seth, the phrase's immediate antecedent.

[129]"The Original Text of CD," 385.

[130]"The Original Text of CD," 386. Both quotations are now
introduced by אשר כתוב, but Murphy-O'Connor ("The Original Text
of CD," 380,n.4, following Rabin, *Zadokite Documents,* 30-31)
claims that the quotation of Zechariah was introduced by אשר אמר,
the regular formula that precedes ביד (Cf. 3:21, 4:13, 19:14).

[131]"The Original Text of CD," 385.

[132]The same phrase occurs at CD 12:23, 14:19, 20:1.

[133]At least according to MT. BH^3 supposes that כוכב אלהיכם
is an addendum. In the LXX (=Acts 7:43) the order is altered
such that Μολοχ and Ραιφαν (the star god) are described as idols.
Syr. has a different order again.

[134]If the phrase כוכב אלהיכם אשר עשיתם לכם is taken as a whole,
then it may have been omitted purposely because of its negative
significance.

[135]*Zadokite Documents,* 28; followed by Vermes, *Scripture and
Tradition,* 2nd ed., 45.

[136]"The Ideology of the Temple in the Damascus Document," 300.

[137]*APOT 2,* 816. Charles concedes that the change of verbs at
the beginning of the line is deliberate; but this is negated if
we allow some such description of the matter as proposed here:
it is 5:27 that is quoted, not 5:26.

[138]Nowhere is the סוכת identified with the Temple or Tabernacle
par excellence, yet the two may be linked because one was kept
in the other.

[139]In the same form as in 4QFlor 1:12 though with a different
introductory formula.

[140]The king and the assembly are equated somewhat in
2 Chr 29:23, 30:2, 4, but not sufficiently for these verses to
provide the basis of the identification.

[141]*Zadokite Documents*, 29.

[142]"The Ideology of the Temple in the Damascus Document," 300.

[143]Gen 42:23, Job 33:23, Isa 43:27. Charles (*APOT 2*, 309)
noticed in *T. Levi* 8:14 that τύπος translating צלם may rather
stand for מליץ. מליץ is used for the Righteous Teacher in
4QpPss[a] 1:19.

[144]A possible allusion to Num 15:31, 2 Sam 12:9, 2 Chr 36:16
or even *1 Enoch* 99:2, 104:9.

[145]*Les écrits esséniens*, 149 and n.1.

[146]Cf. *T. Levi* 18:2-3, *T. Judah* 24:1-6, wherein the star is
the priest to come. For נשיא as the royal prince cf. 1QSb 5:20,
CD 5:1, 1QM 3:3, 15, 4:1. It is also the most frequent title
for the messianic prince in Ezek 44-48. In Ps 2:9 the sceptre
is the symbol of the (messianic) king; cf. Gen 49:10, Isa 11:4.
It is possible that the Interpreter of the Law in CD 6:7 refers
to a past figure whereas in the revision of CD, represented by
the Amos-Numbers midrash, the title refers to a future figure;
in different recensions of CD the one title may have different
referents.

[147]Already observed from the comparative study of the Qumran
texts; see, e.g., J. Starcky, "Les quatre étapes du messianisme
à Qumran," *RB* 70 (1963), 481-505; R. E. Brown, "J. Starcky's

Theory of Qumran Messianic Development," *CBQ* 28 (1966), 51-57.

[148]Cf. plural suffix written without *yôd*: CD 10:9, 1QS 1:26,
3:1, 1QH 5:4, 5.

[149]*Zadokite Documents,* 8, 20.

[150]E.g., Vermes, *Dead Sea Scrolls in English,* 98, 102;
Dupont-Sommer, *Les écrits esséniens,* 139, n. 1; 145. n. 8. Yadin
("Three Notes on the Dead Sea Scrolls," *IEJ* 6 1956 , 158-59)
was the first to read this phrase correctly.

[151]משיח (מ)אהרן ו(מ)ישראל: CD 19:10, 20:1, A^2 (CD 9-16) also
looked for only one Messiah: CD 12:23, 14:19 (supported by $4QD^b$).
None of this is appreciated by A. Caquot in his treatment of the
phrase ("Le messianisme qumrânien," *Qumrân: Sa piété, sa
théologie et son milieu*, BETL 46, 240-41).

[152]E.g., E. A. Wcela, "The Messiah(s) of Qumran," *CBQ* 26
(1964), 340-49.

[153]Argued most cogently by A. S. van der Woude, *Die
messianische Vorstellungen,* 38-66; more recently by R. Deichgräber,
"Zur Messiaserwartung der Damaskusschrift," *ZAW* 78 (1966), 333-43;
on CD 7:10-21, see esp. 338-39. For further exposition on the
messianism of this passage see my article "The Amos-Numbers
Midrash (CD 7,13b-8,1a) and Messianic Expectation," esp. 402-4.

[154]Allegro first published the text in "Further Messianic
References in Qumran Literature," *JBL* 75 (1956), 182-87, and
later definitively in DJD V, 57-60, No. 175 and Plate XXI. See
further the corrective work of J. Strugnell, "Notes," 225-29.

[155]*Testimonies I-II*, Cambridge: Cambridge University, 1916-20.

[156]"'4QTestimonia' and the New Testament," *TS* 18 (1957), 513-37;

reprinted in *Essays on the Semitic Background of the New Testament,* 59-89; see 89 n.78 for more recent bibliographical information. Also see Fitzmyer's bibliographical article on 4QTest generally, *CBQ* 30 (1969), 68-70.

[157]E.g., P. Prigent, *Les Testimonia dans le Christianisme primitif: L'épitre de Barnabé I-XVI et ses sources* (EBib; Paris: Gabalda, 1961), 27-28.

[158]The combination of MT Deut 5:28-29 and 18:18-19 was first pointed out by P. Skehan, "The Period of the Biblical Texts from Khirbet Qumrân," *CBQ* 19 (1957), 435.

[159]"Further Messianic References," 187; followed by E. A. Wcela, "The Messiah(s) of Qumran," 346 among others.

[160]*Les écrits esséniens,* 330-31.

[161]*Die messianische Vortsellungen,* 184.

[162]*Dead Sea Scrolls in English,* 247.

[163]F. M. Cross (*The Ancient Library of Qumran,* revised 1961, 147-49) sees Deut 33:8-11 as probably referring to the Righteous Teacher, though he does not totally exclude possible reference to the priestly Messiah.

[164]*Essays on the Semitic Background,* 84. M. Treves ("On the Meaning of the Qumran Testimonia," *RQ* 2 1959-60 , 569-71) denies any messianism in 4QTest and supposes the text to celebrate John Hyrcanus I as prophet, ruler, son of Levi and high priest: he offers no cogent support for his assessment.

[165]*Ten Years of Discovery,* 61.

[166]*Dead Sea Scrolls in English,* 248. R. E. Brown ("The Teacher of Righteousness and the Messiah(s)," 39) also understands

a reference to only two people; for him the accursed man is
Jonathan (arrested 143 B.C.) and the other vessel of violence
is his brother Simon. This view was expressed earlier by
P. Skehan, "Two Books on Qumran Studies," *CBQ* 21 (1959), 75;
and by implication, P. Winter ("Two Non-Allegorical Expressions
in the Dead Sea Scrolls," *PEQ* 91 1959 , 40-42) who relates the
building of 4QTest to that of CD 4:19, 8:12, 13, 18=19:24-26 and
1QpHab 10:9-10 and refers such activity to Jonathan and Simon
(*1 Macc.* 10:10-11:45, 12:36-37, 13:10, 48).

[167]"Further Messianic References," 187; supported by Dupont-
Sommer, *Les écrits esséniens,* 366-68, and perhaps by
Gaster (*Dead Sea Scriptures in English Translation,* 350, n.18)
who lets the reader decide between Allegro's "ingenious" proposal
and a further suggestion of Phasael and Herod as the two brothers
and either Antipater or Mark Anthony as the accursed man.

[168]*Ten Years of Discovery,* 61-64; criticized and refuted by
Cross (*The Ancient Library of Qumran,* revised 1961, 149-52, n.84).

[169]*The Ancient Library of Qumran,* revised 1961, 147-55; now
supported by H. Burgmann, "Antichrist-Antimessias. Der
Makkabäer Simon?" *Judaica* 36 (1980), 152-74.

[170]"Donnersöhne, Menschenfischer und der Davidische Messias,"
RQ 3 (1961-62), 42, n.4; also, Brownlee, *Meaning,* 103-4.

[171]J. Starcky ("Les Maîtres de Justice et la chronologie de
Qumrân," *Qumrân: Sa piété, sa théologie et son milieu,* BETL 46,
253) identifies the men of violence as Antigonus and his brother
Aristobulus I.

[172]Brownlee sees the same act of building in 1QpHab 10:9-10
from which he concludes that John Hyrcanus and his sons are the

persecuting wicked priests; this highlights the antithesis
between Righteous Teacher=Prophet and cursed man=false prophet.
The Qumran covenanters reached the conclusion for the former
identification after the death of the Teacher, upon reading
1QH 3:7-10.

[173]Cf., *4Q 158* frg. 6 for a similar combination of MT
Deuteronomy 5 and 18 (DJD V, 3).

[174]*Scripture and Tradition,* 2nd ed, 56-66. From a study of
the MT alone H. Kosmala concludes ("The Term *Geber* in the Old
Testament and in the Scrolls," *Congress Volume, Rome 1968,*
SupVT 17; Leiden: E. J. Brill, 1969, 168) that גבר in 1QH 3
is not messianic but simply refers to the spiritual re-birth
of the author of the hymns.

[175]*Scripture and Tradition,* 2nd ed, 65. Brownlee ("The
Servant of the Lord in the Qumran Scrolls. II," *BASOR* 115 [1954],
35) points out that Bo Reicke and J.-P. Audet seem to have been
the first to recognize the messianic significance of גבר in
1QS 4:20.

[176]E.g., the Targum of Jer 31:21. The Targum of Mal 3:1-3
implies that the messenger is the one to be purified, i.e.,
Elijah is given the same mission of purification and teaching
as גבר in 1QS. Among those denying גבר in 1QH 3:10 any messianic
significance are P. W. Skehan ("A New Translation of Qumran
Texts," *CBQ* 25 1963 , 120) and L. H. Silberman ("Language and
Structure in the Hodayot [1QH 3]", *JBL* 75 1956 , 106).

[177]"The Servant of the Lord . . . II," 36, n.30.

[178]*Meaning,* Appendix A, 261-70; Appendix C, 274-81.

[179]*Meaning,* 270.

[180]"The Significance of 'David's Compositions'," *RQ* 5
(1964-66), 569-74.

[181]"Whence the Gospel According to John?" *John and Qumran,*
ed. J. H. Charlesworth; London: G. Chapman, 1972, 175-77.

[182]For other possible biblical support that גבר is used of
a prophet, cf. Jer 23:9.

[183]Along with the word נביא in line 7 which is in neither
Sam. nor MT but is in the LXX text-type.

[184]4QTest 7: אשר לוא ישמע אל דברי; 4QTest 10: שומע אמרי אל.

[185]E.g., *Tg. Ps.-J.* and *Frg. Tg.* to Num 24:17; cf., *y. Ta^c an.*
68d, Rev 22:16 (Vermes, *Scripture and Tradition,* 2nd ed, 165).

[186]*T. Levi* 18:3-4 talks of the expected priest as a shining
star (like that of the king) whose knowledge is illumination.

[187]The relation of the messianic priest to the prince has
already been described in Chapter III with reference to 1QSb,
1QM and 4QpPs^a.

[188]J. Amusin ("4Q Testimona, 15-17," *Hommages à André Dupont-
Sommer,* eds. A. Caquot and M. Philonenko; Paris: Maisonneuve,
1971, 357-61) has stressed this section concerning denial of
family in the Deuteronomy quotation, especially in relation to
the similar aspect of Christian discipleship.

[189]Cf. T. H. Gaster ("A Qumran reading of Deuteronomy XXXIII
10," *VT* 8 1958 , 217-19) who comments upon the interplay between
יאר and ירה, the latter represented in MT at this point; he points
to LXX Ben Sira 45:17 for a similar wordplay (also LXX 2 Kgs 12:3,

17:28). Gaster's work was furthered in relation to the targumic
understanding of MT light as the Law by Vermes ("The Torah is
a Light," *VT* 8 1958 , 436-38).

[190]Not surprisingly the same three figures occur in 1QS 9:11.
It appears that 1QS was written by the same scribe as 4QTest;
the similarity with respect to eschatological expectations bears
this out.

[191]First published by A. S. van der Woude, "Melchisedek als
himmlische Erlösergestalt in den neugefundenen eschatologischen
Midraschim aus Qumran-Höhle XI.," *OTS* 14 (1965), 354-73;
reprinted with revisions, M. de Jonge and A. S. van der Woude,
"11Q Melchizedek and the New Testament," *NTS* 12 (1965-66), 301-26.
Reprinted with assorted restorations: J. A. Fitzmyer, "Further
Light on Melchizedek from Qumran Cave 11," JBL 86 (1967), 25-41;
J. Carmignac, "Le document de Qumrân sur Melkisédeq," *RQ* 7 (1969-
71), 343-78; J. T. Milik, "Milkî-ṣedeq et Milkî-rešaᶜ dans les
anciens écrits juifs et chrétiens (I)," *JJS* 23 (1972), 95-144.

[192]Line 24 according to Milik, "Milkî-ṣedeq et Milkî-rešaᶜ," 99.

[193]The general similarity between 4QFlor and 11QMelch has been
commented upon in particular by Fitzmyer ("Further Light on
Melchizedek," 26).

[194]Fitzmyer, "Further Light on Melchizedek," 29.

[195]Vermes, *Dead Sea Scrolls in English*, 118.

[196]Vermes, *Dead Sea Scrolls in English*, 105-6.

[197]Alternatively, God sets the few לברית עם לאור גוים (Isa
42:6; cf. 49:8). Note the reading of this verse in 4QIsa[h]: "I
have formed you and given you as an eternal covenant" (Text:

P. Skehan, "The Qumran Manuscripts and Textual Criticism,"
Volume du Congrès, Strasbourg 1956, VTSup 4; Leiden: E. J. Brill,
1957, 151).

[198]"11Q Melchizedek and the NT," 304.

[199]"11Q Melchizedek and the NT," 306.

[200]"11Q Melchizedek and the NT," 308.

[201]"Further Light on Melchizedek," 29; followed by Milik,
"Milkî-ṣedeq et Milkî-rešaᶜ," 100-01.

[202]"The Function of Isa 61:1-2 in 11Q Melchizedek," *JBL* 88
(1969), 467-69; taking up Y. Yadin's earlier remark ("A Note on
Melchizedek and Qumran," *IEJ* 15 1965 , 153).

[203]"The Function of Isa 61:1-2," 467.

[204]"From Isaiah 61 to Luke 4," *Christianity, Judaism and Other
Greco-Roman Cults 1* (Studies for Morton Smith at Sixty; SJLA 12;
ed. J. Neusner; Leiden: E. J. Brill, 1975), 90-91.

[205]T. H. Gaster Festschrift; ed. D. Marcus; *JANESCU* 5 (1973),
374-76.

[206]In "Milkî-ṣedeq et Milkî-rešaᶜ," 97-100; designated as
11QMelch 3 II.

[207]Lev 25:9 in 11QMelch 7, Isa 61:3 and Ps 7:8 in line 14,
Isa 52:7 in line 17, Dan 9:25 in line 18 and Isa 61:2-3 in line 19.
If Milik's restoration is correct, it is no longer possible to
uphold the suggestion of D. F. Miner ("A Suggested Reading for
11Q Melchizedeq 17," *JSJ* 2 1971 , 144-48) that line 17 contains
an abbreviated citation of Isa 56:7. Both reconstructions,
however, remain possible.

[208]See especially "11QMelch and the OT," 380-81: *gĕzērâ šāwâ* and *'asmaktâ*.

[209]Isa 61:1-2 is thus a "haftarah portion" ("From Isaiah 61 to Luke 4," 92).

[210]*Exégèse biblique et Judaïsme* (ed. J.-E. Ménard; Strasbourg: Palais Universitaire, 1973), 170-86.

[211]The literary influence of such liturgical texts together with the possibility that Luke understood Jesus' mission to have started in a jubilee year has been pointed out by A. Strobel ("Das apokalyptische Terminproblem in der sogen. Antrittspredigt Jesu [Lk 4, 16-30]," *TLZ* 92 1967 , 251-54). Interestingly, W. Zimmerli ("Das „Gnadenjahr des Herrn"," *Archäologie und Altes Testament,* eds. A. Kuschke and E. Kutsch; Tübingen: J.C.B. Mohr, 1970, 321-32) proposes that Isa 61:1ff. is in its very origin a sermonic treatment of Lev 25:10 and various parts of Deutero-Isaiah, including Isa 52:7.

[212]"Luc 4, 16-30 et la lecture biblique," 173.

[213]*The Bible as Read and Preached in the Old Synagogue* I, 282-89.

[214]"Luc 4, 16-30 et la lecture biblique," 178.

[215]If these readings are those of the Day of Atonement (or possibly one of the days of Tabernacles), then these psalms could be among the thirty festival songs which David composed: 11QPs[a] 27:8. Cf., J. A. Sanders, DJD IV, 91; W. H. Brownlee, "The Significance of 'David's Compositions'," 570-71.

[216]And rests, anyway, on the reading of a *dālet* and a partial *nûn* proposed by Fitzmyer, and followed by Milik. None of the

text of Dan 9:25 is actually present. For a detailed
treatment of 11QMelch 18-19, see D. E. Aune, "A Note on
Jesus' Messianic Consciousness and 11HQ Melchizedek," *EvQ* 45
(1973), 161-65.

Chapter IV

CONCLUSIONS

In Chapter I the study of Jewish texts that were demonstrated as very probably belonging to the first centuries B.C.
and A.D. showed that in using authoritative scripture the Jew
made it relevant through the application of certain exegetical
principles. These are dimly perceived by modern scholarship,
but in relation to both indirect and direct use of the scriptures
they formed the basis whereby a Jew talked validly of and with
the scriptural text; often the use of such principles may have
been subconscious. The study of passages from Philo and the
Targums has shown the diversity and universality of these
principles. With some hesitancy the later rabbinic designations
for such principles have been used throughout.

Study of 4QFlor with such a background understanding has
demonstrated several times the worth of being able to presuppose
a particular exegetical principle at work. Although such a presupposition was based primarily on the study of the use of
language rather than on particular comparisons of content, study
of the text itself proceeded in terms of traditional higher
criticism. At the start the perspective of the use of certain
exegetical principles helped with textual restorations, e.g., at

4QFlor 1:1 ([יו]אויב) in relation to 1:7, at 1:14 (חטאים) in relation to Psalm 1, and at 1:19 (וה]וסי בוא) in relation to Psalm 2.

After the provision of an adequate text, a structural analysis enabled, above all, the intention of the fragments to come to light. Recognition of certain principles at work aided in such an analysis too: e.g., in discussing how 4QFlor 1:7 (2 Sam 7:11aᵝ) related to the whole context of 4QFlor but particularly 1:1-2 (2 Sam 7:10-11aᵅ). Again, though not ultimately determinative of it, the principles aided in the discussion of the genre of the parts of the text and also of the whole, for in examining the midrash as a whole the principles pointed to an overall unity within 4QFlor based on a combination of texts that historically almost certainly belonged in the liturgy (of the Feast of Tabernacles).

In discussing the theology of 4QFlor, the structural outline helped demonstrate the eschatological aspect of the whole as each major subsection contained the phrase "the latter days." More interestingly, for 4QFlor 1:1-9, the analysis revealed a certain ambiguity concerning the sanctuary and the community; neither is stressed to the ultimate denial of the other, nor is the language purely metaphorical. Rather, the explanation based on the structural outline maintained the ambiguity of the terms through concluding that the community understood itself as being the eschatological sanctuary in anticipation.

As regards the actual use of scripture in 4QFlor, it was noted that while exegetical principles are used throughout, they do not of necessity require that one particular verse always be interpreted in the same way. Thus Amos 9:11 is used differently

in 4QFlor 1:10-13 from its use in CD 7:13b-8:1a, just as the
technique of *gĕzērâ šāwâ* is applied differently in each case.
Conversely, that does not deny that certain scriptural passages
were used consistently, at least for a while, to support theological views that were reached through the application of
certain principles to such texts. For example, the messianism
present in 4QFlor in the persons of the Shoot of David and the
Interpreter of the Law is best understood in light of the
occurrence of similar phrases in relation to scriptural passages
in other Qumran scrolls, notably the later recension of CD.
Indeed the similarity of certain texts to 4QFlor allowed some
tentative traditio-historical remarks to be made.

The concluding illustrations examined in Chapter III have
shown that, apart from the mere recognition of exegetical
principles at work in the Qumran texts, such recognition can
lead to fresh interpretations of those Qumran texts that cite
scripture explicitly or implicitly. The examples from 11QtgJob,
1QpHab, 1QM and 1QS have provided examples of midrashic
techniques at work in a wide variety of genres. The most noteworthy aspect of the study of CD 7:13b-8:1a was the conclusion
that principles of exegesis had been used in the redaction of
CD as well as in the actual composition of the Amos-Numbers
Midrash. From the structural analysis of 4QTest could be
determined the reasons for the order of the texts cited therein;
also, the ambiguity of גבר and כוכב was left intact by the
editor of the texts. The brief remarks on 11QMelch support
firstly the conclusion reached in relation to the use of Amos
9:11 at Qumran, that the same biblical quotation (in this case
Isa 8:11) can be used in a variety of ways depending upon the

manner in which it is cited and the principles of exegesis
involved; secondly, the combination of the major biblical texts
in 11QMelch may originally have had a liturgical setting.

This study has shown that one cannot approach the use
of the Bible at Qumran presupposing that such use was guided,
for instance, by an overall eschatological perspective. Biblical
exegesis at Qumran, and 4QFlor has shown this admirably, depended
upon a correct use of certain principles by the interpreter.
Some such quality as Qumran eschatology can only be discussed as
it is derived from the texts. The scholar's primary task,
therefore, is to understand the method of composition that lies
behind the texts. It is hoped that this study has provided a
somewhat exhaustive treatment of 4QFlor with such a primary
concern in mind. The application of such an understanding to
the treatment of most of the other Qumran scrolls has as yet
hardly been overworked.

INDEXES

Plato	265	Ber.		
		13a	62	
Pliny	8	28b	338	
Plutarch	265	'Erub.		
		54a	227	
Porphyry	8			
		Menah.		
Ps. -Clem. Hom.		36b-37a	34,74	
8:11-15	70			
		Nid.		
Ps. -Philo	32,71	61a	69	
Sifra	12	Sanh.		
Lev		34a	291	
23:40	251	90b	327	
		97a	251	
Sifre				
Num		Šabb.		
6:25	339	63a	251,328	
27:7-11	65	105a	20,21,61	
		115a	51	
Deut				
22:23-27	65	Yebam.		
23:12	230	11b	57	
33:12	269	11b-12a	292	
		24b	261	
Solinus	8			
		Yoma		
Symmachus	32,282	67b	69	

TALMUD (BABYLONIAN)
'Abod. Zar.
3b 261

TALMUD (JERUSALEM)
Pesah
6a 52

Full bibliographical details of works cited are given in the text and the notes.

The following author index is therefore a substitute for a bibliography.

INDEX OF AUTHORS

DATE DUE

5/21/14			

The Library Store   #47-0103

Lightning Source UK Ltd.
Milton Keynes UK
UKOW05f0059211113

221480UK00001B/127/A

9 781589 832374